Business Intelligence with Databricks SQL

Concepts, tools, and techniques for scaling business intelligence on the data lakehouse

Vihag Gupta

BIRMINGHAM—MUMBAI

Business Intelligence with Databricks SQL

Group Product Manager: Reshma Raman
Publishing Product Manager: Heramb Bhavsar
Senior Editor: Nazia Shaikh
Technical Editor: Sweety Pagaria
Copy Editor: Safis Editing
Project Coordinator: Farheen Fathima
Proofreader: Safis Editing
Indexer: Rekha Nair
Production Designer: Vijay Kamble
Marketing Coordinator: Nivedita Singh

First published: September 2022
Production reference: 1260822

Published by Packt Publishing Ltd.
Livery Place
35 Livery Street
Birmingham
B3 2PB, UK.

ISBN 978-1-80323-533-2

www.packt.com

This book came into life with the eternal blessings from Dada Ji & Dadi Ji
&
Love from Mom, Dad, Utkarsh, Suteja, Toffee
&
Love for the One who is arriving.

– Vihag Gupta

Contributors

About the author

Vihag Gupta is a solutions architect with a specialization in cloud data platform architecture and design. He has a background in data engineering and a professional interest in machine learning. He loves getting hands-on and solving real business problems with technology. He graduated with a degree in information technology from PES University, Bengaluru, in 2011 and earned a degree in information systems management from Carnegie Mellon University, Pittsburgh, in 2016. He has worked at companies including Deloitte Consulting, DataSpark, and Qubole. He currently works at Databricks, helping clients bring their lakehouse platforms for analytics to life.

Originally from Jharkhand, India, Vihag currently lives in Singapore with his wife and dog.

About the reviewers

Jerrold Law currently works at Databricks as a specialist solutions architect, specializing in data engineering and streaming. He helps organizations all over the world to adopt scalable big data processing use cases with the Lakehouse architecture. Prior to Databricks, he worked for Confluent, helping enterprise organizations to enable their real-time streaming use cases as part of the solutions engineering field team.

Ivan Tang is a solutions architect at Databricks, helping enterprises in the ASEAN region in their cloud transformation journey. Previously, he worked with Confluent Professional Services, where he helped enterprises from the APAC region to design, build, operate, and maintain event streaming platforms using Apache Kafka and Confluent. Prior to that, he was wrangling data and building models while being an architect, builder, and user of distributed systems, including Hadoop, Storm, Kafka, and Spark. Prior to that, he worked for Confluent, GIC (Singapore's sovereign wealth fund), and other firms.

With over 15 years of experience working as a solutions architect for some of the largest and most innovative companies in the world, including Amazon, Bridgewater, and Bloomberg, **Tomasz Kurzydym** is a strong supporter and advocate for constant learning, experimentation, and curiosity. His work has taken him from his native country of Poland to the USA and UK, and he now lives with his family in Singapore working for Databricks – a data and AI company. In his spare time, Tomasz enjoys traveling, skiing, and photography.

Mahdi Askari is a lead solutions architect at Databricks. He is a software engineer at heart, and has been working in the data and big data space since 2010. He has worked across different industries with customers and prospects using Databricks Lakehouse to derive insight from their data.

Roja Boina is an engineering senior advisor. She provides data-driven solutions to enterprises. She takes pride in her get-it-done attitude. She enjoys defining requirements, designing, developing, testing, and delivering backend applications, and communicating data through visualizations. She is very passionate about being a **Women in Tech** (**WIT**) advocate and being a part of WIT communities. Outside of her 9-5, she loves to volunteer for non-profits and mentor fellow women in STEM. She believes in having a growth mindset.

Table of Contents

Preface   xiii

Part 1: Databricks SQL on the Lakehouse

1

Introduction to Databricks   3

Technical requirements   4   An overview of the Databricks
An overview of Databricks,   Lakehouse platform   9
the company   4   Summary   10
An overview of the
Lakehouse architecture   5

2

The Databricks Product Suite – A Visual Tour   11

Technical requirements   12   The SQL persona view   15
Basic navigation with the sidebar   12   The Machine Learning persona view   26
The top of the sidebar   13   The Data Science and
The bottom of the sidebar   14   Engineering persona view   29
The middle of the sidebar   15   Summary   30

3

The Data Catalog   33

Technical requirements   33   Understanding the data organization
                                                 model in Databricks SQL   34

Apache Hive Metastore   34
Unity Catalog   35
Implications of choosing
a cataloging technology   37
An example of the data organization model   38

Exploring data visually with
the Data Catalog   41
Exploring the data programmatically
with SQL statements   51
Summary   61

4

The Security Model   63

Technical requirements   64
The Databricks SQL security model   64
Access control with Apache Hive Metastore   65
Access control with Unity Catalog   66
Query execution model   67

User-facing table access control   69
Users, groups, and service principals   69
Securable objects   71
Operations   72
Privileges   72
Bringing everything together   73
The security model in practice   75
Ownership   77
Sharing the database   77

Exploring the database   78
Exploring asset metadata   80
Revoking access   82
Denying access   83
Going beyond read access – part 1   83
Going beyond read access – part 2   85
Going beyond read access – part 3   86
Summarizing the security model   86
UI-based user-facing table access control   87

The internals of cloud
storage access   89
Cloud storage access in Microsoft Azure   92
Cloud storage access in
Amazon Web Services   97
Summary   101

5

The Workbench   103

Technical requirements   103
Working with queries   103
Developing queries   104

Visualizing query results   120

Creating and publishing dashboards   139
Administering and
governing artifacts   148
Summary   149

6

The SQL Warehouses   151

Technical requirements	151	Rules for query routing, queuing, and cluster autoscaling	159
Understanding the SQL Warehouse architecture	152	Sizing the SQL Warehouse	162
Creating and configuring SQL Warehouses	154	**Organizing and governing SQL Warehouses**	**168**
Cluster size	156	SQL Warehouse assignment strategy	169
Scaling	157	Access control in SQL Warehouses	170
Spot instance policy	158	Chargeback	173
Auto Stop	158	**Using Serverless SQL**	**175**
The art of SQL Warehouse sizing	159	**Summary**	**176**

7

Using Business Intelligence Tools with Databricks SQL   177

Technical requirements	178	Step 2 – install the driver	185
Connecting from validated BI tools	178	Step 3 – configure the SQL Warehouse connection	186
SQL Warehouse details	180		
Authentication details	182	**Connecting programmatically**	**187**
Connecting from non-validated BI tools	184	**Databricks Partner Connect**	**187**
		The internals of a data source file	190
Step 1 – download the driver	184	**Summary**	**191**

Part 2: Internals of Databricks SQL

8

The Delta Lake   195

Technical requirements	195	Data engineering before Delta Lake	196
Fundamentals of the Delta Lake storage format	196	The Delta Lake storage format	201
		Data engineering after Delta Lake	204

Built-in performance-boosting
features of Delta Lake   207

Automatic statistics collection   207
Automatic Compaction and
Optimized Writes   211
Automatic caching   212

Configurable performance-boosting
features of Delta Lake   214

Z-ordering   214
Bloom filter indexes   217
CACHE SELECT   218

Summary   218

9

The Photon Engine   221

Technical requirements   221
Understanding Photon Engine   221
What is Photon?   222
The Apache Spark execution model   223

Understanding vectorization   227
Volcano model   228

Code generation   228
Vectorization   229

Discussing the Photon
product roadmap   234
Summary   237
Further reading   237

10

Warehouse on the Lakehouse   239

Technical requirements   239
Organizing data on the Lakehouse   240
Components of a warehouse system   240
The Medallion architecture   241

Implementing data modeling

techniques   244
The bronze layer   245
The silver layer   245
The gold layer   247

Summary   249

Part 3: Databricks SQL Commands

11

SQL Commands – Part 1   253

Technical requirements   253
Working with data definition
language commands   254

DDL for catalogs   254
DDL for external locations   255
DDL for Delta Sharing   258

Working with data manipulation
language commands   262
MERGE INTO   262
COPY INTO   268

Working with the inbuilt functions in

Databricks SQL   269
JSON   269
Lambda functions   272

Summary   273

12

SQL Commands – Part 2   275

Technical requirements   275

Working with Delta Lake
maintenance commands   276
Vacuuming your Delta Lake   276
Time -traveling in your Delta Lake   278
Repairing your Delta Lake   279
Optimizing your Delta Lake   279

Working with data
security commands   280

Dynamic view functions   280
Controlling access to columns   281
Controlling access to rows   283

Working with metadata commands   284
Listing data assets   284
Describing data assets   285
Analyzing Delta tables   285

Summary   287

Part 4: TPC-DS, Experiments, and Frequently Asked Questions

13

Playing with the TPC-DS Dataset   291

Technical requirements   291
Understanding the TPC-DS dataset   292
Generating TPC-DS data   293
Building the spark-sql-perf library   293
Installing the spark-sql-perf library   295
Creating a data generation cluster   296
Importing the spark-sql-perf repository   298
Running the data generation notebook   298

Running automated benchmarks   300

Experimenting with
TPC-DS in Databricks SQL   302
Case study 1 – the effect of file formats 303
Case study 2 – the effect of specialized
data types   303
Case study 3 – the effect of NULLs   303
Case study 4 – ZORDER and partitions   304
Case study 5 – Bloom filter indexes   304

Summary   304

14

Ask Me Anything   305

Frequently asked questions   305   Summary   311

Index   313

Other Books You May Enjoy   326

Preface

It is a new era in the design of data platform systems. Disparate data lakes and data warehouses are giving way to a new type of data platform system – the lakehouse. It promises to unify all data analytics into a single platform. Databricks, with its Databricks SQL product suite, is the hottest lakehouse platform out there. It harnesses the power of Apache Spark™, Delta Lake™, and other innovations that enable data warehousing capabilities on the lakehouse with data lake economics.

This book is a comprehensive hands-on guide that lets you explore all the advanced features, use cases, and technology components of Databricks SQL. You will start with the fundamentals of the lakehouse architecture and how Databricks SQL fits into it. Next, you will learn how to use the platform – exploring data, executing queries, and building reports and dashboards. Moving on, you will learn about the administrative aspects of the lakehouse – data security, governance, and managing the computation power of the lakehouse. You will delve into the core technology enablers of Databricks SQL – Delta Lake™ and Photon. Finally, you will get hands-on with advanced SQL commands for ingesting data and maintaining the lakehouse.

By the end of this book, you will have mastered Databricks SQL and be able to deploy and deliver fast, scalable business intelligence on the lakehouse.

Who this book is for

This book is for business intelligence practitioners, data warehouse administrators, and data engineers who are new to Databricks SQL and want to learn how to deliver high-quality insights, unhindered by the scale of data or infrastructure. This book is also perfect for anyone who wants to study the advanced technologies that power Databricks SQL.

Basic knowledge of data warehouses, SQL-based analytics, and optionally, the ETL processes is recommended to effectively learn the concepts introduced in this book and appreciate the innovation in the platform.

What this book covers

Chapter 1, *Introduction to Databricks*, introduces Databricks along three dimensions. First, it will introduce Databricks, the company. Second, it will introduce the Data Lakehouse architecture – the core data Platform design pattern enabled by Databricks. Third, it will introduce the Databricks Lakehouse Platform. Essentially, this is the platform that Databricks provides for your organization to implement the data lakehouse architecture.

Chapter 2, The Databricks Product Suite – A Visual Tour, presents a visual tour of Databricks SQL and the rest of the Databricks platform. It will teach you how to navigate the platform and locate features of interest with ease.

Chapter 3, The Data Catalog, introduces the data catalog of the Databricks Lakehouse platform. It will teach you how the data objects – catalogs, schemas, tables, and views – are represented in the data catalog. Finally, it will teach you how to navigate and explore the data catalog with UI interfaces and SQL commands. Generated and populated by data engineers and consumed by data analysts, the data catalog is the central pillar of all your data operations.

Chapter 4, The Security Model, discusses the Databricks data security model and teaches how to use it to secure the data. Databricks provides a very fine-grained, yet easily programmable data security model to secure all data and data-related assets.

Chapter 5, The Workbench, introduces the Databricks workbench. The workbench is a set of capabilities that enable a simple, intuitive, and intelligent experience in query building and dashboarding. The Databricks SQL workbench provides users on the unified lakehouse platform an instant way to query the data and extract insights from it.

Chapter 6, The SQL Warehouses, introduces the compute power behind Databricks SQL. SQL Warehouses provide the elastic, scalable compute power that can execute **Business Intelligence** (**BI**) queries with ease, no matter the scale of the data. The cloud philosophy says storage and compute power should scale independently so that we can drive the maximum **Return on Investment** (**ROI**). This is exactly what the SQL Warehouses in Databricks SQL do.

Chapter 7, Using Business Intelligence Tools with Databricks SQL, teaches you how to connect your business intelligence tool of choice to Databricks SQL. This allows you to harness the power of Databricks SQL from the comfort of your favorite business intelligence tool.

Chapter 8, The Delta Lake, deep dives into the default storage format of Databricks – Delta Lake. It adds a layer of transactional intelligence to the otherwise simple data lake. This chapter will discuss the Delta Lake storage format and how it enables superior out-of-the-box query performance.

Chapter 9, The Photon Engine, deep dives into the Photon engine. It is the query engine that powers Databricks SQL. It is written from the ground up in native C++ and uses the Apache Spark API. This chapter deep dives into what makes Photon so fast.

Chapter 10, Warehouse on the Lakehouse, addresses one of the biggest mental leaps that must be taken when adopting the data lakehouse architecture. This chapter discusses how to implement popular warehousing patterns on the lakehouse.

Chapter 11, SQL Commands Part–1, introduces Databricks-specific SQL commands that are used for data definition and data manipulation operations.

Chapter 12, SQL Commands Part–2, introduces Databricks-specific SQL commands that are used for data security and metadata operations.

Chapter 13, *Playing with the TPC-DS Dataset*, introduces the TPC-DS dataset. It is a popular dataset for benchmarking decision support systems such as data warehouses. The chapter shows how to generate the TPC-DS dataset in Databricks and test the various concepts learned in the past chapters at scale.

Chapter 14, *Ask Me Anything*, presents and answers the frequently asked questions about Databricks SQL.

To get the most out of this book

This book is about Databricks SQL as an enabler for your business intelligence practice. Hence, the book assumes knowledge of standard SQL and business intelligence concepts. Basic knowledge of data warehouses and data lakes is recommended, but it is not mandatory. Some chapters, such as *Chapter 8*, *The Delta Lake*, and *Chapter 9*, *The Photon Engine*, assume some familiarity with Apache Spark and some data engineering constructs. That said, they are optional, deep-dive chapters and do not affect your learning of Databricks SQL.

Software/hardware covered in the book	Operating system requirements
Databricks SQL	Windows, macOS, or Linux

Databricks SQL is a **Platform-as-a-Service** (**PaaS**) offering and is accessible via any modern internet browser. It does not require any installation on your machine.

If you are using the digital version of this book, we advise you to type the code yourself or access the code from the book's GitHub repository (a link is available in the next section). Doing so will help you avoid any potential errors related to the copying and pasting of code.

Download the example code files

You can download the example code files for this book from GitHub at `https://github.com/PacktPublishing/Business-Intelligence-with-Databricks-SQL-Analytics`. If there's an update to the code, it will be updated in the GitHub repository.

We also have other code bundles from our rich catalog of books and videos available at `https://github.com/PacktPublishing/`. Check them out!

Download the color images

We also provide a PDF file that has color images of the screenshots and diagrams used in this book. You can download it here: `https://packt.link/vXWLg`.

Conventions used

There are a number of text conventions used throughout this book.

`Code in text`: Indicates code words in text, database table names, folder names, filenames, file extensions, pathnames, dummy URLs, user input, and Twitter handles. Here is an example: "Mount the downloaded `WebStorm-10*.dmg` disk image file as another disk in your system."

A block of code is set as follows:

```
OPTIMIZE table_name [WHERE predicate]
  [ZORDER BY (col_name1 [, ...] ) ]
```

Bold: Indicates a new term, an important word, or words that you see onscreen. For instance, words in menus or dialog boxes appear in **bold**. Here is an example: "To do so, we can click on the **SQL Editor** icon on the left-hand sidebar to bring up the **SQL Editor** page."

> **Tips or Important Notes**
> Appear like this.

Get in touch

Feedback from our readers is always welcome.

General feedback: If you have questions about any aspect of this book, email us at `customercare@packtpub.com` and mention the book title in the subject of your message.

Errata: Although we have taken every care to ensure the accuracy of our content, mistakes do happen. If you have found a mistake in this book, we would be grateful if you would report this to us. Please visit `www.packtpub.com/support/errata` and fill in the form.

Piracy: If you come across any illegal copies of our works in any form on the internet, we would be grateful if you would provide us with the location address or website name. Please contact us at `copyright@packt.com` with a link to the material.

If you are interested in becoming an author: If there is a topic that you have expertise in and you are interested in either writing or contributing to a book, please visit `authors.packtpub.com`.

Share Your Thoughts

Once you've read *Business Intelligence with Databricks SQL*, we'd love to hear your thoughts! Scan the QR code below to go straight to the Amazon review page for this book and share your feedback.

https://packt.link/r/1803235330

Your review is important to us and the tech community and will help us make sure we're delivering excellent quality content.

Part 1: Databricks SQL on the Lakehouse

This part focuses on the features and functions of the Databricks SQL product suite, which enables the day-to-day workflows of business intelligence practitioners and warehouse administrators.

This part comprises the following chapters:

- *Chapter 1, Introduction to Databricks*
- *Chapter 2, The Databricks Product Suite – A Visual Tour*
- *Chapter 3, The Data Catalog*
- *Chapter 4, The Security Model*
- *Chapter 5, The Workbench*
- *Chapter 6, The SQL Warehouses*
- *Chapter 7, Using Business Intelligence Tools with Databricks SQL*

1
Introduction to Databricks

Databricks is one of the most recognizable names in the big data industry. They are the providers of the lakehouse platform for data analytics and **artificial intelligence** (**AI**). This book is about Databricks SQL, a product within the Databricks Lakehouse platform that powers data analytics and business intelligence.

Databricks SQL is a rapidly evolving product. It is not a traditional data warehouse, yet its users are the traditional data warehouse and business intelligence users. It claims to provide all the functionality of data warehouses on what is essentially a data lake. This concept can be a bit jarring. It can create resistance in adoption as you might be wondering if your skills are transferrable, or if your work might be disrupted as a result of a new learning curve.

Hence, I am writing this book.

The primary intent of this book is to help you learn the fundamental concepts of Databricks SQL in a fun, follow-along interactive manner. My aim is that by the time you complete this book, you will be confident in your adoption of Databricks SQL as the enabler of your business intelligence.

This book does not intend to be a definitive guide or a complete reference, nor does it intend to be a replacement for the official documentation. It is too early for either of those. This book is your initiation into business intelligence on the data lakehouse, the Databricks SQL way.

Let's begin!

In this chapter, we'll cover the following topics:

- An overview of Databricks, the company
- An overview of the Lakehouse architecture
- An overview of the Databricks Lakehouse platform

Technical requirements

There are no technical requirements for this chapter. However, familiarity with the concept of databases, data warehouses, and data lakes will help.

An overview of Databricks, the company

Databricks was founded in 2013 by seven researchers at the University of California, Berkeley.

This was the time when the world was learning how the **Meta, Amazon, Netflix, Google, and Apple (MANGA)** companies had built their success by scaling up their use of AI techniques in all aspects of their operations. Of course, they could do this because they invested heavily in talent and infrastructure to build their data and AI systems. Databricks was founded with the mission to enable everyone else to do the same – use data and AI in service of their business, irrespective of their size, scale, or technological prowess.

The mission was to democratize AI. What started as a simple platform, leveraging the open source technologies that the co-founders of Databricks had created, has now evolved into the lakehouse platform, which unifies data, analytics, and AI in one place.

As an interesting side note, and my opinion: To this date, I meet people and organizations that equate Databricks with Apache Spark. This is not correct. The platform indeed debuted with a cloud service for running Apache Spark. However, it is important to understand that Apache Spark was the enabling technology for the big data processing platform. It was not the product. The product is a simple platform that enables the democratization of data and AI.

Databricks is a strong proponent of the open source community. A lot of popular open source projects trace their roots to Databricks, including MLflow, Koalas, and Delta Lake. The profile of these innovations demonstrates the commitment to Databricks's mission statement of democratizing data and AI. MLflow is an open source technology that enables **machine learning (ML)** operations or MLOps. Delta Lake is the key innovation that brings reliability, governance, and simplification to data engineering and business intelligence operations on the data lake. It is the key to building the lakehouse on top of cloud storage systems such as Amazon Web Service's **Simple Storage Service (S3)**, Microsoft Azure's **Azure Data Lake Storage (ADLS)**, and **Google Cloud Storage (GCS)**, as well as on-premises HDFS systems.

Within the Databricks platform, these open source technologies are firmed up for enterprise readiness. They are blended with platform innovations for various data personas such as data engineers, data scientists, and data analysts. This means that MLflow within the Databricks Lakehouse platform powers enterprise-grade MLOps. Delta Lake within the Databricks Lakehouse platform powers enterprise-grade data engineering and data governance. With the Databricks SQL product, the Databricks Lakehouse platform can power all the business intelligence needs for the enterprise as well!

Technologies and Trademarks

Throughout this book we will refer to trademarked technologies and products. Some notable examples are Apache Spark™, Hive™, Delta Lake™, Power BI™, Tableau™ and others that are inadvertently mentioned.

All such trademarks are implied whenever we mention them in the book. For the sake of brevity and readability, I will omit the use of the ™ symbol in the rest of the book.

An overview of the Lakehouse architecture

If, at this point, you are a bit confused with so many terms such as databricks, lakehouse, Databricks SQL, and more – worry not. We are just at the beginning of our learning journey. We will unpack all of these throughout this book.

First, what is Databricks?

Databricks is a platform that enables enterprises to quickly build their Data Lakehouse infrastructure and enable all data personas – data engineers, data scientists, and business intelligence personnel – in their organization to extract and deliver insights from the data. The platform provides a curated experience for each data persona, enabling them to execute their daily workflows. The foundational technologies that enable these experiences are open source – Apache Spark, Delta lake, MLflow, and more.

So, what is the Lakehouse architecture and why do we need it?

The Lakehouse architecture was formally presented at the **Conference on Innovative Data Systems Research** (**CIDR**) in January 2021. You can download it from `https://databricks.com/research/lakehouse-a-new-generation-of-open-platforms-that-unify-data-warehousing-and-advanced-analytics`. This is an easily digestible paper that I encourage you to read for the full details. That said, I will now summarize the salient points from this paper.

Attribution, Where it is Due

In my summary of the said research paper, I am recreating the images that were originally provided. Therefore, they are the intellectual property of the authors of the research paper.

According to the paper, most of the present-day data analytics infrastructures look like a two-tier system, as shown in the following diagram:

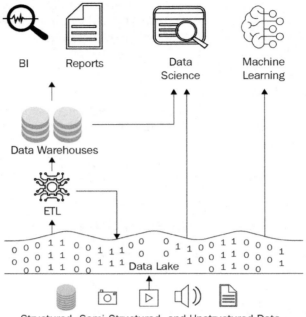

Figure 1.1 – Two-tier data analytics infrastructures

In this two-tier system, first, data from source systems is brought onto a data lake. Examples of source systems could be your web or mobile application, transactional databases, ERP systems, social media data, and more. The data lake is typically an on-premises HDFS system or cloud object storage. Data lakes allow you to store data in big data-optimized file formats such as Apache Parquet, ORC, and Avro. The use of these open file formats enables flexibility in writing to the data lake (due to schema-on-read semantics). This flexibility enables faster ingestion of data, which, in turn, enables faster access to data for end users. It also enables more advanced analytics use cases in ML and AI.

Of course, this architecture still needs to support the traditional BI workloads and decision support systems. Hence, a second process, typically in the form of **Extract, Transform, and Load (ETL)**, is built to copy data from the data lake to a dedicated data warehouse.

Close inspection of the two-tier architecture reveals several systemic problems:

- **Duplication of data**: This architecture requires the same data to be present in two different systems. This results in an increased cost of storage. Constant reconciliation between these two systems is of utmost importance. This results in increased ETL operations and its associated costs.

- **Security and governance**: Data lakes and data warehouses have very different approaches to the security of data. This results in different security mechanisms for the same data that must always be in synchronization to avoid data security violations.

- **Latency in data availability**: In the two-tier architecture, the data is only moved to the warehouse by a secondary process, which introduces latency. This means analysts do not get access to fresh data. This also makes it unsuitable for tactical decision support such as operations.

- **Total cost of ownership**: Enterprises end up paying double for the same data. There are two storage systems, two ETL processes, two engineering debts, and more.

As you can see, this is unintuitive and unsustainable.

Hence, the paper presents the Lakehouse architecture as the way forward.

Simply put, the data lakehouse architecture is a data management system that implements all the features of data warehouses on data lakes. This makes the data lakehouse a single unified platform for business intelligence and advanced analytics.

This means that the lakehouse platform will implement data management features such as security controls, ACID transaction guarantees, data versioning, and auditing. It will implement query performance features such as indexing, caching, and query optimizations. These features are table stakes for data warehouses. The Lakehouse architecture brings these features to you in the flexible, open format data storage of data lakes. A Lakehouse is a platform that provides data warehousing capabilities and advanced analytics capabilities for the same platform, with cloud data lake economics.

> **What is the Formal Definition of the Lakehouse?**
> *Section 3* in the CIDR paper officially defines the Lakehouse. Check it out.

The following is a visual depiction of the Lakehouse:

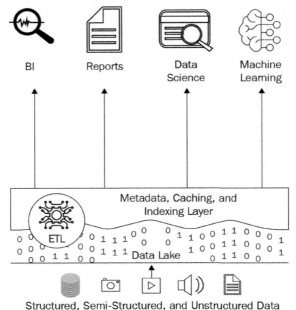

Figure 1.2 – Lakehouse architecture

The idea of the Lakehouse is deceptively simple – as all good things in life are! The Lakehouse architecture immediately solves the problems we highlighted about present-day two-tier architectures:

- A single storage layer means no duplication of data and no extra effort to reconcile data. Reduced ETL requirements and ACID guarantees equate to the stability and reliability of the system.

- A single storage layer means a single model of security and governance for all data assets. This reduces the risk of security breaches.

- A single storage layer means the availability of the freshest data possible for the consumers of the data.

- Cheap cloud storage with elastic, on-demand cloud compute reduces the total cost of ownership.

- Open source technologies in the storage layer reduce the chances of vendor lock-in and make it easy to integrate with other tools.

Of course, any implementation of the Lakehouse will have to ensure the following:

- **Reliable data management**: The Lakehouse proposes to eliminate (or reduce) data warehouses. Hence, the Lakehouse implementation must efficiently implement data management and governance – features that are table stakes in data warehouses.

- **SQL performance**: The Lakehouse will have to provide state-of-the-art SQL performance on top of the open-access filesystems and file formats typical in data lakes.

This is where the Databricks Lakehouse platform, and within it, the Databricks SQL product, comes in.

An overview of the Databricks Lakehouse platform

The Databricks Lakehouse platform enables enterprises to build their Lakehouse by providing simplified data engineering and data management techniques. The Databricks Lakehouse platform also provides one of the best ML experiences for data scientists and ML engineers.

Finally, Databricks SQL brings in the last piece of the puzzle – a home for the business intelligence and data analyst personas with a first-class workbench that allows query editing, building visualizations, and publishing dashboards. It also allows plug-and-play with downstream business intelligence tools such as Power BI, Tableau, Looker, and more. All of this is backed by state-of-the-art SQL query performance.

The following diagram represents the Databricks Lakehouse platform:

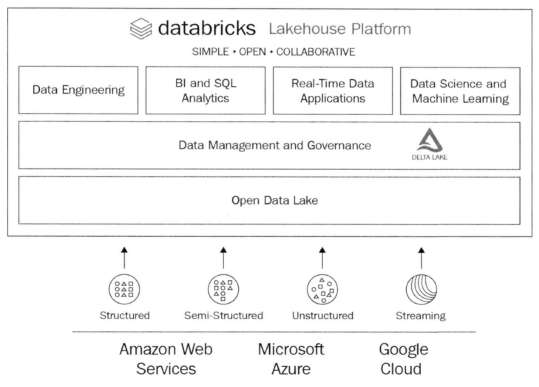

Figure 1.3 – The Databricks Lakehouse platform

The lakehouse platform by Databricks is a simple, open, and collaborative platform that combines the reliability, performance, and governance capabilities of data warehouses with the openness, flexibility, and economies of cloud data lakes.

Summary

In this chapter, we learned about Databricks as a company and the Databricks Lakehouse platform as the product of this company, which enables the democratization of data and AI for all organizations. We are now ready to begin exploring Databricks SQL.

In the next chapter, *Chapter 2, The Databricks Product Suite – A Visual Tour*, we will start with a tour of the Databricks Lakehouse platform.

2
The Databricks Product Suite – A Visual Tour

The Databricks Lakehouse platform is an expansive product that caters to personas such as data engineers, data scientists, and business analysts. It also caters to administrator personas such as platform administrators and database administrators. As we discuss core concepts in subsequent chapters, we will have to refer to other persona-specific features. Familiarity with the platform will allow us to navigate to the correct feature or function when referred.

In this chapter, we will take a visual tour of the Databricks Lakehouse platform, with an emphasis on the Databricks SQL product. We will use the official Lakehouse infographic from *Figure 1.3* as our guiding light to navigate through the Databricks Lakehouse platform and introduce, at a very high level, the features and functionalities and how they fit together.

We will use screenshots throughout, and you are encouraged to navigate accordingly in your instance of Databricks for the best orientation possible. Please note that the Databricks platform is regularly updated and refined, so the visuals may have evolved by the time you read this book. Once we have this orientation and context, we will be better placed to dive into the details of the Databricks SQL product suite.

In this chapter, we will cover the following topics:

- Basic navigation with the sidebar
- The SQL persona view
- The Machine Learning persona view
- The Data Science and Engineering persona view

Technical requirements

To get the most out of this chapter, you will need to have access to the following resources:

- A Databricks workspace. Databricks SQL requires a Premium or higher level of subscription. Databricks SQL is currently available on **Amazon Web Services (AWS)**, Microsoft Azure, and **Google Cloud Platform (GCP)**. Provisioning a Databricks workspace is beyond the scope of this book. You can get started here: `https://databricks.com/try-databricks`.

- Any modern internet browser. Databricks workspaces are accessed via browsers. Command-line interface and REST API-based access is also possible, but these are beyond the scope of this book. You can explore the CLI and REST API at your own pace by following the guide at `https://docs.databricks.com/reference/command.html`.

> **Note**
> The documentation links contain a switcher that allows you to navigate to the documentation links for the cloud of your choice. The core functionality of Databricks SQL is the same across all clouds. I will call out any cloud-specific nuances as required.

Basic navigation with the sidebar

In this section, we will learn how to navigate the Databricks platform using the left-hand sidebar. The left-hand sidebar contains links to all the user-facing features and functions on the platform.

First things first, we must log in to our Databricks platform. Whether you created a Databricks account for yourself or are using a Databricks account that your organization uses, you should have a workspace URL. Visit the workspace URL and log in with your credentials. For **Azure Databricks** users, the URL should be of the `https://adb-<an_alphanumeric_string>.azuredatabricks.net/` form. For Databricks on **AWS**, the URL should be of the `https://dbc-<an_alphanumeric_string>.cloud.databricks.com/` form. Finally, for Databricks on GCP, the URL should be of the `https://<an_alphanumeric_string>.gcp.databricks.com/` form.

Upon successfully logging in, you should see a sidebar on the left-hand side. This sidebar is the key to navigating the Databricks platform. The sidebar can be divided into three main sections. Let's have a look.

The top of the sidebar

When a Databricks workspace is launched, the user lands on their *pinned* persona experience. There are three persona experiences:

- **Data Science & Engineering**
- **Machine Learning**
- **SQL**

Each of these persona experiences enables access to tools and features relevant to that persona's daily workflow. The top of the sidebar primarily allows you to switch between these persona experiences. The following screenshot shows the persona dropdown:

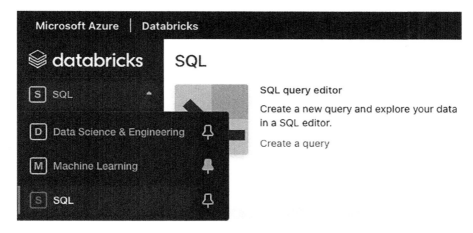

Figure 2.1 – The persona experience dropdown

Note

The landing page may differ based on how you have gained access to the Databricks workspace. If you have created a new trial account on either AWS or Azure, you will land on the **Data Science & Engineering** experience. If you are part of an organization that already has Databricks, you may have to ask them for access to the **SQL** experience. Once enabled, you can *pin* it so that you always land on the **SQL** experience upon logging in.

Since we will be primarily working with the **SQL** experience, it is a good idea to go ahead and pin the SQL persona experience as our default landing page.

The bottom of the sidebar

Let's discuss the options available at the bottom of the left-hand sidebar, as shown in the following screenshot:

Figure 2.2 – The Settings section

As shown in the preceding screenshot, the following options are available:

- **Partner Connect**: This provides a portal where you can select the partner tool or solution you want to connect to. Partner Connect simplifies and accelerates the integration. We will cover this in *Chapter 7, Using Business Intelligence Tools with Databricks SQL*.

- **Help**: This provides navigation to the documentation, release notes, service status page, knowledge base, and more.

- **Settings**: This provides navigation to various management capabilities, depending on your privilege level:

  - **User Settings**: This is where you can generate access tokens, toggle visual settings, and configure personal Git integrations. We will cover this in future chapters when we discuss programmatic access to Databricks SQL.

  - **Admin Console**: This is where users and groups can be created. It also provides access to self-service customization of the Databricks workspace. Any discussion on this is beyond the scope of this book, so you are encouraged to go through the options with the help of the documentation from the Help Center (`https://help.databricks.com/`).

  - **Manage Account**: This leads to global settings that can be used to manage all the workspaces under your Databricks account. A discussion on the enterprise deployment architecture of Databricks is beyond the scope of this book. However, as a quick note – once you've purchased Databricks, you can create an account, and within that account, you can launch any number of workspaces. Workspaces can be aligned to projects, teams, sandboxes, business units, or any logical division that the organization may employ. You can learn more about enterprise deployment patterns at `https://docs.databricks.com/getting-started/overview.html`.

- **Workspace selector**: This is the part in Figure 2.2 that says **databricks-sql-book**. This allows the user to seamlessly switch between various workspaces that they are part of.

The middle of the sidebar

At this point, you must be wondering why we skipped the middle of the sidebar. This is because the middle of the sidebar is where the *persona experience* really comes in. The options that we see in this section of the sidebar are dependent on the persona we are currently in. Hence, we will explore it as we deep dive into the different personas. We will start with the SQL persona and experience.

The SQL persona view

The SQL persona is the focus of this book, so let's start with that first. The following screenshot shows the home page of the SQL persona. The now-familiar left-hand sidebar should be visible, with SQL persona-specific options in the middle section. The landing page itself should show quick links to daily workflow features such as Query Editor, BI Connectors, and Data Explorer. Once the Databricks SQL product has seen some usage, links to recent work such as queries, dashboards, and others will also be populated on the main page for fast access:

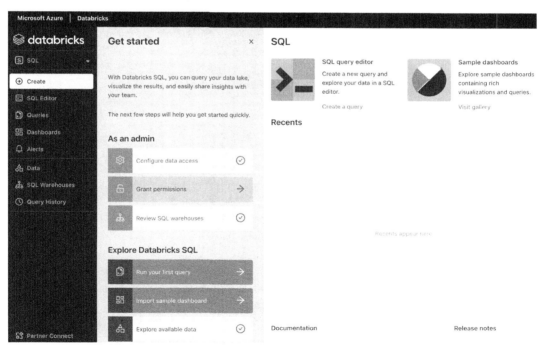

Figure 2.3 – The SQL persona home page

> **Note for New Workspaces**
>
> The interface shown in the preceding screenshot has an additional sidebar called **Get started**. You will see this if this is the first time Databricks SQL has been accessed in the workspace. Depending on the user's privileges, certain options will be provided to help them get started with Databricks SQL from an admin or end user perspective.
>
> You are not discouraged from exploring the guided **Get started** journeys. However, we promise that those journeys will be explored in detail in subsequent chapters.

Recall the Lakehouse infographic that we introduced in *Chapter 1, Introduction to Databricks* (*Figure 1.3*). To begin the visual tour, let's start from the **Open Data Lake** layer with Delta Lake on top of it for **Data Management & Governance**. This is highlighted in the following diagram:

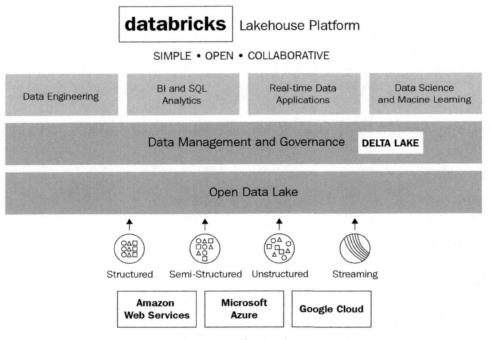

Figure 2.4 – The data layer

The data in the Lakehouse is sourced from various sources, including structured, relational data sources, semi-structured data sources, unstructured data sources, and streaming data sources. This is the Open Data Lake layer. This is powered by the Delta Lake technology (https://delta.io/), which abstracts the nuances and complexity of handling data on cloud object stores such as AWS S3, Azure ADLS, and GCP GCS.

The Data Explorer, which we will cover in the following subsections, is a visual tool that we can use to discover the data in the lakehouse platform.

Data Explorer

To navigate to Data Explorer, click the **Data** icon, , on the left-hand sidebar to bring up the **Data Explorer** page. The following screenshot shows a section of the **Data Explorer** page:

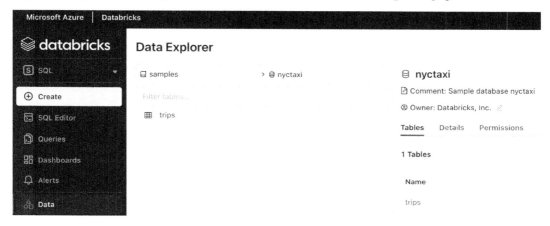

Figure 2.5 – The Data Explorer page

The **Data Explorer** page has a three-level hierarchy – the *catalog*, the *database*, and the *tables and views within the database*. Here, database is synonymous with schema. Traditional databases or warehouses have a hierarchy of `database.schema.table`. However, in Databricks, the top level is a container of schemas, hence we have `catalog.database/schema.table`. Data Explorer lets us visually explore these objects. For example, in the preceding screenshot, we have navigated to the `nyctaxi` database in `samples`, where we are viewing the `trips` table.

> **Note on Incidental Charges**
>
> Upon opening the **Data Explorer** page, the catalog will be set to **Hive Metastore** by default and the database will be set to **default** by default.
>
> Databricks provides sample datasets for getting started. They are available in the `samples` catalog. The preceding screenshot shows how to explore the sample data.
>
> Bear in mind that at the time of writing, Data Explorer requires a SQL Warehouse to be up and running. This will incur cloud costs, including Databricks costs and cloud compute costs (AWS EC2 or Azure VM). This will change soon with the introduction of a new cataloging technology called Unity Catalog. We will discuss Unity Catalog in *Chapter 3, The Data Catalog*.

Data Explorer is the portal to visually exploring the data in a Lakehouse. As we can also see, it provides a visual view of data management and governance as well – with **Access Control Lists** (**ACLs**), comments, and more. We will explore these in detail in *Chapter 3, The Data Catalog*.

SQL Warehouses

Data Explorer provides features and functions for visually exploring the data available to analysts. Since Databricks leverages the economies and elasticity of the cloud, the storage and compute layers are decoupled. This means that the data in the Lakehouse (visible in Data Explorer) is sitting on the cloud object storage, so computation resources must be acquired to execute queries against the data when needed. In Databricks SQL, this compute power is acquired with **SQL Warehouses**. They run a query processing engine called the Photon engine that works with the Delta Lake layer to provide a seamless query experience in the Databricks SQL product.

> **Note**
> The Photon Engine and the Delta Lake are transparent to the end user/analyst. They can query the data as if it were just another relational database.

If we refer to our guiding reference architecture, we are at the bounding box, as shown here:

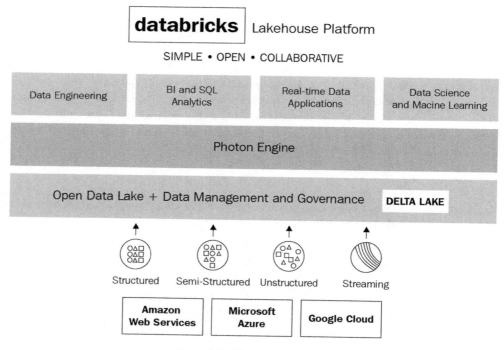

Figure 2.6 – The compute layer

To configure a SQL Warehouse, click on the **SQL Warehouses** icon on the left-hand sidebar, ⁂, to bring up the **SQL Warehouses** page:

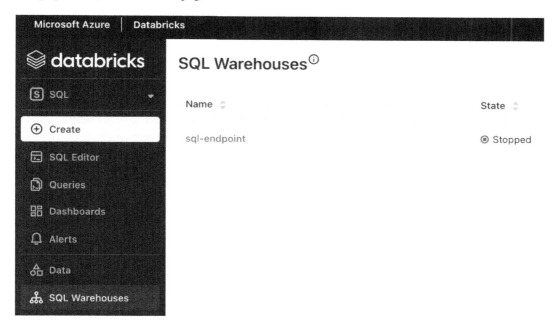

Figure 2.7 – The SQL Warehouses page

Here, we can see a warehouse named `sql-warehouse`. We can see that it is in a **Stopped** state. We can have multiple SQL Warehouses in our instance of Databricks. We will learn how to create and configure them in *Chapter 6, The SQL Warehouses*.

Query Editor

So far, we have learned how to explore the data visually and acquire the computation power to run queries against the data. The logical next step is to write some queries.

Going back to our reference architecture, we are at the consumption layer, where analysts and end users have access to features and tools that enable their daily workflows. The consumption layer is highlighted in red in the following diagram:

> **Note**
>
> The rest of the visual tour of the Databricks SQL product suite will be concerned with the consumption layer, and hence the bounding box highlighted in the diagram.

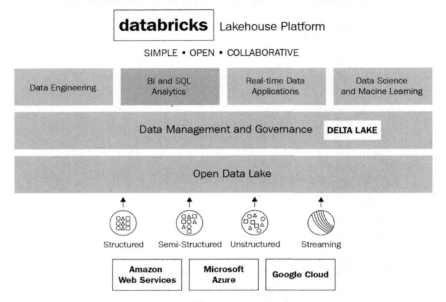

Figure 2.8 – The consumption layer

To do so, we can click on the **SQL Editor** icon on the left-hand sidebar, 🔲, to bring up the **SQL Editor** page:

Figure 2.9 – The SQL Editor page

The **SQL Editor** page provides an intelligent workbench to quickly author queries with typeahead and other features. It also provides built-in visualization capabilities for query results. Finally, it has an integrated view of the **Schema browser**, which provides a view of the catalog namespace for faster exploratory data analysis.

In the preceding screenshot, we are sampling some data from the `trips` table in the `nyctaxi` database. This Query Editor is running queries on the SQL Warehouse called `sql-warehouse`, which we visited in the previous section (not visible in the preceding screenshot).

The SQL Editor provides many more daily workflow features and functions, all of which we will explore in *Chapter 5, The Workbench*.

The Queries page

In the previous section, you may have noticed we had created a "named" query called `Sample trips Taxi`, as is visible in the **Query** tab. In Databricks SQL, queries can be named and saved for use with other features, such as dashboards and alerts.

The named, saved queries can be explored on the **Queries** page as follows. Click the **Queries** icon, , in the left-hand sidebar to bring up the **Queries** page. The following screenshot shows a portion of the **Queries** page:

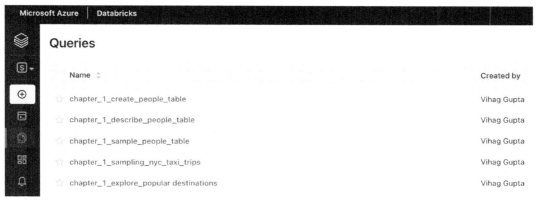

Figure 2.10 – The Queries view

The Queries view helps you discover existing queries authored by the user or by others in the team, hence promoting reuse and collaboration. The Queries view also provides metadata about the queries for better search capabilities. More on this in *Chapter 5, The Workbench*.

The Query History page

The Queries view allows the user to discover or revisit named/saved queries. However, it is an unreasonable expectation that all the queries that are written or executed will be named or saved. Hence, the **Query History** page fills the gap in discovering past query executions. To visit the **Query History** page, click on the **Query History** icon, ⏱, as shown in the following screenshot:

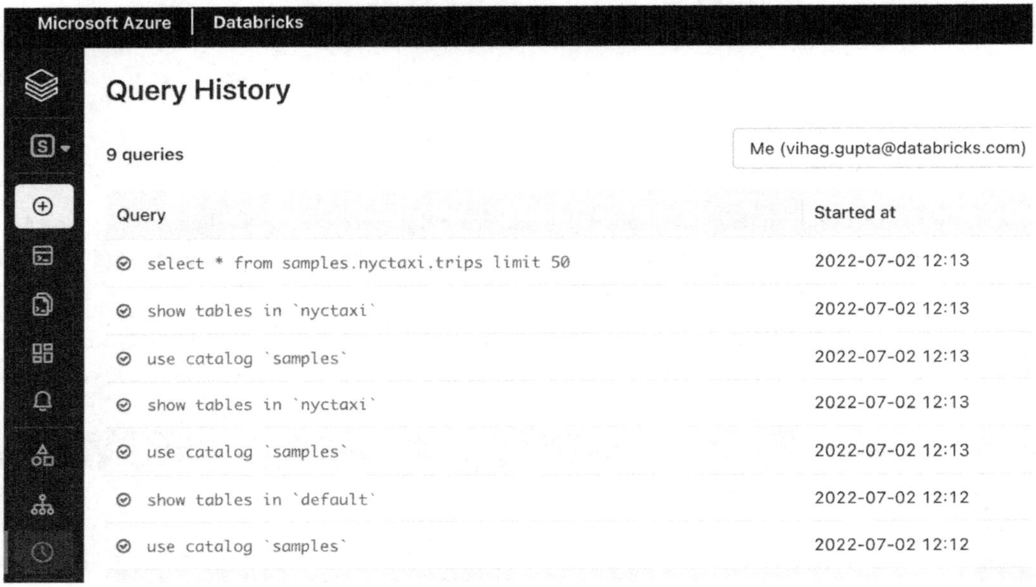

Figure 2.11 – The Query History page

Here, we can see that the **Query History** page maintains a history of all the queries that have been executed in the SQL persona view. There are smart filters that can be applied to sift through the history. We will cover practical applications of this feature in *Chapter 5, The Workbench*.

The Dashboards page

The queries that we author in the Databricks SQL product can be composed into dashboards. These dashboards can then be shared with other teams and stakeholders for their consumption. Click on the **Dashboards** icon, 🔡, on the left-hand sidebar to bring up the **Dashboards** page, as shown in the following screenshot:

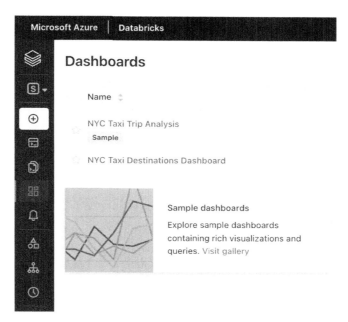

Figure 2.12 – The Dashboards page

The preceding screenshot shows a section of the **Dashboards** landing page where we have two dashboards. The first one, **NYC Taxi Trip Analysis**, is a sample dashboard that you can import from the Dashboards Gallery.

Users can create a new dashboard using the **Create Dashboard** button in the top right-hand corner. The following screenshot shows a section of the Creation view of the **NYC Taxi Trip Analysis** sample dashboard:

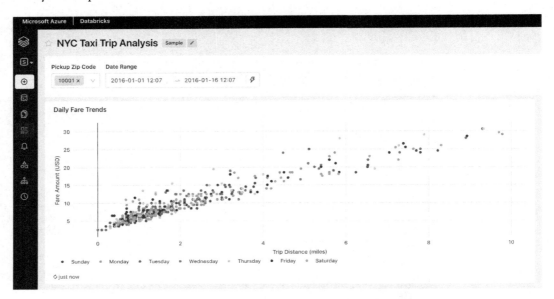

Figure 2.13 – Sample dashboard (Databricks Dashboard Gallery)

In the Dashboard Composer, we can add visualizations based on existing queries, parameterize them for interactivity, and compose them into useful dashboards.

More on building dashboards will be covered in *Chapter 5, The Workbench*.

The Alerts page

Queries are an amazing way to look at events in a retrospective manner. However, we are talking about the Lakehouse today, where real-time events are consumable and actionable. In this scenario, queries can also enable proactive analysis and mitigation. For this reason, Databricks SQL provides an **Alerts** function. Alerts can be configured to trigger when some value threshold on a named, saved query is breached. To reach the **Alerts** page, click the **Alerts** icon, 🔔 , on the left-hand sidebar:

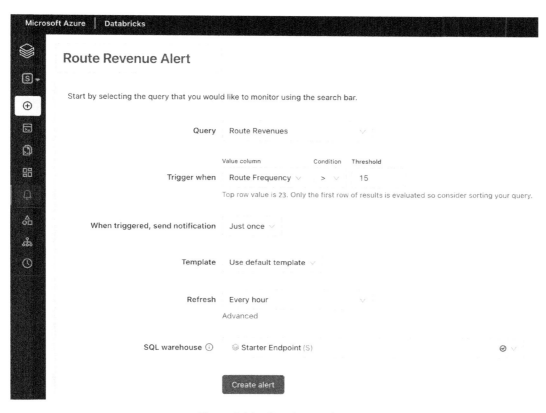

Figure 2.14 – Creating an alert

In the preceding screenshot, we are setting an alert when the revenue frequency exceeds a value of 15.

This example shows the alert behavior and the template of the alert. More on this will be covered in *Chapter 5, The Workbench*.

The Create menu

Databricks SQL also provides a handy **Create** menu that allows you to quickly navigate so that you can create the following items. We looked at these in the previous sections:

- Query
- Table
- Dashboard
- SQL Warehouses
- Alert

The **Create** menu can be accessed by clicking on the **Create** icon, ⊕ , in the left-hand sidebar. It will open a drop-down, as shown in the following screenshot:

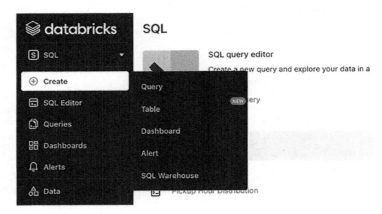

Figure 2.15 – The Create menu

The user can quickly navigate to the *creation* aspect of the available options with this menu.

> **Note on the Create Button**
>
> The **Create** menu is a persona/experience-specific menu. The **Creation** options will be different for the Machine Learning persona and the Data Science & Engineering persona.

This concludes our tour of the SQL persona. Moving on, we will take a brief tour of the Machine Learning persona and the Data Science & Engineering persona to complete our visual tour of the lakehouse platform.

The Machine Learning persona view

In this section, we will cover the Machine Learning persona. To switch to the Machine Learning persona, click on the **Machine Learning** option in the persona switching menu, as shown in the following screenshot:

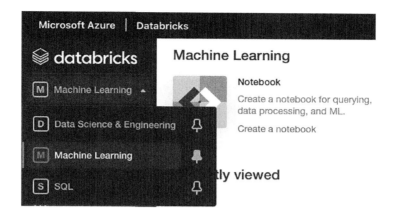

Figure 2.16 – Switching to the Machine Learning persona

Switching to the Machine Learning persona will bring up the landing page for **Machine Learning**. The following screenshot shows a section of the landing page:

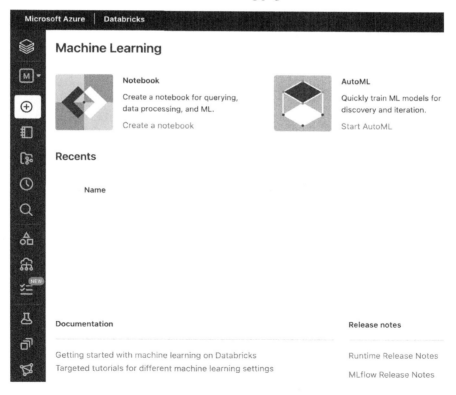

Figure 2.17 – The Machine Learning persona landing page

The first thing that should stand out is the familiarity of experience. The left-hand sidebar brings up familiar icons, such as the following:

- **Create** ⊕ : Like the SQL persona, the **Create** button provides easy navigation to creating artifacts relevant to the Machine Learning persona. These artifacts can be divided into two groups:

  - **Machine Learning**: Databricks AutoML Experiments, MLflow Experiments, and MLflow Models

  - **Developer Tools**: Notebooks, Tables, Clusters, and Jobs

- **Data** : Exactly like the SQL persona, Data Explorer allows you to explore the data on the Lakehouse. This is in keeping with Lakehouse's mission for a single source of truth for all data teams.

- **Clusters** : Like the SQL Warehouses in the SQL persona, the clusters allow data scientists to provision computation resources in the form of clusters with Delta Engine to execute their machine learning code and pipelines. It is important to note that clusters differ from SQL Warehouses in terms of their topology, performance, and concurrency characteristics. This is in keeping with Lakehouse's mission to bring the correct computation power to the task at hand – be it business intelligence, machine learning, or data engineering.

Apart from the familiar Lakehouse unification features – the data and the clusters/warehouses – the Machine Learning experience also exposes other data science and machine learning-oriented features. A detailed discussion of these features is outside the scope of this book. I encourage you to explore these at your own pace with official product guides and the latest documentation (`https://docs.databricks.com/applications/machine-learning/index.html`). However, here is a quick rundown of the major available tools:

- **Workspace** : This is like a shared space or workbench where users and teams can create shared projects with arbitrary folder structures and author code in them with Databricks Notebooks and other files. **Workspace** also allows you to create shared code libraries and experiments.

- **Repos** : This option allows users and teams to connect their choice of version control system (for example, GitHub, Bitbucket, GitLab, and so on) to their Databricks workspace. It allows you to author code in Databricks Notebooks and sync them with project repositories. This enables seamless **continuous integration and continuous deployment (CI/CD)** pipelines.

- **Workflows** : This option allows you to execute code in a non-interactive, scheduled way. We can think of **Workflows** as a way of creating data or task pipelines. It also allows you to author jobs with multiple tasks and arbitrary dependencies from the UI and via APIs. A practical example would be creating a job for a model pipeline involving feature engineering, model training, model validation, and model deployment. Another example would be a job for monthly predictions using a model. You can also use **Workflows** to schedule a periodic refresh of a Databricks SQL query or dashboard.

- **Experiments** 🧪: Databricks provides a managed MLflow service (`https://databricks.com/product/managed-mlflow`) that data scientists and machine learning engineers can use for MLOps. Experiments are a high-level concept in MLflow that corresponds to a machine learning project within which data scientists can record and organize their "experiments" while developing a model.

- **Feature Store** ⬜: Machine learning algorithms take a set of input data (features) and try to create a mathematical model that best explains its characteristics. These features can be raw or derived data. In large enterprises, features can often be reused. **Feature Store** enables cataloging, discovery, governance, and reuse of features across data science projects.

- **Model Registry** ⬛: Like **Feature Store**, **Model Registry** aims to catalog all the models that are developed by various teams, as well as enable their discovery and reuse.

This concludes a very brief visual tour of the Machine Learning persona. You are encouraged to follow the official guides and the latest documentation if you wish to explore the Machine Learning persona in depth.

Next, we will quickly cover the Data Science & Engineering persona in Databricks.

The Data Science and Engineering persona view

The Data Science & Engineering persona caters to data engineering personnel. It allows them to develop, run, and maintain data engineering pipelines that keep the Lakehouse data catalog up to date. These data engineering pipelines feed the data catalog with the latest data, which, in turn, is consumed by the SQL and **Data Science & Engineering** personas. In this section, we very briefly cover this persona.

To switch to the Data Science & Engineering persona, click on the **Data Science & Engineering** option in the persona menu:

Figure 2.18 – Switching to the Data Science & Engineering persona

Switching to the Data Science & Engineering persona will bring up the following landing page:

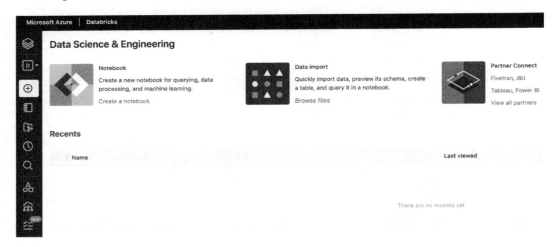

Figure 2.19 – The Data Science & Engineering persona landing page

In keeping with the other views, we can see that we have the now-familiar **Create**, **Workspace**, **Repose**, **Data**, **Compute**, and **Jobs** options.

These features are the same as what we saw in the previous section, *The Machine Learning persona*. As we can see, the only thing that's different is a lack of machine learning-specific toolsets. This is because this persona is primarily concerned with data wrangling, data ingestion, and data quality and access. Therefore, tools such as Repos, Notebooks, and Jobs are enough for them to carry on with their daily workflow.

For the sake of brevity and elimination of redundancy, we will conclude this very brief visual tour of the data engineering experience. For details on the various left-hand sidebar menu options, please go to the *The Machine Learning persona* section.

Summary

In this chapter, we took a visual tour of the Databricks Lakehouse platform. We focused on the lakehouse platform primarily from the perspective of a business intelligence user – that is, the SQL persona. We familiarized ourselves with the various features and toolsets that the Databricks SQL product provides to enable the daily activities of users.

We also briefly examined the Data Science & Engineering and Machine Learning persona views of the Databricks Lakehouse platform, which we will not revisit as they are not the focus of this book.

Finally, while looking at the various features and toolsets, we learned how they map to the various layers of the Lakehouse architecture and how the same data is leveraged for all users of the data in the Lakehouse.

In the next chapter, we will start our deep dive into the features and toolsets in the Databricks SQL product, starting with the data catalog.

3
The Data Catalog

The data catalog is the portal to the data layer of the Lakehouse. It exposes the various catalogs, databases, and tables to the end user for their consumption. In this chapter and the next, we will deep dive into the various facets of the data catalog.

In this chapter, we will explore the data catalog from the perspective of an end user. Here, *end user* refers to business intelligence analysts, data analysts, and users who are interested in exploring data and performing **exploratory data analysis (EDA)**.

In this chapter, we will cover the following topics:

- Understanding the data organization model in Databricks SQL
- Exploring data visually with the data catalog
- Exploring data programmatically with SQL statements

Technical requirements

For this chapter, you will need the following tools and functions:

- A Databricks workspace that has a premium or higher subscription level.
- Any modern internet browser.
- VM quotas for creating a SQL Warehouse. The default small-size SQL Warehouse requires a minimum VM quota. If you are using your cloud account, ensure that your account has service limits to meet these. Having an insufficient quota will prevent the SQL Warehouses from starting up. You can review the required quotas at `https://docs.databricks.com/sql/admin/sql-endpoints.html#cluster-size`.

Understanding the data organization model in Databricks SQL

In this section, we will learn about how data assets are organized in Databricks SQL. We call this the data organization model.

The open data lake, which is the foundation of the Databricks Lakehouse platform, relies on cloud object storage for storing data. This data is stored in human-readable formats such as CSV, TSV, and JSON, or big data-optimized formats such as Apache Parquet, Apache ORC, or Delta Lake.

> **A Note on Data Engineering**
>
> The data in the data lake is ingested by data engineering processes. Data engineers create data pipelines that bring data from source systems, clean them, transform them, and write them to the designated destinations in the data lake. These destinations are directories in the data lake. The data within the directory can be further arranged in some fashion – for example, by date.

These file formats are structured and have a defined schema. Having a schema means these files (or a directory of files within the same schema) can be conceptualized as a **table**. These tables are usually part of an organized collection of structured information. Hence, directories that contain data can be conceptualized as **databases** or **schemas**. Due to this, we have the makings of a traditional database-like system on the data lake. Once we have these, we must **catalog** these databases and their tables so that SQL users can discover and query these tables with standard SQL.

Databricks provides two cataloging technologies: Apache Hive Metastore and Unity Catalog.

Apache Hive Metastore

Apache Hive Metastore is a popular open source catalog for data lakes. It is part of the larger Apache Hive system that revolutionized the big data processing scene when it was launched in 2010. You can read more about Metastore's design and concepts here: `https://cwiki.apache.org/confluence/display/hive/design#Design-Metastore`.

At the time of writing, Apache Hive Metastore is the default cataloging technology in Databricks. However, it will soon give way to Unity Catalog.

Unity Catalog

Unity Catalog (`https://databricks.com/product/unity-catalog`) is a new data cataloging technology developed by Databricks that aims to meet the requirements of the Lakehouse (compared to a vanilla data lake). It provides significant benefits over Hive Metastore in general and within the context of Databricks. For example, it provides audit logging, inbuilt access control, and the ability to control access to cloud storage. At the time of writing, Unity Catalog is in preview in Databricks. It may become generally available by the time you read this book.

> **Note**
>
> I will introduce the differences between Hive Metastore and Unity Catalog as we proceed. However, I will say this – within the context of our discussion of Databricks SQL, the core concepts and our interactions with the data catalog will remain the same, irrespective of whether you are using Hive Metastore or Unity Catalog. So, you can read ahead without the fear of missing out. If, however, you are a data engineer, Databricks administrator, or just generally inquisitive about the Unity Catalog product, you can head over to `https://docs.microsoft.com/en-us/azure/databricks/data-governance/unity-catalog/key-concepts`.

Regardless of the data cataloging technology, each instance of Databricks SQL is associated with an instance of a **Metastore**.

> **Note**
>
> The instance of a Metastore is not to be confused with the technology Apache Hive Metastore!

A **Metastore** is a container that organizes the metadata for the databases and tables in a high-level object called a **catalog**.

One instance of Databricks SQL (a workspace in Databricks parlance) can only be associated with one Metastore.

So, bringing it all together, we have a three-level data organization model of Databricks SQL:

- **Tier 1**: Catalogs
- **Tier 2**: Databases (equivalent to Schema)
- **Tier 3**: Tables (as well as views and functions based on the tables)

Officially, this is called the three-level namespace and can be visualized as follows:

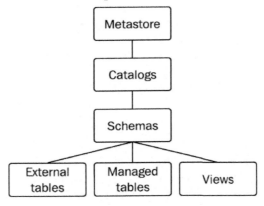

Figure 3.1 – Three-level namespace

The three-level namespace fits into the data catalog as follows:

- One organization can have any number of Metastores (1:n).
- One Metastore can have any number of catalogs (1:n).
- Each catalog can have any number of databases/schemas (1:n).
- Each database can have any number of tables, views, and functions (1:n).
- Each table points to directories in cloud storage (1:n).

The following alternative visualization should make things clearer:

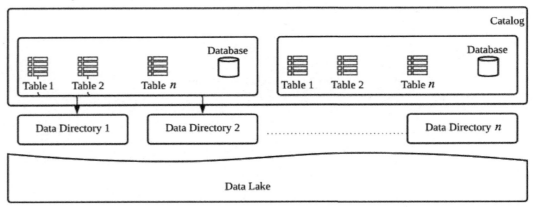

Figure 3.2 – Data lake data abstraction hierarchy

We will bring this organization model to life with an actual example shortly. However, before we do so, let's quickly look at the nuances that arise from choosing between Apache Hive Metastore and Unity Catalog.

Implications of choosing a cataloging technology

Let's look at the preceding diagram from the perspective of Apache Hive Metastore:

- You cannot create a new Metastore at will. Each instance of the Databricks SQL workspace will come with an instance of Hive Metastore.

- You cannot create new catalogs in the Metastore. You will be provided with an out-of-the-box catalog called `hive_metastore` that you must use.

- The Metastore associated with the Databricks SQL workspace cannot be shared with other Databricks SQL workspaces in your organization. To circumvent this, you can have a central, self-maintained Apache Hive Metastore (`https://docs.microsoft.com/en-us/azure/databricks/data/metastores/external-hive-metastore`) or you can switch to Unity Catalog.

Now, let's look at the preceding diagram from the perspective of Unity Catalog:

- You can create any number of Metastores.

- You can create any number of catalogs within each Metastore.

- A Databricks workspace can be associated with only one Metastore at a time. You can change this association if required. The same Metastore can be shared across multiple Databricks workspaces.

- You will still see the `hive_metastore` catalog in your list of catalogs. This is to enable a smooth migration for organizations using Apache Hive Metastore to Unity Catalog.

You might be wondering why we need to provision multiple Metastores and multiple catalogs within Metastores. Well, the answer lies in how Databricks is deployed as an organization-wide data platform. For example, if your enterprise spans multiple countries, each country may want to organize its data separately for data privacy and data residency reasons. In this case, you can have a Metastore for each country, where all the Databricks workspaces in that country will be associated with this Metastore. Within a Metastore, you can have multiple catalogs. You can use catalogs as a way of aligning to your information architecture. For example, a catalog can correspond to a business unit, a team, or a project. You could have a production catalog, a staging catalog, and a development catalog. You could even have a business unity-specific catalog per environment, such as a production catalog for sales.

After this brief detour regarding the implications of choosing a data catalog, we are ready to bring the data organization model to life.

> **Note**
>
> The examples and figures in the following sections have been built with Apache Hive Metastore since Unity Catalog is in preview at the time of writing. If you are using Unity Catalog, you can simply replace any occurrence of Apache Hive Metastore with Unity Catalog and any occurrence of the `hive_metastore` catalog name with the catalog name that you are using.

An example of the data organization model

Databricks provides example datasets out of the box. One such dataset is the `people` dataset, which is stored at the following location in Delta format:

```
dbfs:/databricks-datasets/learning-spark-v2/people/people-10m
```

> **About DBFS**
>
> **DBFS** is a **distributed filesystem** that provides an abstraction on top of any cloud object storage. You can read more about it here: `https://docs.databricks.com/data/databricks-file-system.html`. The path mentioned in the preceding snippet is cloud agnostic, so it will work irrespective of which cloud you are on.

To get started, follow these steps:

1. Create a database that will logically bind all the data assets to the `people` dataset.

Execute the following code in the SQL Editor to create a database:

```
CREATE DATABASE people_db;
```

This command will create a new database called `people_db` and register it in our data catalog. This will be the `hive_metastore` catalog if you are using Apache Hive Metastore.

If you are using Unity Catalog, it will be a catalog of your choice in the Metastore associated with your Databricks SQL workspace. The command will be in the following form:

```
CREATE DATABASE <catalog-name>.people_db
```

> **How to Execute the Snippets**
>
> In *Chapter 2, The Databricks Product Suite – A Visual Tour*, in the *Query Editor* section, we briefly touched on how to navigate to the SQL Editor and execute queries. This includes associating the editor with a SQL Warehouse. If you have not already gone through that chapter, please do so now, as it introduces some of the features and functions that will be referenced in this chapter.

2. Next, we can create a TABLE in this database with the following SQL code:

```
CREATE TABLE people_db.people OPTIONS (PATH 'dbfs:/databricks-
datasets/learning-spark-v2/people/people-10m.delta');
```

As we learned earlier, TABLE is nothing but a relational abstraction of files with a defined schema. Using the PATH option, we are specifying that the table abstraction, called people, points to the data contained in the given PATH. You will also notice that this command creates this table in the people_db database that we just created.

Now, the data catalog is aware of a database named people_db and a table named people in this database.

Do I Always Need a Location?

No, you do not. The preceding example is an example of an unmanaged table, which means that you are just applying the abstraction of a table to some dataset at some location. The data at this location is being managed by some other process or entity. The other option is that of a managed table, which creates a brand-new table at a location defined by Hive Metastore or Unity Catalog. You can read more about unmanaged tables at https://docs.databricks.com/data/tables.html#managed-and-unmanaged-tables.

So, if we were to visualize our database and table as per *Figure 3.2*, it would look like this:

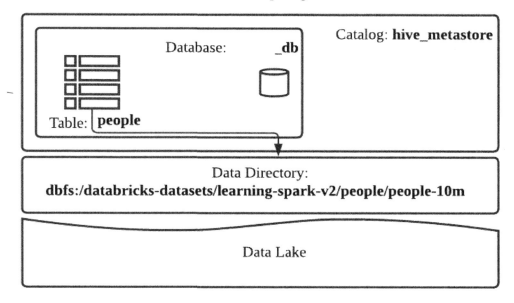

Figure 3.3 – Data lake data abstraction hierarchy for people_db

It is important to remember that the catalog, which is `hive_metastore` in this case, merely holds the metadata about the schema. It does not store the actual data. It only hosts metadata, such as the physical location, schema, partitioning schemes, and data statistics, about the databases and tables that are registered with it.

The following diagram shows a very simplified version of the execution model of a query in Databricks SQL:

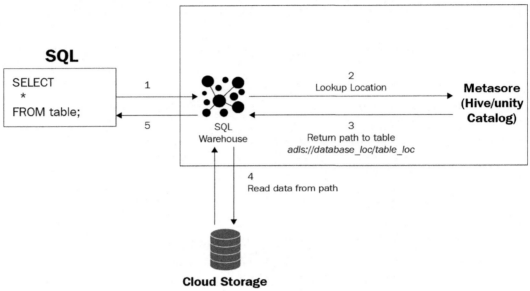

Figure 3.4 – The execution model of a query

In the preceding diagram, the following process is occurring:

1. The user submits a query in Databricks SQL.

2. The query engine of Databricks SQL, running on a SQL Warehouse, transparently queries the Metastore for the location of the objects referred to in the user query.

3. The Metastore returns the locations of the data that needs to be read by the query submitted by the user.

4. The query engine reads the data at the received physical locations and performs the required query.

5. The results are returned to the user.

As you can see, from the end user's perspective, working with Databricks SQL is like working with any traditional data warehouse or database system. You have a catalog of available data assets. You write queries against them and Databricks SQL gets you the results of the query.

At this point, you might be thinking – if Databricks SQL hides all the underlying operations and exposes a familiar SQL experience, then why did the author burden me with the knowledge of all the underlying mechanics? I did so because, as with all software systems, if we have a firm handle on the mechanics and resulting nuances, we can get the best user experience from the software system.

Now that we understand how data is organized in the Lakehouse (and hence Databricks SQL), we are ready to start exploring. Let's start by looking at the visual exploration tool in the Databricks SQL platform – **Data Explorer**.

Exploring data visually with the Data Catalog

Data Explorer is a feature of Databricks SQL that allows users to visually navigate and explore the data assets that are available in the data catalog.

As we saw in *Chapter 2, The Databricks Product Suite – A Visual Tour*, we can navigate to Data Explorer by clicking the **Data** icon, 🔲, on the left-hand sidebar.

Data Explorer requires a running SQL Warehouse to be associated with it to be able to display the data catalog. If the associated SQL Warehouse is not running, it will prompt you to start the Warehouse or associate the explorer with a SQL Warehouse that is running.

> **Note**
>
> If you are using Unity Catalog, then a running SQL Warehouse is not required.

The SQL Warehouse association can be controlled using the dropdown highlighted in the following screenshot:

Figure 3.5 – Associating a SQL Warehouse with Data Explorer

At this point, you can create a new SQL Warehouse or use the default out-of-the-box SQL Warehouse as the associated SQL Warehouse. Start the SQL Warehouse if it is not already running.

In *Chapter 2*, *The Databricks Product Suite – A Visual Tour*, we briefly saw the `samples` catalog and the databases and tables present in it. In this chapter, we will create our own database, tables, views, and functions.

We will use the `people` dataset, which comes bundled with Databricks, to do the following:

1. Create a database named `people_db`.
2. Create a table named `people`.
3. Create a view named `gender_distribution`.
4. Create a function named `full_name`.

The following minimal starter SQL code builds the preceding process for us:

```sql
--CREATE DATABASE
CREATE DATABASE people_db;


--CREATE TABLE
CREATE TABLE people_db.people OPTIONS (PATH 'dbfs:/databricks-datasets/learning-spark-v2/people/people-10m.delta');


--CREATE VIEW
CREATE VIEW people_db.gender_distribution AS SELECT gender,
count(*) AS count FROM people_db.people GROUP BY gender;


--CREATE FUNCTION
CREATE FUNCTION people_db.full_name(
  firstName STRING,
  middleName STRING,
  lastName STRING
) RETURNS STRING RETURN concat(firstName, ' ', middleName, ' ',
lastName);
```

> **A Note on Creativity**
>
> Feel free to be creative when naming the data objects and even with the definition of views and functions. The preceding SQL snippet is a minimal starter and, let's be honest, not very creative. However, it serves the purpose of creating data assets that will allow us to learn about Data Explorer, which is the true focus of this chapter.

Data Explorer consists of two view panes. The left-hand view pane contains the navigation controls. Let's call it the *navigation pane*. The right-hand view pane is dynamic and shows content based on the data asset that we have navigated to. Let's call it the details pane. For example, if we have navigated up to a database, the details pane will populate information about the database. Then, if we navigate to a table or a view in the database, the details pane will populate information about the table or the view.

So, let's begin our navigation and exploration, starting with Tier 1, the **catalog**.

Navigating the catalogs

In the navigation pane, click on the catalog blade, which is denoted by the ⊟ icon. This will open a dropdown showing the available catalogs. Since we looked at the `samples` catalog in *Chapter 2, The Databricks Product Suite – A Visual Tour*, let's select the `hive_metastore` catalog. The `hive_metastore` catalog comes with a default database, creatively named `default`:

Data Explorer

Data   ︿

>   ⊟ hive_metastore

>   ⊟ samples

Figure 3.6 – Navigating the available catalogs

The preceding screenshot shows the currently available catalogs.

Navigating the databases

Once we have selected (or decided upon) a catalog to explore, the databases, denoted by the ⊟ icon, will populate the databases available in this catalog. If we select the `samples` catalog, we will see the available databases/schemas:

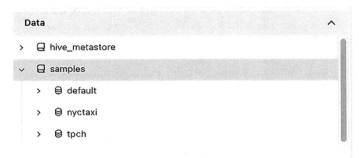

Figure 3.7 – Navigating the databases in a catalog

Selecting a database will do two things:

- The details pane will populate the details about the selected database.
- The navigation pane will populate the list of tables and views available in the database.

The following screenshot shows how the details pane gets populated when we select the `people_db` database:

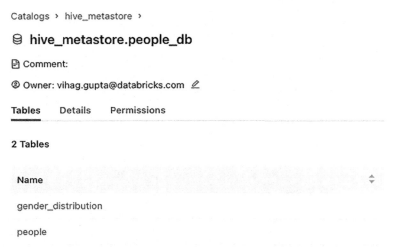

Figure 3.8 – Exploring a database – database details

Click on the **Permissions** tab, as shown in the following screenshot, to see the permissions associated with the database:

Figure 3.9 – Exploring a database – database permissions

Exploring databases

When we navigate to a database, the details pane shows the following four items:

- **Owner** (⊛): This lists the owner of the database (if any). The owner has full privileges on the database and has the power to grant or revoke privileges on the database for other users. See *Figure 3.8*.

- **Comment** (▤): This is a metadata field and contains free-form text describing the database. See *Figure 3.8*. In our example, it is empty. We can modify our CREATE DATABASE statement (https://docs.databricks.com/sql/language-manual/index.html#ddl-statements) so that it includes a comment.

- The **Details** tab: In *Figure 3.8*, the **Details** tab, which can be found in the details pane, shows two things:

- **Location**: The location of the database on cloud storage. If you are using Unity Catalog, a location will only be displayed if the table is external.

- **Properties**: Any additional properties that were set with the CREATE DATABASE statement.

- The **Permissions** tab: The **Permissions** tab, which can be found in the details pane, shows all the principals (users, groups, and service principals) that have any explicit or inherited privilege on the database. We will discuss principals, privileges, and the Databricks security model in depth in *Chapter 4, The Security Model*. The **Permissions** tab is shown in *Figure 3.9*.

> **Note**
>
> *Editable Fields*: The preceding screenshots show the possibility of editing owners and permissions using the UI. We will cover these from a database administrator's perspective in *Chapter 4, The Security Model*, where we will discuss the security and governance of these assets. This section is all about exploring, not governing, the data assets.
>
> *Permissions*: I have kept the **Permissions** tab empty on purpose. My reasoning behind not showing samples of permissions is to avoid introducing new terms that can potentially derail the learning objective of this chapter. That said, we will circle back to these tabs and complete the picture in *Chapter 4, The Security Model*.

Exploring tables

Once you navigate to a database, the navigation pane lists all the available tables and views.

First, let's click on the `people` table. The details pane should now populate with the following view:

Figure 3.10 – Exploring a table – basic details and schema

As we can see, we get the following nine pieces of information:

- **Data Format**: The **Delta** symbol next to the table's name in the Details pane specifies that this table is a Delta table and that the underlying data files are in Delta format.

- **Comment** (📄): This is a metadata field and contains free-form text describing the table. In our example, it is empty. We can modify our `CREATE TABLE` statement so that it includes a comment.

- **Owner** (👤): This lists the owner of the table (if any). The owner has full privileges on the table and has the power to grant or revoke privileges on the table for other users.

- **Size** (#): This lists the total size of the data (that is, the underlying files) and the total number of files across which the data is spread.

- The **Schema** tab: This tab shows the schema of the table – that is, the various available columns, their data types, and any metadata comments for each column.

- The **Sample Data** tab: This tab shows a sample of the dataset. This is very a very helpful feature to quickly get a feel of the data in the table without running any commands. See *Figure 3.11*.

- The **Details** tab: As seen in *Figure 3.12*, the **Details** tab shows three things:

  - **Location**: The location of the database on cloud storage.

  - **Type**: The type of the table. It could be **Managed** or **Unmanaged**. See the *Do I always need a location?* note in the preceding section for a discussion on managed versus unmanaged tables. Here, we can see that the type is **EXTERNAL**, which implies it's an unmanaged table.

  - **Table Properties**: This indicates any additional properties that were set with the CREATE TABLE statement.

- The **Permissions** tab: As seen in *Figure 3.13*, the **Permissions** tab shows all the principals (users or groups) who have any explicit or inherited privilege on the database. We will discuss principals, privileges, and the Databricks security model in depth in *Chapter 4, The Security Model*.

- The **History** tab: See *Figure 3.14*. The **History** tab shows a history of transactions on the table. For every transaction, you will be able to see very granular details. For end users, **Data Version** is the most pertinent column. Users can query the data as of a particular version or time. The rest of the columns facilitate audit and governance on the table. The following are the most important ones to keep in mind:

  - **Version** and **Timestamp**: These two columns uniquely identify every transaction. They can be used to query the snapshot of the data as it existed at that version or timestamp.

  - **User Id** and **Username**: These two columns identify the user who performed this transaction. This is very helpful for audit use cases.

  - **Operation**: This identifies the type of operation.

  - **Job**, **Notebook**, and **Cluster ID**: These identify whether the transaction originated from a scheduled job or workflow (https://docs.databricks.com/data-engineering/jobs/jobs.html) and, if so, the code/notebook that committed the transaction, as well as the cluster that the transaction was executed on.

  - **Operation Metrics**: This provides useful statistics, such as the number of output rows.

Let's look at some screenshots to visualize what we've just discussed. The following screenshot shows a section of the **Sample Data** tab for the `people` table:

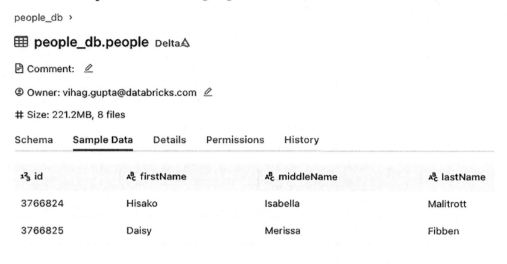

Figure 3.11 – Exploring a table – the Sample Data tab

The following screenshot shows the **Details** tab for the same table:

Figure 3.12 – Exploring a table – the Details tab

The following screenshot shows the **Permissions** tab for the same table:

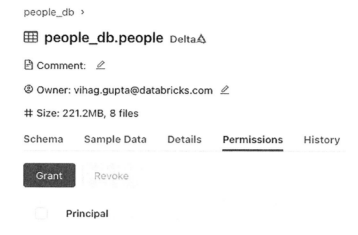

Figure 3.13 – Exploring a table – the Permissions tab

The following screenshot shows a section of the **History** tab for the same table:

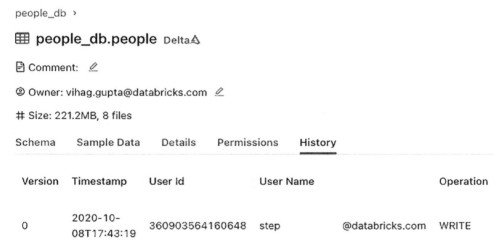

Figure 3.14 – Exploring a table – the History tab

Note on the Rest of the History Details

The **History** tab of the table shows a lot of additional information about the DeltaLake transaction. It is not very relevant to the current discussion, so you should not be concerned about this. However, if you want, you can read more about it here: `https://github.com/delta-io/delta/blob/master/PROTOCOL.md`.

Exploring views

Views are listed along with tables in the navigation pane. To distinguish between tables and views, views are depicted with the **Sunglasses** icon: 👓.

The **Details** tab for views is the same as that for tables. Hence, for the sake of brevity, we will only mention the notable differences here:

- **Size** (#): At the time of writing, Databricks SQL does not support materialized views (https://en.wikipedia.org/wiki/Materialized_view). Hence, views are just, well, views. Therefore, they do not have a computed size associated with them. You should see **Unknown** in the **size** field.

- The **History** tab: Similar to the **Size** tab, since these are not materialized views, no transactions can be performed on them. Hence, the **History** tab will always be empty.

- The **Details** tab: This tab shows additional information about the view. The following important details are populated:

  - Created Time

  - Last Access

  - View Text: The underlying SQL query

  - View Query Output Columns

> **Note on the Rest of the View Details**
>
> The **Details** tab for the view shows a lot of additional information about Apache Hive, such as serialization/deserialization libraries and their formats. I do not think they are very relevant to the current discussion, so you should not be concerned about this either. However, if you want, you can read more about them here: https://cwiki.apache.org/confluence/display/Hive/SerDe.

Exploring functions

At the time of writing, functions are not visible in Data Explorer. We will learn how to explore functions in the next section, where we'll learn how to explore the data catalog programmatically.

Exploring the data programmatically with SQL statements

Databricks SQL provides familiar SHOW and DESCRIBE commands that allow users to query the data catalog and discover the various databases, tables, views, and functions available to them. For a detailed SQL reference on the same, please see https://docs.databricks.com/sql/language-manual/index.html#auxiliary-statements.

Let's look at some examples of how we can use these commands to explore the data available to us. We will continue to use the people_db database we created in the preceding section on visual exploration (see *Figure 3.8*).

Broadly, we will use two groups of SQL statements:

- Show statements
- Describe statements

As we saw in *Chapter 2, The Databricks Product Suite – A Visual Tour*, we will use the SQL Editor to execute our queries. Navigate to the SQL Editor by clicking the **SQL Editor** icon, ▦. Associate your editor with a SQL Warehouse, as highlighted in the following screenshot:

Figure 3.15 – Associating a SQL Warehouse with the Query Editor

> **Note on the SQL Editor's Features**
>
> The SQL Editor will be covered in depth in *Chapter 5, The Workbench*. For this chapter, we only need to know how to execute a query.

The preceding screenshot also shows the familiar navigation pane on the left-hand side, which allows us to browse through the catalogs, databases, tables, and views.

On the right-hand side is the Query Editor. This is where we will type in our SQL code. The **Run** button in the top right-hand corner runs the SQL code in the Query Editor. Below the Query Editor is the results section.

We will begin navigating and exploring by looking at databases.

> **Note**
>
> If you are using Unity Catalog, you can also explore the catalogs that are available in your workspace by executing SHOW CATALOGS and DESCRIBE CATALOG.

Exploring the databases

The following SHOW statement lists all the databases that we have access to:

```
SHOW  DATABASES;
```

Executing the preceding command produces the following output:

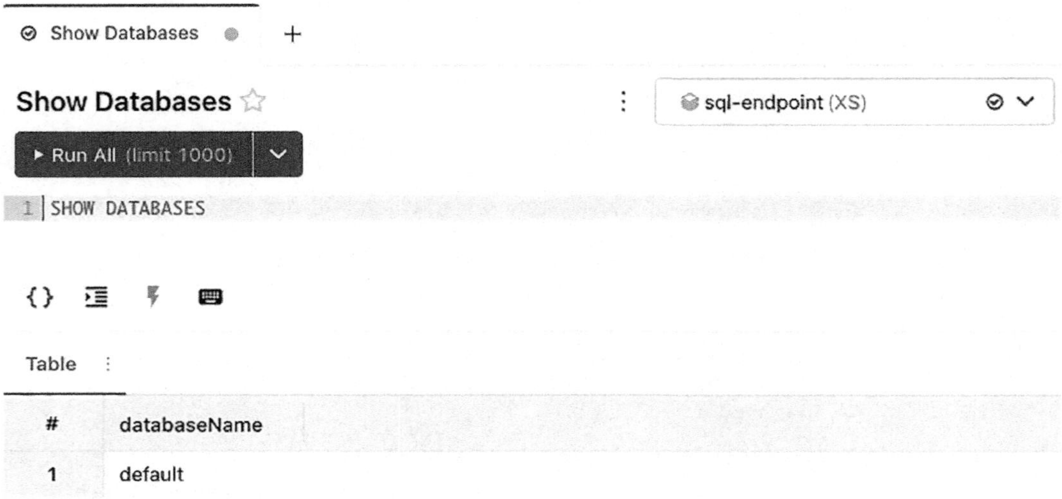

Figure 3.16 – Showing databases in the Data Catalog

As we can see, once the SQL statement has been keyed in, we can click the **Run** button. The query results are then returned. As we saw previously, here, the databases are listed in the results section.

To see the details about a database, we can run the DESCRIBE statement, like so:

```
DESCRIBE DATABASE EXTENDED people_db;
```

Executing the preceding command produces the following output:

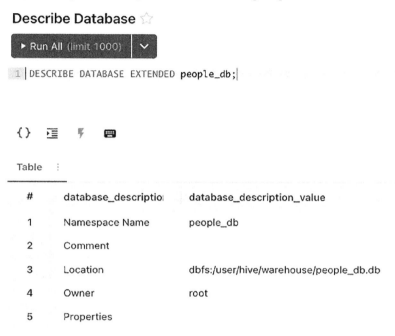

Figure 3.17 – Describing a database

As we can see, the results contain the following fields:

- **Namespace Name**
- **Comment**
- **Location**
- **Owner**
- **Properties**

These are the same description fields that we saw when visually exploring the data catalog in the preceding section.

> **A Note on the Owner Field**
>
> In Data Explorer, the **Owner** field shows the creator of the database as the owner. However, in the preceding screenshot, you will see that the owner is set to `root`. This is very likely due to some quirks of the underlying Apache Hive Metastore. In the Hive world, the owner is supposed to be the owner of the directory **Hadoop Distributed File System (HDFS)**. However, there is no direct equivalent of the owner on cloud storage systems. Hence, it defaults to `root`. This is one of the advantages of Unity Catalog. Unity Catalog comes bundled with table ownership and access control tracking.

The Data Explorer UI also shows the permissions associated with the database. We can achieve the same programmatically by running the SHOW GRANT statement, like so:

```
SHOW GRANT ON DATABASE people_db;
```

The preceding command produces the following output:

Figure 3.18 – Showing permissions on the database

As we can see, each row lists a privilege (**ActionType**), the recipient of the privilege (**Principal**), and the object upon which the privilege is granted (**ObjectType** and **ObjectKey**). This is the same information we get when using Data Explorer.

Exploring tables

We can list all the tables available in a database using the SHOW statement, like so:

```
SHOW TABLES IN people_db;
```

The preceding command produces the following output:

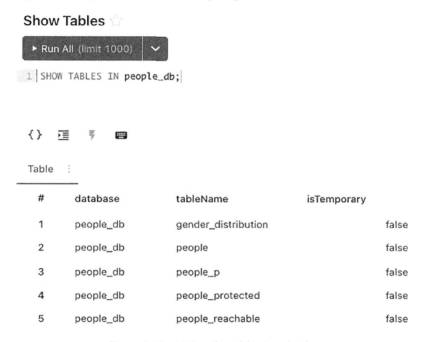

Figure 3.19 – Listing the tables in a database

As we can see, the aforementioned command returns the available tables in the **tableName** column.

> **Note**
> If you have been following this example carefully, you will notice that the gender_
> distribution view is also listed as a table in this example. Views are only treated as tables
> in Apache Hive Metastore.

To retrieve the details about a table, we can run the DESCRIBE statement, like so:

```
DESCRIBE TABLE EXTENDED people_db.people;
```

The preceding command produces the following output:

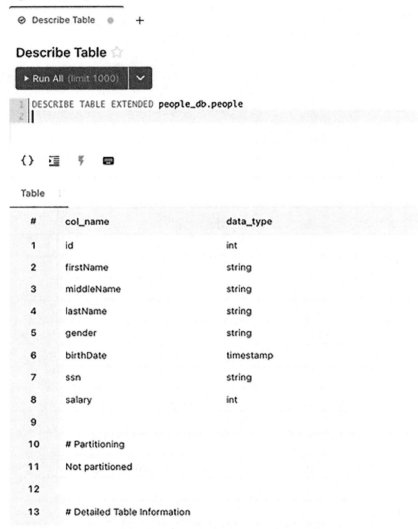

Figure 3.20 – Retrieving details about a table

Here, we can see that the results are divided into three sections (each separated by a blank row):

- Section 1: This is equivalent to the **Schema** tab in the Data Explorer UI. It provides the schema of the table.

- Section 2: This is the partitioning section. This relates to the underlying directory and file structure. If the data is divided into folders based on a field, such as birthDate, then that field becomes a partition column. The partition column is used by Query Engine to smartly read only the required data files. We will cover this in detail in *Chapter 8, The Delta Lake*. Our table does not have any partitions.

- Section 3: This is equivalent to the **Details** tab in the Data Explorer UI.

The Data Explorer UI also shows the permissions associated with the table. We can achieve the same programmatically by running the SHOW GRANT statement, like so:

```
SHOW GRANT ON TABLE people_db.people;
```

The preceding command produces the following output:

Figure 3.21 – Showing permissions on the table

The Data Explorer UI also shows the **History** tab, which displays all the transactions that have been committed on the table. We can achieve the same programmatically by running a DESCRIBE statement, like so:

```
DESCRIBE HISTORY people_db.people;
```

The preceding command produces the following output:

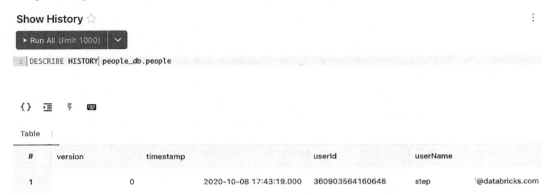

Figure 3.22 – Showing the transaction history of the table

Exploring views

The methods of exploring views are the same as they are for tables. Hence, for the sake of brevity, we will just list the SQL commands here. You are encouraged to run them in your workspace and observe the results.

We can list the views that are available in a database by executing the following SHOW statement:

```
SHOW VIEWS IN people_db;
```

To retrieve details about a view, we can run the following DESCRIBE statement:

```
DESCRIBE TABLE EXTENDED people_db.gender_distribution;
```

Note that we are using the DESCRIBE TABLE statement to describe the view. This is because the DESCRIBE statement does not accept the VIEW keyword and, as you may recall, views are treated as equivalents of tables in Apache Hive Metastore.

To retrieve the permissions on a view, execute the SHOW GRANTS statement:

```
SHOW GRANTS ON people_db.gender_distribution;
```

Unlike tables, views do not support writes, which is they do not have an associated history.

Exploring functions

Functions can only be explored programmatically.

There are two categories of functions in Databricks SQL:

- System functions
- User-defined functions

To list all the available system functions, execute the following SHOW statement:

```
SHOW SYSTEM FUNCTIONS;
```

Databricks SQL supports a lot of functions. You should refer to the official documentation (https://docs.microsoft.com/en-us/azure/databricks/sql/language-manual/) for a comprehensive list of functions.

To list all the available functions in a database, execute the following SHOW statement:

```
USE people_db;
SHOW USER FUNCTIONS;
```

The preceding code produces the following output:

Figure 3.23 – Showing the available user-defined functions

To get details about the function, we can execute the following DESCRIBE statement:

```
DESCRIBE FUNCTION people_db.full_name;
```

The preceding code produces the following output:

Figure 3.24 – Details of a function

As we can see, the details are not pretty printed, but they get the job done. We can quickly get the signature of the function with the **Input** and **Output** sections of the results.

Finally, we can get the permissions on the function by executing the following SHOW GRANTS statement:

```
SHOW GRANTS ON FUNCTION people_db.full_name;
```

Programmatic Access from Code

At this point, if you are a developer, you might be wondering whether you can execute these commands from your code in Java or Python, for example. Or, if you are an analyst with a preference for a specific tool, you might be wondering whether you are bound to using the workbench that Databricks SQL provides. The answer is that you can use any tool you want. We will cover access from external tools in *Chapter 7, Using Business Intelligence Tools with Databricks SQL*.

Summary

In this action-packed chapter, we learned how data assets are arranged in the data catalog with the data organization model. After that, we learned how to explore and discover the data assets in the data catalog with the Data Explorer UI. Finally, we learned how to explore and discover the data assets in the data catalog with standard (and familiar) SHOW and DESCRIBE statements.

In the next chapter, we will continue looking at the data catalog. However, this time, we will put on the lens of a database administrator, who is responsible for the governance and security of the data assets.

4

The Security Model

In *Chapter 3, The Data Catalog*, we saw how the data catalog is the portal to the data layer of the Lakehouse. It exposes the various catalogs, databases, and tables to the end user for their consumption. This raises an important question of how to secure these data assets.

The data catalog represents all the data of your organization and it should be protected with the relevant and necessary controls. Securing and governing data assets in a data lake is a significant undertaking. Furthermore, uniform access control must be applied to all the data assets for reasons such as auditability and scalability. Typically, the **database administrators** (**DBAs**) are responsible for implementing the controls for the security and governance of the data assets.

However, as we discussed in *Chapter 3, The Data Catalog*, unlike traditional databases and data warehouses, the DBAs will have to consider that the tables in a data lake are abstractions over files in cloud object storage. This means they must ensure that while access control is programmed on these tables, these access controls are translated to the underlying cloud object storage access.

This chapter will introduce the data security model of Databricks SQL. We will discuss how the security model accounts for both user-facing table access control and cloud object storage. We will also discuss the mechanisms to program it for all current and future data assets at scale and with simplicity.

In this chapter, we will cover the following topics:

- The Databricks SQL security model
- User-facing table access control
- The internals of cloud storage access

Technical requirements

To follow this chapter effectively, ensure that you have the following:

- A Databricks workspace. Databricks SQL requires a premium or higher subscription level.
- A basic understanding of standard SQL statements for data access control, such as GRANT, DENY, and REVOKE.
- A fundamental understanding of cloud object storage, cloud **Identity and Access Management** (**IAM**), and the data lake architecture.
- Enough VM/EC2 quotas for creating a SQL Warehouse.

The Databricks SQL security model

The Databricks SQL security model is based on the well-established security model in SQL databases, which allows you to set fine-grained access permissions using standard SQL statements such as GRANT and REVOKE.

In *Chapter 3*, *The Data Catalog*, in the *Understanding the data organization model in Databricks SQL* section (see *Figure 3.1*), we established the existence of the following data assets:

- Catalog
- Databases
- Tables
- Views
- Functions (named and anonymous)
- Any files (that is, the underlying files of a table)

These are the **securable objects** in the data catalog.

In *Chapter 3*, *The Data Catalog*, we also learned that we have a choice of two data cataloging technologies:

- Apache Hive Metastore (current default)
- Unity Catalog (future default)

Regardless of the catalog that you use, from a usage perspective, the security model and the means to program it remain the same. The difference lies in the internals of how each technology implements the security model. We will discuss the differences in this chapter. That said, keep in mind that while the underlying implementation is different, the effects and commands are the same.

The data catalog is responsible for storing the table **access control lists (ACLs)** – that is, the programmed permissions for users on various securable objects.

Let's revisit our diagram of *The execution model of a query* from *Figure 3.4* and see how the two cataloging technologies handle ACL information.

Access control with Apache Hive Metastore

The following diagram shows the execution of a query when Apache Hive Metastore is used. We will discuss the steps shortly. For now, let's take note of the authorization flow:

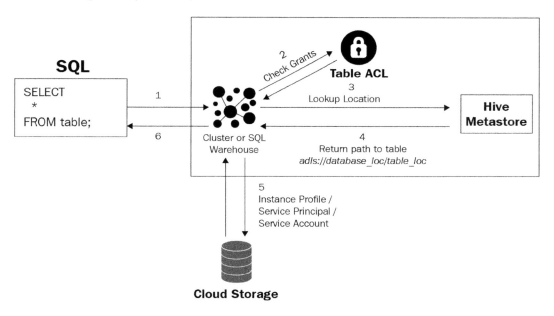

Figure 4.1 – The execution model of a query with Hive Metastore

Apache Hive Metastore is only a data catalog. It does not have any built-in authorization mechanisms for either the tables or the underlying data storage locations. It depends on auxiliary systems to enable authentication and authorization. Databricks provides a separate table ACL store that complements Apache Hive Metastore and contains the programmed ACLs.

In *Chapter 3, The Data Catalog*, we also discussed how the table ACLs and the instance of Apache Hive Metastore are unique to each Databricks SQL workspace. This means the ACLs must be programmed anew for every workspace.

Finally, Hive Metastore does not have objects representing cloud storage paths and cloud storage credentials such as IAM profiles or service principals. Hence, you must separately program direct user access to the cloud storage using the cloud's respective IAM controls. This scenario is less likely for the users of Databricks SQL, but still possible. For example, if someone requests an external table on a cloud storage location, your cloud IAM team may have denied the user access to that location, so you permit them to access it via the external table. Hence, you must keep in sync with the cloud IAM team at all times.

Access control with Unity Catalog

The following diagram shows the execution of a query when Unity Catalog is used. We will discuss the steps shortly. For now, let's take note of the authorization flow:

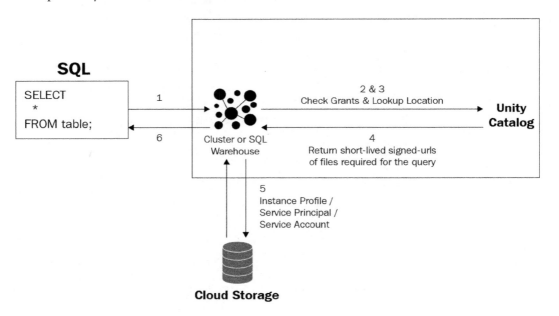

Figure 4.2 – The execution model of a query with Unity Catalog

Unity Catalog contains the table ACLs within itself, along with the metadata about the securable objects.

In *Chapter 3, The Data Catalog*, we learned how Unity Catalog allows you to create multiple Metastores. These can be assigned to one or more workspaces, allowing different projects or business units to access the same data catalog. This also means that the ACLs are carried over seamlessly into the workspace that the Metastore has been assigned to, so there is no need to reprogram the ACLs in every workspace.

Finally, Unity Catalog also contains objects that represent cloud storage locations and cloud storage credentials. Hence, Unity Catalog allows you to program access to cloud storage locations with familiar security statements such as GRANT, DENY, and REVOKE instead of cloud-specific IAM implementations.

Query execution model

Irrespective of the data cataloging technology, you will notice that there are two distinct authorization events:

- The access control on catalogs and objects in the catalog such as databases, tables, and views. This access control is user-facing – that is, it will affect the user's permissions to interact with data assets (*Steps 2* and *3* in *Figure 4.1* and *Figure 4.2*).

- The SQL Warehouse uses its authorization on the physical data locations on the cloud storage to fetch the data files and serve the query (*Step 5* in *Figure 4.1* and *Figure 4.2*). The authorization that's given to SQL to access the physical data locations on the cloud storage is a one-time administrative step. We will learn more about it in the *The internals of cloud storage access* section.

Let's look at how authorization happens within the overall query execution flow:

1. The user submits a query in Databricks SQL.

2. The query engine consults the ACLs to confirm whether the user has the necessary privileges to access the table or view referred to in the user query:

    - If the privileges are insufficient, the query is blocked.

    - The query attempt is audit-logged.

3. The query engine transparently queries the Metastore for the location of the objects referred to in the user query.

4. The Metastore returns the locations of the data that need to be read for the query submitted by the user:

    - Hive Metastore will return the paths of the data files on the cloud object storage.

    - Unity Catalog will return signed URLs for the data files on the cloud object storage. A signed URL is a URL to the data file that comes bundled with short-lived authorization to perform some action, such as GET, on the file referred to by the URL.

5.   The query engine reads the data at the locations returned by the Metastore in *Step 4*, performs the computations in the query, and obtains the results:

- With Hive Metastore, the query engine transparently authenticates itself to the cloud IAM system and accesses the data at the location using the configured authorization. For Azure, this is done via Active Directory service principals. For AWS, it will be via instance profiles. For GCP, it will be via service accounts.

- With Unity Catalog, the short-lived signed URLs will be used.

6.   The results are returned to the user.

The DBAs only need to configure the privileges to the objects for users or groups of users with the GRANT, DENY, and REVOKE statements. The complexity of translating the table abstraction into cloud object storage and authenticating the cloud object storage access is handled transparently by the Databricks SQL system during query execution. The following diagram should clarify this further:

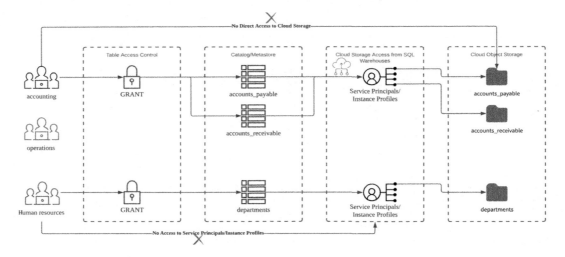

Figure 4.3 – User-facing table access control versus cloud storage access with Hive Metastore

As we can see, the table access control uses the standard database security statement, GRANT, to permit users to operate on data assets such as tables. Similarly, standard database security statements such as REVOKE and DENY (not mentioned in the preceding diagram) can be used to prevent access.

When a user submits a query, the permissions are checked to confirm whether the user is privileged to perform the operations specified in the query, upon the tables specified in the query. If the check goes through, Databricks SQL will use the appropriate means to read the data files of the table – signed URLs with Unity Catalog and a service principal/instance profile/service account with Hive Metastore. This step is transparent to the end user. If the end user is authorized to use the table in the way they have requested, the request will go through; otherwise, they will receive an error in line with GRANT – for example, "*The user does not have* READ *privileges on table departments.*" They will not be burdened with the knowledge of the underlying cloud object permissions.

User-facing table access control

Diving further into the security model, let's discuss table access control. In essence, table access control requires programming a user's privileges to perform operations on a data object/asset. The owners of data objects or administrators will implement this programming with standard database security statements.

First, we will discuss users, objects, operations, and privileges. Then, we will bring them all together and see how we can program them with user-facing table access control.

Users, groups, and service principals

Databricks SQL inherits users and groups from the Databricks Lakehouse platform. Users and groups can be managed from the **Admin Console** area of the Databricks platform.

Note to Administrators

At the time of writing, user and group management is only available from the Data Science & Engineering and the Machine Learning persona experiences.

If you are using Unity Catalog, you should create account-level identities so that the ACLs can be programmed once and carried into different workspaces automatically. See https://docs. databricks.com/data-governance/unity-catalog/manage-identities. html for more information.

A full discussion of user and group management is outside the scope of this book. We will only explore the parts that are relevant to the discussion at hand. Please see the official documentation at https://docs.databricks.com/administration-guide/users-groups/ for detailed user and group administration.

The first thing we must ensure is that the user or user group has the necessary **entitlement** to access Databricks SQL.

An entitlement is a property that allows a user, service principal, or group to interact with Databricks in a specified way. We must select the **Databricks SQL access** entitlement for the user or group.

To provide a user with access to Databricks SQL, go to **Admin Console | Users** and select the **Databricks SQL access** entitlement, as shown in the following screenshot:

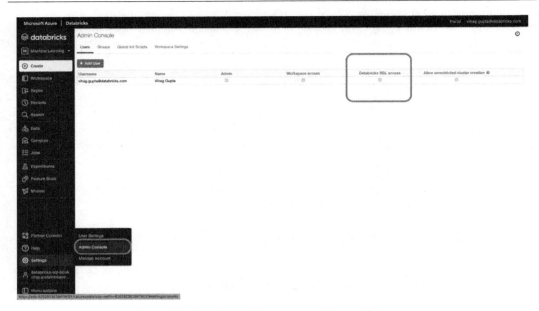

Figure 4.4 – Databricks SQL access entitlement for a user

To provide a user group with access to Databricks SQL, go to **Admin Console | Groups** and select the **Databricks SQL access** entitlement, as shown in the following screenshot:

Figure 4.5 – Databricks SQL access entitlement for a user group

> **Note on Service Principals**
>
> There is a special type of user in Databricks called the **service principal**. The service principal is an API-only identity and is used for executing automated tools, jobs, and applications. This avoids binding a production job to an actual user. You can read more about them in the official documentation at `https://docs.databricks.com/administration-guide/users-groups/service-principals.html`. At the time of writing, the service principal user cannot execute queries on Databricks SQL. It is only used for management APIs. Hence, this user type is not relevant to the discussion at hand.

Securable objects

The second concept is the data objects that users will access. These data objects can be anything in the data catalog. The following list enumerates the available data objects, along with their place in the hierarchy:

- Catalog:
  - Database:
    - Table
    - View
    - Function (named)
- Anonymous function: These are user-defined functions and temporary session-specific functions programmed in Scala, Java, or Python. At the time of writing, they are not supported in Databricks SQL.
- Any file: This is a special data object that represents direct access to the underlying cloud object storage. This allows access to the data files directly if such access is required.
- External location (Unity Catalog only).
- Storage credential (Unity Catalog only).

If you need a refresher, revisit the *Understanding the data organization model in Databricks SQL* section of *Chapter 3*, *The Data Catalog*, for more details on the various objects and the relevant hierarchy.

These are the objects that users (introduced in the *Users, groups, and service principals* section) will access, so they must be secured with access control and governance. Hence, we call all of them **securable objects**.

We can define securable objects as all the elements in the data catalog that must be protected and governed. In effect, securable objects are the data catalogs, and the data objects within those catalogs must be secured by the table access control system.

Operations

Users can execute operations on securable objects. There are different varieties, as follows :

- **Data Definition Language (DDL)** statements such as CREATE, DROP, ALTER, COMMENT, and TRUNCATE

- **Data Manipulation Language (DML)** statements such as INSERT, UPDATE, DELETE, and MERGE

- Data retrieval statements such as SELECT

- Auxiliary statements such as SHOW, DESCRIBE, ANALYZE, and EXPLAIN

- Security statements such as GRANT, REVOKE, and DENY

> **Note**
>
> Refer to the official documentation to learn more about individual commands: https://docs.databricks.com/sql/language-manual/ for details.

Privileges

To be able to execute operations on securable objects, users require the necessary **privileges**. The following is a list of available privileges:

- ALL_PRIVILEGES: A blanket privilege that gives the recipient all the privileges in this list in one go.

- USAGE: This is a catalog/database-level privilege that is a must-have requirement for a user or group to be able to make use of any other privilege discussed in this list:

  - If a user is an admin or the owner of a catalog/database either directly or via a group, then the user has USAGE privileges.

  - For any other case, USAGE privileges must be explicitly granted. For example, to create a table, users should either own the database or have USAGE and CREATE privileges on the database.

- SELECT: The ability to have read access to a data object:

  - Supported on databases, tables, views, and named functions.

  - If you are using Unity Catalog, SELECT does not apply to catalogs and databases. SELECT must be applied at the table level.

- CREATE: The ability to create a data object:

  - **Supported on a catalog object**: This allows you to create a database in the catalog.

  - **Supported on a database object**: This allows you to create tables, views, and functions in the database.

- MODIFY: The ability to add data to an object, delete data from an object, and modify data in an object. This allows standard commands such as INSERT, DELETE, UPDATE, MERGE, and TRUNCATE. It also allows Delta Lake commands such as RESTORE, OPTIMIZE, VACUUM, and REPAIR:

  - Supported in catalogs, databases, tables, and views. However, the MODIFY privilege is very specific to data manipulation, which is why it's only effective on the table object.

  - If you are using Unity Catalog, MODIFY does not apply to catalogs and schemas.

- READ_METADATA: The ability to view an object's metadata. This allows you to execute commands to EXPLAIN a query or DESCRIBE a database, table, or function:

  - Supported on databases, tables, views, and functions.

  - If you are using Unity Catalog, READ_METADATA is not required

- MODIFY_CLASSPATH: The ability to add files to the Spark classpath. This allows you to create user-defined functions from a resource file such as a **JAR** file that your team will build. Since the resource needs to be loaded into the execution classpath, the MODIFY_CLASSPATH privilege is required:

  - Supported on the catalog object only

- READ FILES, WRITE FILES, and CREATE TABLE: The ability to read files, write files or create external tables on a cloud storage location. These are specific to Unity Catalog and are supported on external location and storage credential objects. We will learn about them in the *Going beyond read access – part 1* section.

Bringing everything together

Now, let's tie the four concepts that we just learned about together to achieve a coherent access control on the data in Lakehouse while following the principle of least privilege.

Users and groups must be provided with only the **privileges** on **securable objects** that are required by them to execute **operations** concerning their daily workflow.

Assigning privileges to data objects can be done by two people:

- A Databricks workspace administrator
- The owner of the object

Object ownership can be achieved in three ways:

- By creating the object – that is, the database, table, view, or function. Here, the user becomes the owner of the object.
- The Databricks workspace administrator or owner transfers ownership of the data object to the user or user group. Databricks recommends assigning ownership to groups rather than users as a best practice.
- The user is a part of a group that has received ownership of the object.

An object owner (or administrator) can assign privileges with the help of the following operations:

- GRANT: Grants a privilege on an object to a principal (user or group)
- DENY: Ensures that the principal *cannot* access the specified object, irrespective of implicit or explicit GRANTs
- REVOKE: Rolls back an explicit GRANT or DENY on an object for the principal
- SHOW GRANT: Displays all inherited, denied, and granted privileges on the object

The rules of privilege inheritance should also be kept in mind:

- With table access control on Hive Metastore, GRANTs and DENYs are cascaded to child objects – that is, GRANT or DENY on CATALOG is propagated to all databases and all objects within the database – tables, views, and functions. A GRANT or DENY on a database is propagated to all the objects within the database. This cascade is not applicable in Unity Catalog.
- REVOKE is not cascaded. It is strictly scoped to the object specified in the command.
- An explicit DENY on an object overrules inherited GRANTs. For example, consider that a user has been granted the SELECT privilege on a database and an explicit DENY on a table in this database. If the user lists all the tables in the database, the table that has been denied to the user will not be shown in the listing. This behavior is true for all securable objects. DENY is not applicable in Unity Catalog as we learnt that Unity Catalog does not support cascading/inheriting permissions.
- A GRANT, DENY, or REVOKE applies to one object at a time. The first two cascading rules can be used to propagate privileges to multiple objects in one go.

At this point, you might be overwhelmed with the theoretical brain dump. So, let's log in to our Databricks SQL workspace and try out these concepts with some practical examples.

> **Note on Unity Catalog**
> The examples in the following sections have been built using Hive Metastore since Unity Catalog is in preview at the time of writing. I will call out any applicable differences as we go.

The security model in practice

In the spirit of novelty and exploration, let's create new data assets based on the `airlines` dataset that comes bundled with Databricks.

Use the following SQL code snippets to create the data assets to work with in this chapter:

1. Create the database. If you are using Unity Catalog, consider adding the catalog's name. Otherwise, the database will be created in the default catalog:

```
CREATE DATABASE airlines;
```

2. Set `airlines` as the default database:

```
USE airlines;
```

3. Create an external table on the source `planes` data, which is in CSV format:

```
CREATE TABLE planes_csv
USING csv
OPTIONS(
  path '/databricks-datasets/asa/planes/',
  header true,
  inferSchema true
);
```

4. Create a managed delta table using the source `planes` data for better performance:

```
CREATE TABLE planes USING DELTA AS SELECT * FROM planes_csv;
```

5. Create an unmanaged table on the source `flights` data, which is in CSV format:

```
CREATE TABLE flights_csv
USING csv
OPTIONS(
  path '/databricks-datasets/asa/airlines/',
  header true,
```

```
    inferSchema true
);
```

6. Create a managed delta table using the source flights data for better performance:

```
CREATE TABLE flights USING DELTA AS SELECT * FROM flights_csv;
```

7. Create a view that shows valid planes records:

```
CREATE VIEW airlines.clean_planes_data
AS
SELECT * FROM airlines.planes
WHERE model IS NOT NULL AND year IS NOT NULL;
```

8. Create a function that creates date strings from individual columns:

```
CREATE FUNCTION airlines.create_date_string(year_num INT,
month_num INT, day_num INT) RETURNS STRING RETURN concat(year_
num, '-', month_num, '-', day_num);
```

In the preceding code snippet, we are creating a tables abstraction over the source data, which is in CSV format. These are the planes_csv and flights_csv tables, respectively.

We are using these tables to create our final tables, which are managed and are in delta format. These are the planes and flights tables, respectively.

For our examples, we want our users to interact with the planes and flights tables only.

We will create two other data assets:

- A view called clean_planes_data on the planes table that filters our rows. These contain null values for important fields such as model and year.

- A function called create_date_string that combines individual columns for year, month, and day into a string in yyyy-MM-dd format.

We will need one more user in our account. We will use this user as the guinea pig for our experiments with the security model. In my account, I have a user with an email ID of suteja@dbsql.com.

> **Note**
>
> In our examples, we are showing the programming of the security model on a user. In real life, Databrick's best practices recommend programming the security model at the group level.

Now, we are ready to work with the security model on our airlines database.

Ownership

We are the owners of the `airlines` database and the data assets within it on account of having created the `airlines` database and the data assets within it.

We can verify this ownership via Data Explorer:

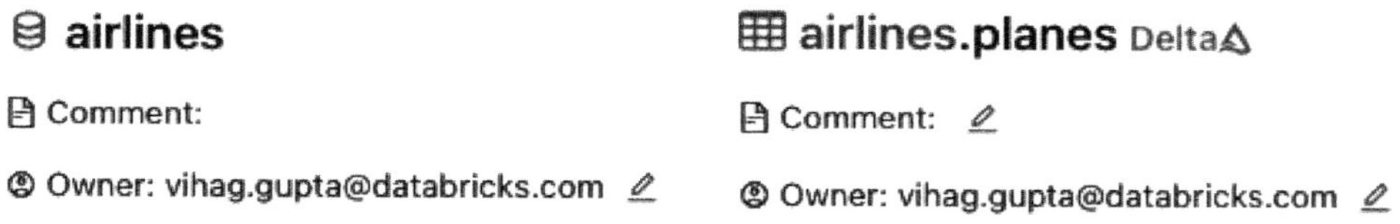

🗄 airlines

📄 Comment:

⊕ Owner: vihag.gupta@databricks.com ✎

⊞ airlines.planes Delta△

📄 Comment: ✎

⊕ Owner: vihag.gupta@databricks.com ✎

Figure 4.6 – Verifying ownership privilege via the UI

We can also verify the ownership of the database with the following SHOW GRANTS statement:

```
SHOW GRANTS ON DATABASE airlines;
```

The preceding code will return the following output:

Principal	ActionType	ObjectType	ObjectKey
vihag.gupta@databricks.com	OWN	DATABASE	airlines

Figure 4.7 – Verifying database ownership privilege via SQL

Similarly, the ownership of the table can be verified with the following SQL statement:

```
SHOW GRANTS ON TABLE airlines.planes;
```

The preceding code will return the following output:

Principal	ActionType	ObjectType	ObjectKey
vihag.gupta@databricks.com	OWN	TABLE	`airlines`.`planes`

Figure 4.8 – Verifying table ownership privilege via SQL

Sharing the database

With that, the database, the tables, views, and functions are ready. Let's see how we can share these data assets with our teammate, `suteja@dbsql.com,` so that she can query them.

As mentioned in the *Privileges* section, we have the SELECT privilege, which fits the bill here.

Let's grant Suteja the SELECT privilege on the airlines database by running the following statement:

```
GRANT SELECT ON DATABASE airlines to `suteja@dbsql.com`;
```

At this point, if Suteja tries to run the SHOW DATABASES statement, we would expect her to be able to see the airlines database in the result. However, this isn't the case.

If you go back to the *Privileges* section, you will find the USAGE privilege. The USAGE privilege on the database and the catalog is a must-have for any of the other privileges to take effect. So, we must add that privilege:

```
GRANT USAGE ON DATABASE airlines to `suteja@dbsql.com`;
```

Now, if Suteja runs the SHOW DATABASES statement, voila – the airlines database will show up!

Exploring the database

Now that Suteja has a working SELECT privilege on the airlines database, we must provide her with access to the tables and views within the database.

But how do we do this?

Again, recall the rules of privilege inheritance – all GRANTs are cascaded down. This means that Suteja should be able to list the tables and views in the database and be able to retrieve data from them, without us having to provide any further privileges.

> **Unity Catalog Difference**
>
> Privileges are not cascaded down in Unity Catalog! You must grant privileges explicitly. This makes Unity Catalog secure by default. This is a very important distinction from the table access control within Hive Metastore.

Let's try this out!

Let's say that Suteja runs the following statement:

```
SHOW TABLES IN airlines;
```

By doing this, she will see all the tables and views in the `airlines` database, as follows:

Table   :

database	tableName	isTemporary
airlines	clean_planes_data	false
airlines	flights	false
airlines	flights_csv	false
airlines	planes	false
airlines	planes_csv	false

Figure 4.9 – Listing (select) privilege is cascaded

Now, let's say she runs the following statement:

```
SELECT * FROM airlines.flights LIMIT 2;
```

She will be able to sample the `flights` data, as follows:

Table

Year	Month	DayofMonth	DayOfWeek	DepTime	CRSDepTime	ArrTime	CRSArrTime	UniqueCarrier
2,006	12	21	4	1155	1,200	1447	1,457	DL
2,006	12	21	4	1124	1,130	1350	1,359	DL

Figure 4.10 – Select (data) privilege is cascaded

So, how did this happen? We only provided the SELECT privilege on the database. How did this cascade work? To understand that, let's run the following SHOW GRANT:

```
SHOW GRANT ON TABLE airlines.flights;
```

You can choose any table or view that you like for the preceding SQL statement; the following result will be the same:

Table   ⋮

Principal	ActionType	ObjectType	ObjectKey
suteja ⌄⌄ l.com	SELECT	TABLE	`airlines`.`flights`
vihag.gupta@databricks.com	OWN	TABLE	`airlines`.`flights`
suteja ⌄⌄ .com	SELECT	DATABASE	airlines
suteja .com	USAGE	DATABASE	airlines

Figure 4.11 – Cascaded (inherited) privileges

Upon inspection, we can see the explicit GRANTs that we provided to Suteja – SELECT and USAGE (**ActionType**) on the airlines (**ObjectKey**) database (**ObjectType**).

We can also see that Suteja has inherited the SELECT privilege on the flights table, in the airlines database. This inheritance is underlined by the fact that **ObjectKey** provides a fully qualified asset name – that is, airlines.flights.

Also, you can see that, since we created the table, we are the default owners of the table – that is, we have the OWN privilege on the table.

Exploring asset metadata

Now that Suteja has her data access privilege sorted out, she wants to inspect the metadata of these data assets, such as tables and views. In particular, she wants to know more about the flights table.

So, she runs the following statement:

```
DESCRIBE EXTENDED airlines.flights;
```

She expects metadata details. However, what she gets is a nasty error:

Error running query

User does not have permission READ_METADATA on table `airlines`.`flights`.

Figure 4.12 – Lack of metadata privileges

This is because the Databricks SQL security model requires an explicit READ_METADATA privilege for users to be able to retrieve metadata about the asset.

> **Unity Catalog Difference**
>
> The READ_METADATA privilege is only applicable if you are using the table access control with Hive Metastore. It is not required if you are using Unity Catalog.

This can easily be resolved. We, as the owners of this table, can provide her with the privilege:

```
GRANT READ_METADATA ON TABLE airlines.flights to `suteja@dbsql.com`;
```

Now, if Suteja attempts to use DESCRIBE again, she will be presented with the required information:

Table   :

col_name	data_type	comment
Year	int	
Month	int	
DayofMonth	int	
DayOfWeek	int	
DepTime	string	
CRSDepTime	int	
ArrTime	string	
CRSArrTime	int	
UniqueCarrier	string	
FlightNum	int	
TailNum	string	
ActualElapsedTime	string	

Figure 4.13 – Metadata retrieval

> **Note**
>
> You might be tempted to just provide the READ_METADATA privilege on the airlines database and let it cascade. That won't be best practice, though – privileges should always be granted as specifically as possible to avoid data security breaches!

Revoking access

In our example scenario, Suteja has now been granted privileges to explore the tables and views available in our `airlines` database. Since she is working with the data assets, she comes to you with a question – what is the difference between the `flights` table and the `flights_csv` table?

Hearing this question, you remember that the `flights_csv` table is only supposed to be a staging table for internal use, and not to be exposed to end users such as Suteja.

Thankfully, we can run a REVOKE statement, like so:

```
REVOKE SELECT ON airlines.flights_csv FROM `suteja@dbsql.com`;
```

So, all done, right?

Not so fast! This is one of the important gotchas to understand. Suteja's SELECT privilege on the `flights_csv` table is inherited from her SELECT privilege on the `airlines` database. See the *Exploring the database* section to review the permissions given to Suteja. Hence, even though we can REVOKE the SELECT privilege, she will still be able to query data in the table.

> **Unity Catalog Difference**
> Since privileges are not cascaded in Unity Catalog, the preceding gotcha is not applicable if you are using Unity Catalog.

Try it out yourself!

This is in keeping with the **principle of least privilege**. We granted Suteja the SELECT privilege on the entire `airlines` database. What we should have done is give her SELECT access to the data assets that she is privileged to work with!

The following sequence of commands should do the trick:

```
REVOKE SELECT ON DATABASE airlines FROM `suteja@dbsql.com`;
GRANT SELECT,READ_METADATA ON TABLE airlines.flights TO
`suteja@dbsql.com`;
GRANT SELECT,READ_METADATA ON TABLE airlines.planes TO `suteja@
dbsql.com`;
GRANT SELECT,READ_METADATA ON TABLE airlines.clean_planes_data
TO `suteja@dbsql.com`;
```

Here, we revoke the SELECT privilege that we had provided to Suteja on the `airlines` database. Then, we provide the SELECT privilege and the READ_METADATA privilege to the `flights` and `planes` tables and the `clean_planes_data` view.

Now, Suteja should only be able to list and query the aforementioned assets.

> **Remember**
> REVOKE only works on explicitly granted or denied privileges on a securable object from a principal.

Just to drive home the concept of REVOKE, let's say that Suteja complains to you that the planes table has too many missing values, and she must write extra SQL to filter out these rows every time. You remember that you have created a view called clean_planes_data that does just this – it filters out rows that contain empty values. You can REVOKE Suteja's access to the base planes table and ask her to use only the clean_planes_data view:

```
REVOKE SELECT,READ_METADATA ON TABLE airlines.planes FROM
`suteja@dbsql.com`;
```

This REVOKE works because the SELECT and READ_METADATA privileges were explicitly granted to Suteja.

Denying access

Of course, you may not want to always use GRANTs, especially if a schema contains a lot of tables and views. To achieve the same results as we saw in the preceding section – that is, providing select access to a database while selectively revoking access to a few objects – we can use the DENY statement.

Running the following DENY statement has the same effect:

```
DENY SELECT, READ_METADATA ON TABLE airlines.planes TO `suteja@
dbsql.com`;
```

This command makes sure that the table is not visible to Suteja either via Data Explorer or SQL commands.

Going beyond read access – part 1

At times, end users may need to create data assets such as tables, views, or functions. However, CREATE privileges are not implicit to end users.

For example, let's say that Suteja tries to create a new view on the flights table that provides a view of only the flight details and arrival delay:

```
CREATE VIEW airlines.flights_delay AS SELECT year, month,
flightnum, tailnum, arrdelay FROM airlines.flights;
```

She will get the following error:

Error running query

User does not have permission CREATE on database `airlines`.

Figure 4.14 – Missing CREATE privilege

To remedy this, we can simply run the following GRANT statement:

```
GRANT CREATE ON DATABASE airlines TO `suteja@dbsql.com`;
```

> **Note**
>
> The CREATE privilege is applicable at the database level if you are using Hive Metastore, and it provides the privilege to create tables and views only. Functions require the CREATE_NAMED_FUNCTION privilege. If you are creating functions that use code in Scala/Java/Python, an additional MODIFY_CLASSPATH privilege will be required. If you are using Unity Catalog, CREATE is also applicable at the catalog level. However, as we know, the privilege will not cascade down to databases, tables, and views.

Unity Catalog considerations

Unity Catalog introduces a securable object called **external location** that is relevant here. Consider the case where Suteja wants to create an external table for data contained on a cloud storage path. To complete this operation, Suteja needs the CREATE privilege at the database level and access to the cloud storage path.

If we were using Hive Metastore, then granting her the CREATE privilege would have solved the first requirement. However, for the second requirement, she would have to ask the cloud infrastructure team for the necessary permissions. This is less than ideal.

This is where external location comes in. It combines the cloud storage path with the required storage credentials.

As you may have guessed by now, this means that a storage credential is also a securable object.

Consider the following SQL snippet:

```
CREATE EXTERNAL LOCATION airlines_loc URL 'abfss://dbsql/
airlines' WITH (CREDENTIAL airlines_cred);
```

The preceding code highlights how a cloud storage path is combined with the required storage credentials. Since we are using an Azure example, `airlines_cred` CREDENTIAL will be a service principal that grants access to the ADLS path.

Now, Suteja can be granted one of the following privileges on the external location object or the credential object:

- READ_FILES
- WRITE_FILES
- CREATE_TABLE

This will grant her privileges to read, write, or create tables in that location, respectively. Take a look at the following code:

```
GRANT CREATE_TABLE ON EXTERNAL LOCATION airlines_loc TO suteja@
dbsql.com;
```

Now, Suteja can create the required external table with the familiar syntax:

```
CREATE TABLE planes LOCATION 'abfss://dbsql/airlines/planes';
```

This way, DBAs can manage the required credentials across the database and the underlying cloud storage.

For a full reference on creating, altering, and managing external locations and storage credentials, visit `https://docs.databricks.com/spark/latest/spark-sql/language-manual/sql-ref-external-locations.html`.

Going beyond read access – part 2

At times, end users will require permissions to be able to insert, update, or delete data in tables. These *modifications* could be explicit in the sense that the user is trying to actively insert, update, or delete data. They could also be part of optimization commands such as VACUUM, OPTIMIZE, or ALTER TABLE.

> **Optimization Commands**
>
> As an end user, you will rarely encounter the need to use optimization commands. They are primarily in the domain of data engineers, who are creating these datasets and are responsible for optimizing the layout of the data so that you, as the end user, can have the best query experience. In any case, if you are interested, we will be covering this in more detail in *Chapter 8, The Delta Lake*.

In either case, the user running the command must have the MODIFY privilege on the table. Let's say that Suteja tries to INSERT some data into the flights table using the following statement:

```
INSERT INTO airlines.flights VALUES(2006,12,21,4,'1155',1200,'1
447',1457,'DL',1466,'N919DL','172','177','149','-10','-5','FLL'
,'BDL','1173','6','17',0,'',0,'0','0','0','0','0';)
```

She will get the following error:

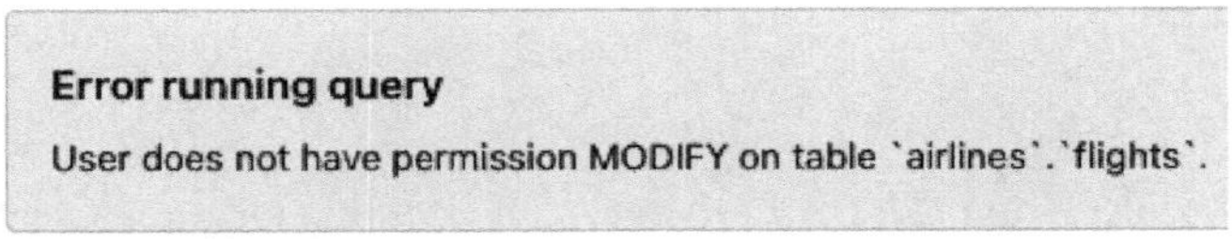

Error running query

User does not have permission MODIFY on table `airlines`.`flights`.

Figure 4.15 – Missing MODIFY privilege

To remedy this, we, as owners of the database, can simply run the following GRANT statement:

```
GRANT MODIFY ON DATABASE airlines TO `suteja@dbsql.com`;
```

Going beyond read access – part 3

Finally, advanced users, such as data engineers, may want to insert data into tables using data from other files, such as CSVs or JSONs. This can be achieved using the COPY INTO statement. We will deep dive into this command in *Chapter 11, SQL Commands – Part 1*. For now, it is sufficient to note that this is the command that requires the SELECT privilege on ANY FILE, along with the MODIFY privilege on the table being inserted into (as we saw in the preceding section).

> **Unity Catalog Difference**
>
> With Unity Catalog, we can use the external location and storage credentials with the READ_FILES, WRITE_FILES, and CREATE_TABLE privileges. This is a more secure way of providing access to cloud storage than ANY FILE.

Summarizing the security model

Hopefully, this theoretical and practical discussion of the Databricks security model (as it pertains to user-facing table access control) has taught you how to navigate and implement the Databricks security model in your organization.

For a comprehensive list of operations, as well as the privileges required to execute them, visit the official documentation at https://docs.databricks.com/security/access-control/table-acls/object-privileges.html.

Programming the security model with standard SQL commands is great. It provides a lot of flexibility. That said, Databricks SQL does provide a UI-based mechanism to program the security model as well. We will learn about it in the next section.

UI-based user-facing table access control

In the preceding sections, we saw many examples of applying table access control with ANSI standard DCL commands such as GRANT and REVOKE.

The Data Explorer UI also enables us to apply table access control to data assets using simple UI controls.

The **Permissions** tab for any data asset (database, table, or view) in the Data Explorer UI does three things. Let's take a look.

Show current permissions

This is equivalent to the SHOW GRANTS statement. In the following screenshot, we have navigated to the **Permissions** tab for the airlines database. Here, we can see the list of applied permissions:

Figure 4.16 – Permissions for the airlines database

Similarly, in the following screenshot, we can see the current permissions for the `flights` table in the `airline` database:

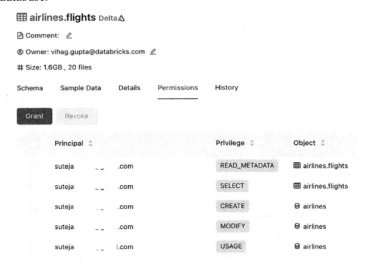

Figure 4.17 – Permissions for the flights table

Granting privileges

Clicking on the **Grant** button for any data asset opens a pop-up window where you can select a user or user group and grant one or more privileges to them, as shown in the following screenshot:

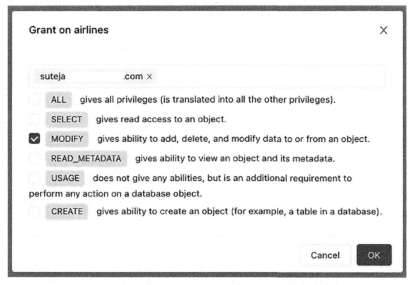

Figure 4.18 – The GRANT permissions from the UI

Revoking privileges

Clicking on an existing privilege and clicking the **Revoke** button revokes that specific privilege from that specific user or user group, as shown in the following screenshot:

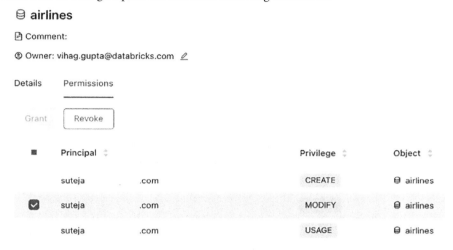

Figure 4.19 – Revoking with the UI

> **Note**
>
> At the time of writing, access control on functions is not available via the UI. Also, note that we cannot perform DENY with the UI.

Now, we are fully equipped to program the access privileges to our data with our preferred method – SQL or UI. This covers the first section of *Figure 4.3*, which represents the user-facing table access control. In the same figure, we can see that the SQL Warehouses must be configured to access the cloud object storage as well. We will discuss this in the next section.

The internals of cloud storage access

In *Figure 4.1* and *Figure 4.2*, we discussed the execution model of a query. In the preceding section on user-facing table access control, we learned how table access control enables user-facing table access control.

This leaves us with one more authorization layer to discuss – the cloud storage access that's given to SQL Warehouses.

Unity Catalog Consideration

If you are using Unity Catalog, or exclusively using managed tables, this section is not relevant. This is because with managed tables, the catalog stores the data in a location dedicated for its use. Further, with Unity Catalog, the query engine is provided signed, short-lived, pre-signed URLs to the relevant data files, even if the tables are unmanaged. This contrasts with Hive Metastore, where the SQL Warehouses use the relevant cloud authorization mechanism – instance profile, service principal, or service account – to access the relevant data files.

To understand why this authorization layer is important, we must unpack *Figure 4.1* and *Figure 4.2* a little bit more. If we look at the overall deployment architecture of Databricks (on either cloud), it will look as follows:

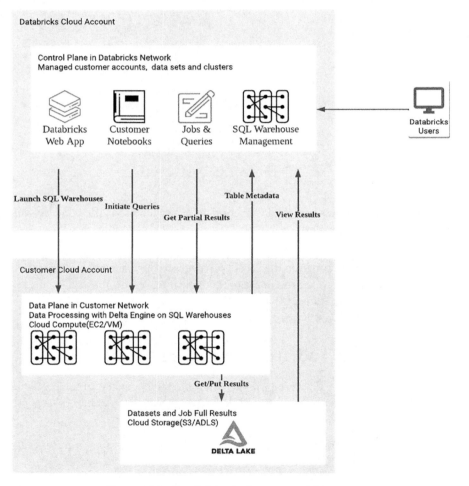

Figure 4.20 – Databricks deployment architecture

What stands out in this reference architecture is that the actual execution layer and storage layer is in your cloud account, not in the Databricks cloud account. This means that to process the query, Databricks creates an instance of the SQL Warehouse (data processing cluster) using EC2 instances, Azure VMs, or GCP VMs in your cloud account. These SQL warehouses (and by association, the instances) will need authorization to access the cloud storage locations required to fulfill the query.

Databricks is responsible for creating and managing these SQL Warehouses in your cloud account, which also means it is responsible for endowing them with the required authorizations to cloud storage locations containing the database files. Therefore, we must authorize Databricks SQL to do so in a secure, governable fashion. Hence, we must learn about the internals of cloud storage access.

Again, Databricks does not receive authorization to interact with these storage locations. It receives authorization to authorize the SQL Warehouses to interact with these storage locations.

Therefore, it is important to make sure that the authorization is restricted to only those buckets that are required to fulfill queries. No more, no less.

> **Remember**
>
> It is important to remember that cloud storage access is not user-facing. We do not have to map a table to a service principal or instance profile explicitly. Databricks SQL will automatically use the appropriate service principal or instance profile based on the cloud storage location of the table. This means that if a query accesses two tables from two storage locations, Databricks SQL will do the heavy lifting of authorizing itself to Microsoft Azure or AWS to gain access to the respective storage locations. Furthermore, it is important to remember that this stage is only relevant if the user submitting the query has been cleared by table access control to be querying these tables in the first place. See *Figure 4.3* for more.

The overall mechanism for this configuration remains the same across clouds. We must create an identity or a proxy in the cloud's IAM system that has privileges to work with the necessary storage locations. Our instance of Databricks SQL should be given the privileges to create SQL Warehouses that will assume this identity or use this proxy to be able to interact with storage locations in a governed and secured way.

> **Technical Requirements**
>
> The *Cloud storage access in Microsoft Azure* section will require familiarity with the Azure Console and concepts such as Azure Active Directory service principals and storage accounts. The *Cloud storage access in Amazon Web Services* section will require familiarity with the AWS Console and concepts such as IAM and S3.

At this point, you might be thinking – *Wait, I already created databases. Where are they stored, then?*

In the examples we've covered so far, we have not specified where on our cloud storage our data should be stored.

If you are using Hive Metastore, it will be a default `warehouse` directory in the following form:

```
dbfs:/user/hive/warehouse/airlines.db
```

On the other hand, if you are using Unity Catalog, the default location will be the location associated with the Metastore being used by your Databricks SQL workspace (see *Chapter 3, The Data Catalog*).

While we are on the topic of Unity Catalog, you may recall that we already created the EXTERNAL LOCATION and CREDENTIAL objects and programmed the user privileges on them. So, why do we have to reauthorize? The reasoning is the same as we discussed earlier in this section. EXTERNAL LOCATION and CREDENTIAL authorize users to use a cloud storage path. The user's queries on this location, however, will be executed by a different entity – the SQL Warehouse, which will also need access to these locations.

Cloud storage access in Microsoft Azure

In Microsoft Azure, access to cloud storage is controlled via **service principals** in **Azure Active Directory**. We introduced service principals in the *Users, groups, and service principals* section.

In our context, we will create a service principal (which is nothing but an Active Directory application) that has the authorization to read data from certain storage accounts (`https://docs.microsoft.com/en-us/azure/storage/common/storage-account-overview`). Our instance of Databricks SQL will use these service principals to get access to the required storage accounts.

Databricks recommends that we configure one service principal per storage account.

Let's walk through an example that's outlined in the official documentation:

- Databricks side configuration: `https://docs.microsoft.com/en-us/azure/databricks/sql/admin/data-access-configuration`

- Azure side configuration: `https://docs.microsoft.com/en-us/azure/databricks/data/data-sources/azure/adls-gen2/azure-datalake-gen2-sp-access`

We will use the same `airlines` dataset that we have been using throughout this chapter.

Step 1 – creating an Active Directory application

Head over to the Azure portal and navigate to **Azure Active Directory**. Select **App Registrations** and create a new app registration. I am naming my app `airlines-app-for-dbsql`. Upon creating the app, copy the **Application (client) ID** and **Directory (tenant) ID** details, as shown in the following screenshot:

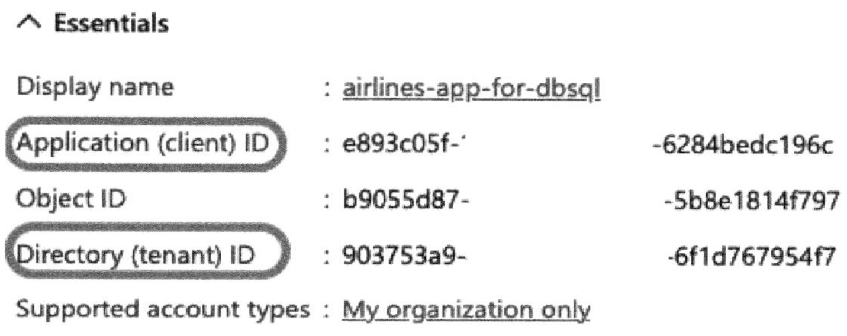

∧ **Essentials**

Display name	: airlines-app-for-dbsql
Application (client) ID	: e893c05f-' -6284bedc196c
Object ID	: b9055d87- -5b8e1814f797
Directory (tenant) ID	: 903753a9- -6f1d767954f7
Supported account types	: My organization only

Figure 4.21 – Creating an app for cloud storage access

The application ID and directory ID collectively identify the service principal that was created by this Azure Active Directory application registration.

> **Note**
> You will require permissions to be able to register an application with your Azure AD tenant and assign the application a role in your Azure subscription.

You must also create a client secret from the **Certificates and Secrets** page for this Active Directory application.

Copy the client secret and add it to Databricks Secrets. See `https://docs.microsoft.com/en-us/azure/databricks/security/secrets/` for more information on Databricks Secrets. On your command line, execute the following code:

```
databricks secrets create-scope --scope airlines-app-secrets
databricks secrets put --scope airlines-app-secrets --key
client-secret
```

Executing the preceding code will open an editor where you should paste the client secret.

Step 2 – creating a storage location on ADLS Gen2

In Azure, we must create a **storage account**, which I am calling `airlinestorageaccount`, and a **container** within that storage account, which I am calling `airlines-container`. Next, we must assign the service principal we created in the preceding step (`airlines-app-for-dbsql`) as a **Storage Blob Data Contributor** to this storage account, as shown in the following screenshot:

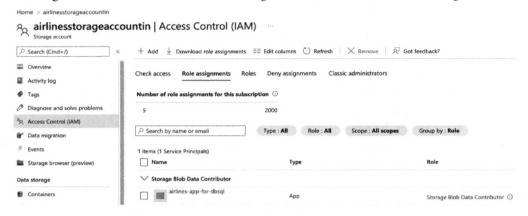

Figure 4.22 – Assigning access to the storage account

> **Caution**
>
> This IAM setting has been done at the storage account level, not at the container level. Setting it at the container level will throw `403 Forbidden` errors during query executions.

Step 3 – creating a service principal in Databricks SQL

Now, we have an Azure Active Directory service principal that will allow our instance of Databricks SQL to work with the ADLS Gen2 storage container that we have dedicated to our `airlines` database.

To configure this service principal, we must navigate to the **SQL Admin Console** area and navigate to the **SQL Warehouse Settings** tab. Click on **Add Service Principal**:

SQL Admin Console

General   Alert destinations   SQL Warehouse settings

Data Security

Define the service principals used by all warehouses to access storage and configure all warehouses with data access metastore properties. Learn more

Data Access Configuration   + Add Service Principal   ⓘ

Figure 4.23 – Add Service Principal

Clicking on **Add Service Principal** opens a popup, in which we must add all the details we collected from *Steps 1* and *2*, like so:

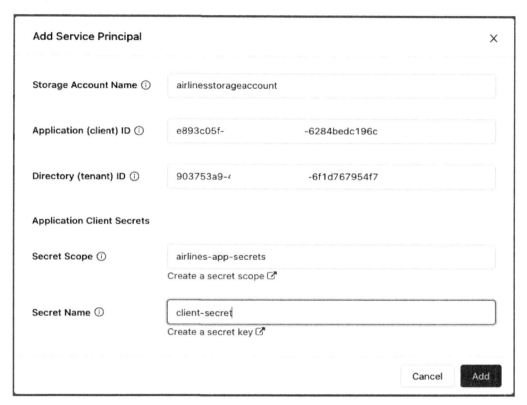

Figure 4.24 – Adding the service principal's details

> **Note**
>
> The **Storage Account Name** field tells Databricks SQL which credentials to use for which storage account. If this field is left blank, then these credentials will be used to access all storage accounts. This is discouraged as it creates security risks.

Do not forget to click on the **Save Changes** button!

Step 4 – taking it out for a test drive

The settings for working with the new storage container dedicated to our `airlines` database are done. So, let's see it in action.

We will execute the same `airlines` starter snippet we introduced in the *The security model in practice* section, but with one difference: the `airlines` database will be located on the storage container that we just created, as shown in the following snippet:

```
--create the database
CREATE DATABASE airlines LOCATION 'abfss://airlines-container@
airlinesstorageaccount.dfs.core.windows.net/';
```

Here, we can see that the `planes` and `flights` tables have been stored in the storage container, as shown in the following screenshot:

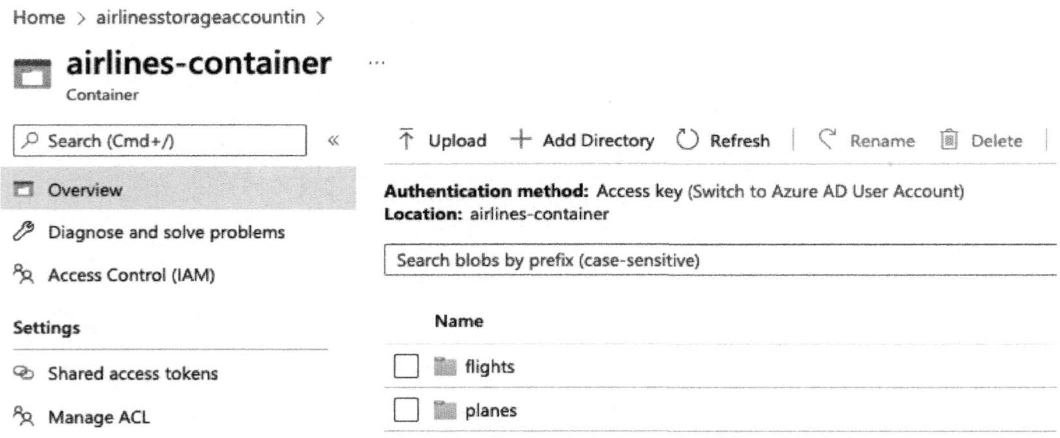

Figure 4.25 – The data in a location of our choosing

> **Unity Catalog Note**
>
> If you are using Unity Catalog, please rework the preceding example so that it uses `EXTERNAL LOCATION` and `STORAGE CREDENTIAL`.

Let's summarize this example:

- We created a container that will be the home of our `airlines` database.

- We created a service principal that is authorized to contribute to this database.

- We authorized our instance of Databricks SQL to assume the identity of this service principal (using the *client secret*) for interacting with this container.

Upon executing the data asset creation script, Databricks SQL transparently uses this authorization to create the `airlines` database on the designated containers.

Cloud storage access in Amazon Web Services

The core principle remains the same when we are working with **Amazon Web Services (AWS)**. We want our instance of Databricks SQL on AWS to assume an identity that has been authorized to interact with the required S3 buckets. In AWS, the mechanism that allows us to do so is the instance profile.

Unlike Azure Databricks, there are three stages to configuring cloud storage access in AWS:

- Create and configure instance profiles on the AWS console: `https://docs.databricks.com/administration-guide/cloud-configurations/aws/instance-profiles.html#secure-access-to-s3-buckets-using-instance-profiles` (*Steps 1* to *4*).

- Configure the instance profiles in Databricks (the data engineering view): `https://docs.databricks.com/administration-guide/cloud-configurations/aws/instance-profiles.html#secure-access-to-s3-buckets-using-instance-profiles` (*Step 5*).

- Configure Databricks SQL to use the instance profiles: `https://docs.databricks.com/sql/admin/data-access-configuration.html`.

We will work with the same `airlines` dataset. However, for the sake of brevity, we will avoid listing out complete IAM policies. I will point you to the official documentation links for picking up the policies.

Step 1 – creating an S3 bucket

Create a new S3 bucket that will host the `airlines` dataset. I am calling it `airlines-bucket`.

Step 2 – creating and configuring the instance profile

Create a new **role** with **EC2** as the trusted entity (`https://docs.databricks.com/administration-guide/cloud-configurations/aws/instance-profiles.html#step-1-create-an-instance-profile-to-access-an-s3-bucket`). I am calling it `airlines-bucket-role`. Attach the IAM policy listed in *Step 1* in the documentation. This IAM policy allows this role (or the user of this role) to perform certain operations on the `airlines-bucket` S3 bucket:

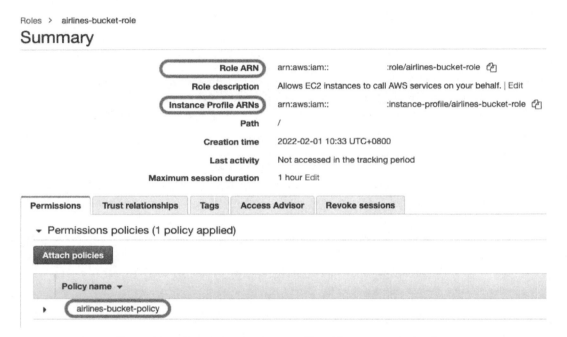

Figure 4.26 – Creating an instance profile with access to the bucket

Copy the **Role ARN** and **Instance Profile ARN** details.

Step 3 – configuring the S3 bucket

Next, we must configure the S3 bucket to accept contributions from the role we created in *Step 2*. This Bucket Policy configuration is required so that this S3 bucket accepts contributions from the holder of the IAM role that we created in *Step 2* (`airlines-bucket-role`). The full policy can be copied from `https://docs.databricks.com/administration-guide/cloud-configurations/aws/instance-profiles.html#step-2-create-a-bucket-policy-for-the-target-s3-bucket`.

Step 4 – configuring your Databricks instance to use this role

When a Databricks workspace is created, it is provided with an IAM role that manages EC2 instances in the customer's account. This IAM role can be found in the **Account Management Console** area.

We must extend this IAM role to be able to *pass along* the S3 access role that we created in *Step 2* to the EC2 instances that Databricks creates in the customer account.

> **Note**
>
> The Databricks SQL Warehouses that execute the queries are a group of EC2 instances that have been organized into a computing cluster. Hence, these EC2 instances should inherit the IAM instance profile to be able to interact with the required S3 buckets.

The modification listed at `https://docs.databricks.com/administration-guide/cloud-configurations/aws/instance-profiles.html#step-4-add-the-s3-iam-role-to-the-ec2-policy` can be a bit wordy. If you are confused by it, all you need to do is add the following snippet to the IAM policy:

```
{
    "Effect": "Allow",
    "Action": "iam:PassRole",
    "Resource": "arn:aws:iam::xxxxxxxxxxxx:role/
airlines-bucket-role"
}
```

Step 5 – configuring Databricks SQL to use this instance profile

Navigate to **Settings**, and then the **SQL Admin Console** tab, as shown in the following screenshot. Click on the **Configure** button to add the instance profile we created in *Step 2* to Databricks SQL. This will navigate you to the dedicated page for managing instance profiles in the Data Engineering persona view. Once done, go back to the **SQL Admin Console** tab, select `airlines-role` from the dropdown, and click **Save**:

Figure 4.27 – Configuring the instance profile in Databricks SQL

Step 6 – taking it out for a test drive

We will execute the same `airlines` starter snippet but with one difference: the `airlines` database will be located in `airlines-bucket` in S3. For the sake of brevity, I am only going to note the `CREATE DATABASE` statement here. The rest of the SQL script remains the same:

```
--create the database
CREATE DATABASE airlines LOCATION "s3://airlines-bucket/";
```

We can also observe that the `planes` and `flights` tables have been stored in the S3 bucket:

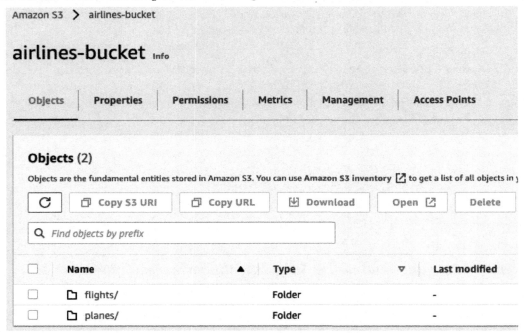

Figure 4.28 – The data in a location of our choosing

> **Unity Catalog Note**
>
> If you are using Unity Catalog, please rework the preceding example so that it uses EXTERNAL LOCATION and STORAGE CREDENTIAL.

Let's summarize this example:

- We created an S3 bucket, which will be the home of our `airlines` database.

- We created an instance profile that is authorized to contribute to this database.

- We authorized our instance of Databricks SQL to assume the identity of this instance profile (using the `PASS ROLE` mechanism) for interacting with this bucket.

Upon executing the data asset creation script, Databricks SQL transparently uses this authorization to create the `airlines` database on the designated buckets.

Summary

In this rather dense chapter, we learned how data assets in the data catalog are secured with the data security model. We learned how user-facing table access control allows for the fine-grained implementation of the data security model using familiar SQL security statements such as `GRANT` and `REVOKE`. We also learned how Data Explorer allows visual, UI-based implementations of the table access control. After that, we learned about the underlying mechanics of authorizing Databricks SQL to cloud storage to access the necessary database files. Finally, we learned about the next-generation data cataloging technology known as Unity Catalog and how it improves upon the security capabilities of table access control with Hive Metastore.

In the next chapter, we will move on to the Databricks SQL workbench itself. Though we introduced the SQL Editor as part of this chapter, we will take this further and see how the SQL Editor, Dashboard Builder, and **Query** tabs all come together as the workbench for a user of Databricks SQL.

5
The Workbench

In the previous chapters, we learned how to organize our data assets, how to secure and govern them, and how to explore the available data assets. This means we are now ready to work on the data.

In this chapter, we will primarily focus on the perspective of the end users: business intelligence users and data analysts. Throughout this chapter, we will learn about workbench in Databricks SQL.

In this chapter, we will cover the following topics:

- Creating and working with queries
- Visualizing query results
- Creating and publishing dashboards
- Administering and governing your work

Technical requirements

To understand this chapter, we should know about the following:

- Standard SQL statements for data retrieval and manipulation such as SELECT, GROUP BY, and others
- The science and math behind analytical techniques and visualizations, including cohort analysis, funnels, pivot tables, and, of course, charts
- The concepts introduced in *Chapter 3, The Data Catalog*

Working with queries

In *Chapter 2, The Databricks Product Suite – A Visual Tour*, in *Figure 2.9*, we briefly introduced the SQL Editor as the intelligent workbench that is at the center of the end user experience for day-to-day work.

In this section, we'll look into the capabilities that the SQL Editor brings to the table.

In the previous chapters, we used the SQL Editor to either program the security model or explore the data assets visually. Hence, I'm not going to introduce the basic layout of the page and dive straight into the most important features.

Continuing within the spirit of the previous chapters, let's start by incorporating another dataset from the bundled databricks-datasets into our data catalog for use in this chapter. Here, we will use the *NYC Taxi Trip* dataset.

Like the previous chapters, execute the following SQL snippet to register this dataset as a database:

```
--create the database
CREATE DATABASE nyc_taxi;
--Set nyc_taxi as the default database
USE nyc_taxi;
--create an unmanaged table on the source nyc taxi trips data
which is in csv format
CREATE TABLE trips USING DELTA OPTIONS(
  path '/databricks-datasets/nyctaxi-with-zipcodes/subsampled/'
)
```

The NYC Taxi Trip dataset is simple, yet it lends to decent statistical computations. This makes it the perfect companion dataset to learn about queries, visualizations, and dashboards.

Now, let's put on our data analyst hat since we've been tasked with building an operational dashboard for the NYC Taxi company. The requirements of the dashboard are as follows:

- *Requirement 1*: A view of Daily Fare Trends
- *Requirement 2*: A view of pickup volumes per hour
- *Requirement 3*: A view of drop-off volumes per hour
- *Requirement 4*: A route to revenue attribution

This dashboard will be used by NYC Taxi to optimize the placement of cabs along various routes at specific times so that revenue can be maximized.

Developing queries

Queries are first-class citizens in Databricks SQL and can be created, read, updated, or deleted. They can also be shared with other people and access controlled. Finally, visualizations on queries are the fundamental building block of dashboards.

Umm... Wait

You might be thinking, hey, we have already written so many SQL queries in the previous chapters. Do I need to go through this chapter after all that?

Well, yes. So far, we have been *writing* queries to learn about concepts such as data asset exploration and security programming. However, those were one-off executions, and we never really explored the tools and techniques available to craft queries in Databricks SQL.

Also, it is the right time to disambiguate something. When we talk about a query in the context of Databricks SQL, we are not referring to the SQL statement within that query. The query is a larger object in Databricks SQL that includes the SQL statement, its associated parameters, and its associated visualizations.

Let's start by considering the case of developing *Requirement 1* – that is, *A view of Daily Fare Trends*.

The development process starts with creating a *query*. This asset will host the SQL statement(s) that we will write to fulfill *Requirement 1*.

To create a query, head to the SQL Editor and click on **Create a new Query**. If you have been working on a query previously, you will see that here. Click on the + symbol in the **Tabbed Editor** area to create a new query.

Provide the query with a logical name by clicking on the text label of the tab. By default, it should be **New Query**. I am naming my work *Daily Fare Trends*:

Figure 5.1 – Creating a named query

It is important to manually save the query asset by clicking the **Save** button. Databricks SQL does not have an auto-save function at the time of writing. This means that Databricks SQL will save your draft and it will be visible to you, but the changes won't be visible to others until you save the query.

Note

Databricks will automatically save a record of every execution of a query. These executions will be visible in the **Query History** tab.

Saving a query asset is a matter of clicking the **Save** button, as shown in the following screenshot:

Figure 5.2 – Saving a named query

Now that we have our development placeholder, we can start developing the SQL statement that fulfills *Requirement 1*.

The first step is inevitably sampling the data to see what we are working with. To this end, we must write a sampling statement:

```
SELECT * FROM nyc_taxi.trips LIMIT 50
```

Live autocomplete – schema hints

The Databricks SQL workbench/SQL Editor provides a feature called **Live autocomplete** that creates typeahead hints for the schemas as you write the preceding SQL statement.

The following screenshot shows how the **Live autocomplete** feature provides hints for selecting a database or table based on the context of a **SELECT** statement being typed:

```
1   SELECT * FROM |
                  FROM airlines_ext.  Database
                  FROM airlines.  Database
                  FROM default.  Database
                  FROM nyc_taxi.  Database
                  FROM people_db.  Database
                  FROM wine_quality.  Database
```

Figure 5.3 – Live autocomplete for the SELECT statement

Selecting the nyc_taxi database opens the next level of typeahead hints for the selection of tables:

```
1   SELECT * FROM nyc_taxi.
                       trips  Table
```

Fig 5.4 – Live autocomplete for table selection

Live AutoComplete can be toggled on or off for the query by clicking the lightning icon in the SQL Editor, as shown in the following screenshot:

Figure 5.5 – Toggling Live autocomplete

UI tools for schema selection and sampling

An alternative to using typeaheads is to use a UI button to insert a table name into the query text. Hovering over a table name in the **Schema Browser** area brings up the **Insert table name into query text** option, as shown here:

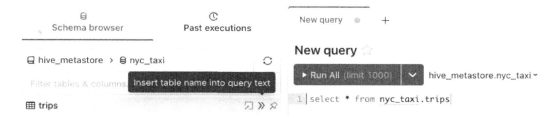

Figure 5.6 – Insert table name into query text

As an alternative to typing out the sampling statement, hovering over a table name in the **Schema Browser** area brings up the **Open a preview of this table in a new tab** option. This is shown in the following screenshot, where clicking the button has opened a new tab and executed the sampling query for us:

Figure 5.7 – Open a preview of this table in a new tab

> **Flashback**
>
> We covered another method of sampling/previewing data in *Chapter 3, The Data Catalog*. The data catalog allows you to preview the data in Data Explorer.

Once we execute the sampling query, we understand the values and transformations that must be done. In this case, we realize that we must extract the day of the week from the pickup time field, `tpep_pickup_datetime`, to build a fare trend based on distance and the day of the week.

Let's return to the Daily Fare Trends query and develop the first cut with the following SQL snippet:

```
SELECT date_format(tpep_pickup_datetime, 'EEEE') as day_of_
week, trip_distance, fare_amount
FROM nyc_taxi.trips
ORDER BY day_of_week
```

If you browse the results in the **results** tab, you will notice that only a subset of the records is displayed. This is by design. Loading humongous volumes of data for display is arguably never required as you will not go through each row manually. Hence, Databricks SQL limits the results of `SELECT` queries to 1,000 rows. This ensures an optimal user experience when browsing through results or visualizing them. This can be toggled off for the query by checking the **LIMIT 1000** checkbox after clicking the **Run** button:

Figure 5.8 – Limiting the results loaded into the browser

> **Note**
>
> The **LIMIT 1000** checkbox is overruled by any explicit `LIMIT` clause in the query.

Live autocomplete – SQL hints

Live autocomplete provides suggestions for applicable SQL commands as well. For example, as you type the preceding SQL statement, you will see **Live autocomplete** hinting at possible, applicable SQL commands. In this case, we can see `ORDER BY`:

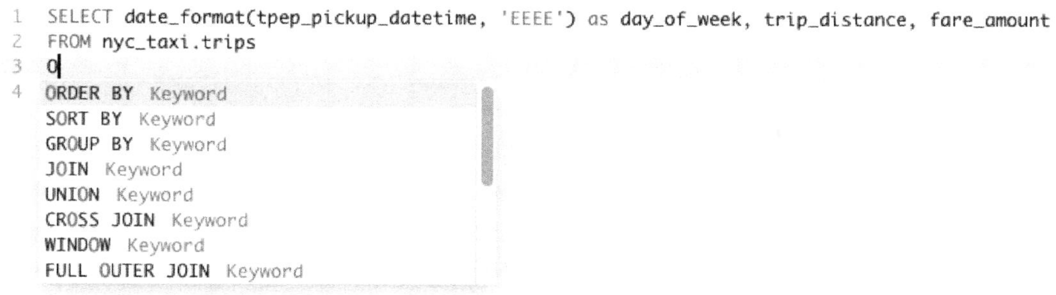

```
1  SELECT date_format(tpep_pickup_datetime, 'EEEE') as day_of_week, trip_distance, fare_amount
2  FROM nyc_taxi.trips
3  o|
4  ORDER BY  Keyword
   SORT BY  Keyword
   GROUP BY  Keyword
   JOIN  Keyword
   UNION  Keyword
   CROSS JOIN  Keyword
   WINDOW  Keyword
   FULL OUTER JOIN  Keyword
```

Figure 5.9 – Live autocomplete for SQL commands

Save Your Work

Now that you have created your first cut of the query, don't forget to save your work!

With that, we have a working base query for *Requirement 1*. However, it is very inflexible – that is, the query does not allow us to choose filtering parameters for our Fare Trends query. For example, the query should provide a mechanism to filter on the desired date or date range. Alternatively, it should provide a mechanism to filter on the ZIP code. It could also provide a mechanism to filter on the day of the week.

We can create such a dynamic view with **query parameters**. A query parameter is a way for the query to receive values during query execution. In Databricks SQL, a query parameter is created by placing a string between double curly braces, { { } }, or by using the *Cmd + P* keyboard shortcut. Creating the double curly braces will automatically create an input widget above the results tab, which is where you set the desired parameter value.

There are three broad categories of query parameters. These are as follows:

- **Free Form Fields**: Text and numbers
- **Temporal Fields**: Date and time
- **User-Defined Choices**

Using query parameters, part 1 – text and numbers

In our working example for *Requirement 1*, we must have the flexibility of seeing fare trends based on a ZIP code. Hence, we will provide a query parameter for users to specify which pickup ZIP code they want to see the fare trends for.

Place your cursor where you want to create the query parameter. Use the *Cmd + P* keyboard shortcut:

```
1  select date_format(tpep_pickup_datetime, 'EEE') as day_of_week, trip_distance, fare_amount
2  from nyc_taxi.trips
3  where pickup_zip in ⟠
4  order by day_of_week
```

+ Add filter

Figure 5.10 – Starting the Add new parameter process

Clicking on the **Add new parameter** button, {}, opens a pop-up where you can configure the query parameter. Three configurations are required, as shown here:

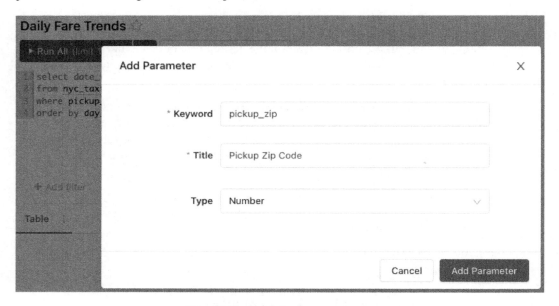

Figure 5.11 – Adding a new parameter

Let's look at these configurations in more detail:

- **Keyword**: The value in this field will represent the parameter in the query text.
- **Title**: The value in this field will be displayed as the title of the widget for this query parameter.
- **Type**: The value in this field defines the acceptable values for this query parameter.

In tune with our example for *Requirement 1*, I have set **Keyword** to pickup_zip, **Title** to Pickup Zip Code, and **Type** to Number. Completing this configuration does two things:

- Inserts the query parameter into the query text

- Creates a corresponding UI widget that receives inputs for the parameter

The following screenshot shows the new state of the query we are building:

Figure 5.12 – A query built with a query parameter

Now, you can insert a value for the **Pickup Zip Code** query parameter and retrieve the fare trends for it.

Default Values

While working in the Query Editor, it is important to provide values for each query parameter via the UI widget. This prompts the question of having default values for query parameters. Databricks SQL allows you to provide default values for query parameters when the query is part of a dashboard. This may seem odd, but think about it – the queries that we develop here will be part of dashboards and ETL flows where these parameterized queries will be provided with dynamic values; otherwise, they will use defaults. They will not be executed in isolation. We will learn how to use default values when we discuss dashboards.

If you are feeling particularly adventurous, you can try executing the query with an empty query parameter value. You will get an error stating **Missing value for pickup_zip parameter**:

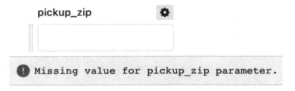

Figure 5.13 – Error due to missing parameter input

> **A Note on Inserting Query Parameters**
>
> It is worth highlighting that when adding a new query parameter, try to keep the cursor at the position where you intend the query parameter to be placed. This is important because if you try to cut and paste the query parameter's text, the settings associated with the query parameter will be lost, which is likely to be frustrating.

To summarize, there are two free-form query parameter types:

- **Text**:

  - Databricks SQL will add quotation marks around the user input for this query parameter type. For example, S123456 will become 'S123456'.

  - Databricks SQL will escape the backslash (\), single quote(') , and double quote (") special characters.

- **Number**:

  - Databricks SQL provides basic sanity checks on the number type – that is, trying to add alphanumeric content for a number query parameter will result in an error.

Using query parameters, part 2 – temporal query parameters

Databricks SQL also allows you to configure temporal query parameters, of which there are two broad categories:

- **Point in time**:

  - Date

  - Date and time

  - Date and time with seconds

- **Range-based**:

  - Range of dates

  - Range of dates and times

  - Range of dates and times with seconds

Let's return to our working example for *Requirement 1*. Here, we should provide the user of the query with the power to filter the fare trends to a specific time window or a specific date.

Creating a temporal query parameter follows the same process as that of free-form text/numbers. Let's insert a new query parameter with **Keyword** set to `pickup_time`, **Title** set to `Pickup Time`, and **Type** set to `Date and Time Range`. The query should look as follows:

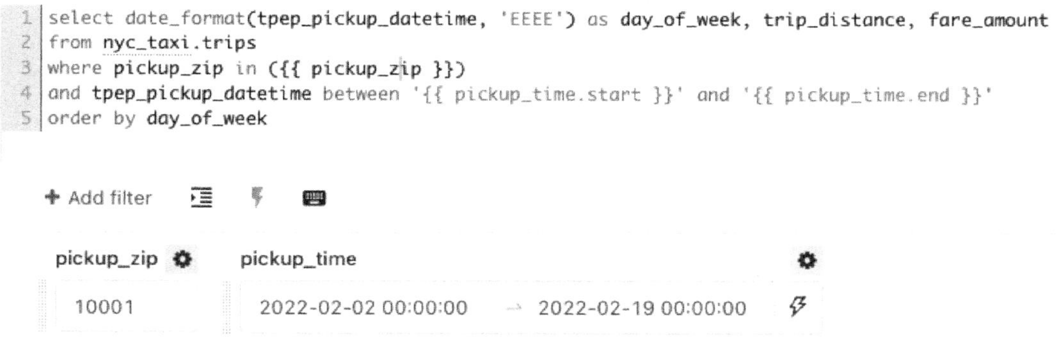

```
1  select date_format(tpep_pickup_datetime, 'EEEE') as day_of_week, trip_distance, fare_amount
2  from nyc_taxi.trips
3  where pickup_zip in ({{ pickup_zip }})
4  and tpep_pickup_datetime between '{{ pickup_time.start }}' and '{{ pickup_time.end }}'
5  order by day_of_week
```

+ Add filter

pickup_zip ⚙	pickup_time	⚙
10001	2022-02-02 00:00:00 → 2022-02-19 00:00:00	⚡

Figure 5.14 – Temporal query parameter with a date and time range

The **Pickup Time** query parameter is a range. Hence, it gets a **Start date** component and an **End date** component. In the query text, **start** and **end** can be accessed with the following syntax:

```
<parameter keyword>.<start/end>
```

> **Important**
>
> For temporal query parameters, the user is responsible for adding the quotes around the parameters in the query text. Failing to do so will result in syntax errors during runtime.

Irrespective of the temporal query parameter type (point in time or ranges), the UI widget provides two components: a calendar-based date-time selection tool and a dynamic tool. Let's learn about them.

Calendar-based selection tool

Clicking on the **Start date** or **End date** field in the UI widget will open a calendar, as shown here:

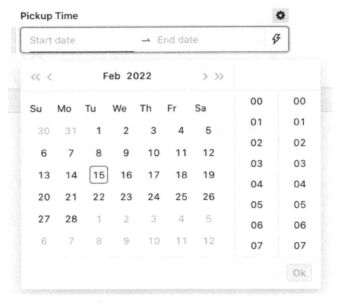

Figure 5.15 – Calendar-base selection tool

Our parameter is the date and time range. Hence, we have three selection fields – the day, the hour, and the minute in that order, respectively.

If our parameter was just the date range, the selection tool would not have the hour and the minute fields. Conversely, if our parameter was the date and time range with seconds, the selection tool would have an additional seconds field.

Here, **Start date** and **End date** would have to be configured individually.

> **So, What about Point-in-Time Query Parameters?**
>
> Great point! If your query parameter is a point in time and not a range – that is, **Type** is either **Date, Date and Time,** or **Date and Time (with Seconds)** – then the query parameter will not have start and end components. Also, the UI widget will not have separate **Start** and **End** selections. It will be just one of **Date/Date and Time/Date and Time (with Seconds)**.

Dynamic value selection tool

Manual selection is great, but often, temporal query parameters are known ranges such as last week, last month, or yesterday. Databricks SQL provides a convenient **dynamic value** selection tool just for this. Clicking on the lightning bolt on the query parameter widget brings up a list of dynamic values that we can select with a click:

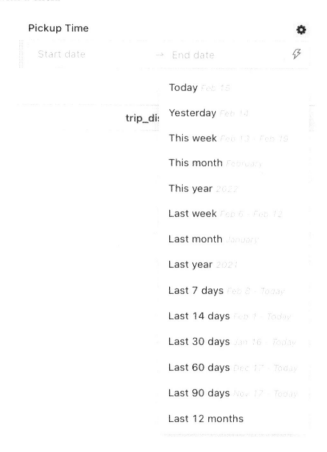

Figure 5.16 – Dynamic value selection

As we can see, the dynamic drop-down provides a range of values for this query parameter. The word *dynamic* comes from the fact that the values of each drop-down option change based on the current date.

> **Again, What About Point-in-Time Parameters?**
>
> Point-in-time parameters also get the dynamic value selection option. However, logically, the only options possible are **Today** and **Yesterday**. Arguably, there can be more, but those options will be wordy. For example, *One week ago* wouldn't look good in a drop-down.

The following screenshot shows the new state of the query we are building:

Figure 5.17 – Query augmented with a parameter to pick up the time range

Using query parameters, part 3 – dropdowns

Databricks SQL provides a third variety of query parameters, which is drop-down lists of valid values. Free-form text/numbers and calendar tools are great, but they can be prone to misuse. For example, someone can enter an invalid value for a text parameter that returns no values. This can result in a bad experience. It also puts the responsibility on the developer to cater to all such edge cases.

The **drop-down query parameter** allows the developer to limit the values that can be provided as input to the query parameter.

There are two ways to specify the allowed list of values:

- **Dropdown List**
- **Query Based Dropdown List**

Optionally, we can also specify that the user is allowed to make multiple selections from the drop-down list by checking the **Allow multiple values** checkbox. If we enable multiple selections, we must choose the **Quotation** mechanism for the selected options – **None**, **Single Quotes**, or **Double Quotes**. This is important because internally, the multiple selections will be translated as an IN clause, as shown here:

```
….WHERE day_of_week IN ('SUNDAY','MONDAY')
```

Let's return to our working example for *Requirement 1*. We should provide the user of the query with the power to filter the fare to a specific day of the week. Let's look at how we can use the two aforementioned options.

Dropdown List

To create a query parameter with a drop-down list, select the **Dropdown List** option in the query parameter's **Type** field:

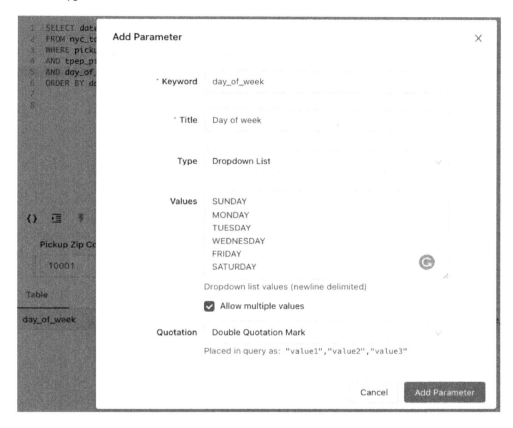

Figure 5.18 – Dropdown List

As you can imagine, utmost care must be taken when specifying the allowed list of values. It is also plausible that manually creating this list is unscalable. This is because the list of allowed values might be long and manually typing them would be error-prone, cumbersome, and, let's be honest, not the best use of your time.

This is where the second option, **Query Based Dropdown List**, comes in.

Query Based Dropdown List

This option works exactly how it sounds. You must create a saved query that returns the list of possible values. Following our example for *Requirement 1*, the following query should do the trick:

```
SELECT
  DISTINCT(date_format(tpep_pickup_datetime, 'EEEE')) AS day
FROM
  nyc_taxi.trips
```

In my instance, I have created a saved query called *List of Days in NYC Taxi*.

Coming back to the query that we are developing; we must add a new **Type** parameter based on **Query Based Dropdown List**. The rest of the options are the same as those for **Dropdown List**, which we discussed in the preceding section.

The following screenshot shows this in action:

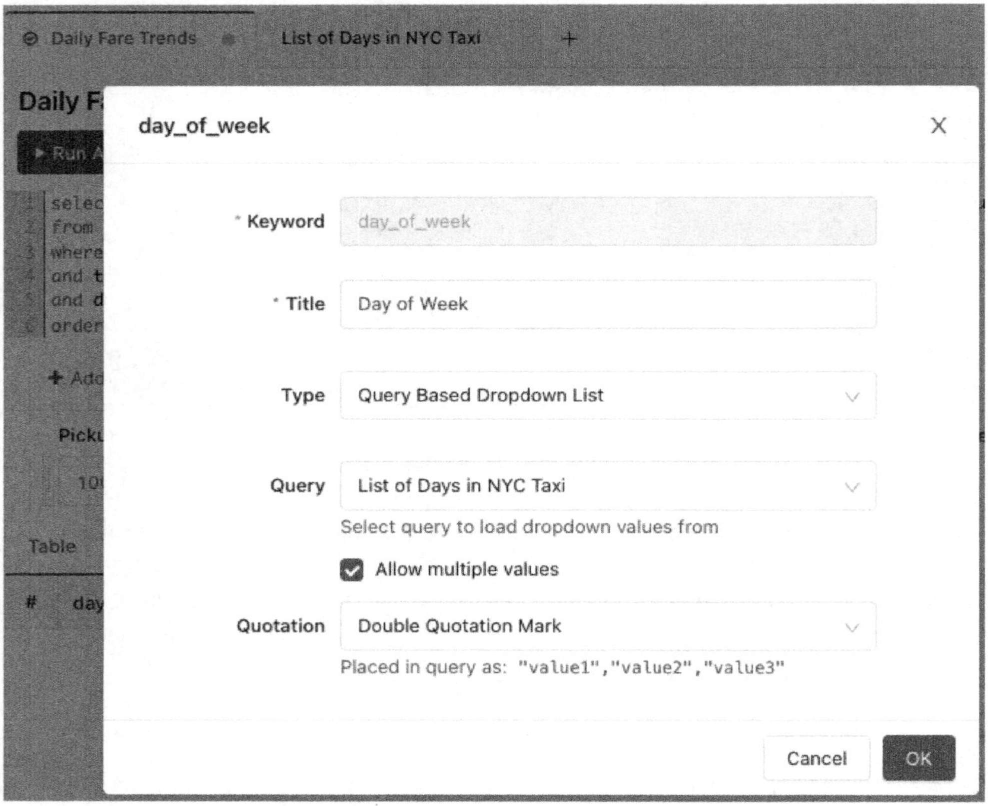

Figure 5.19 – Query Based Dropdown List

Regardless of whether you use **Dropdown List** or **Query Based Dropdown List**, the end state of the query is the same. The only difference is the mechanism to get the list values.

Once the query parameter has been configured, the user will see a UI widget, as shown in the following screenshot:

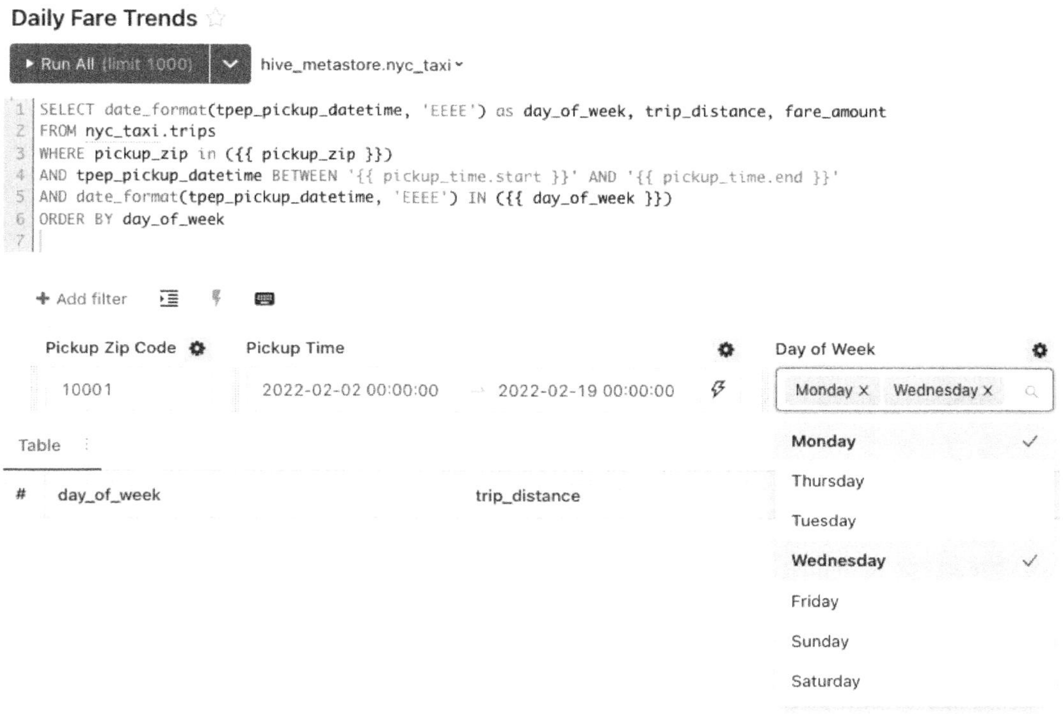

Figure 5.20 – Using a drop-down query parameter

With that, we can conclude our discussion on parameterizing queries. If you have been following along, then you should have arrived at the following SQL query:

```
SELECT date_format(tpep_pickup_datetime, 'EEEE') as day_of_
week, trip_distance, fare_amount
FROM nyc_taxi.trips
WHERE pickup_zip in ({{ pickup_zip }})
AND tpep_pickup_datetime BETWEEN '{{ pickup_time.start }}' AND
'{{ pickup_time.end }}'
AND date_format(tpep_pickup_datetime, 'EEEE') IN ({{ day_of_
week }})
ORDER BY day_of_week
```

This also concludes our discussion of developing queries. In this lengthy section, we covered the following topics:

- The concept of a query as a first-class citizen in Databricks SQL
- Creating SQL statements within a query
- Parameterizing a query for runtime flexibility

Next, we will learn how to work with the results of the SQL statements within these queries.

Visualizing query results

In the previous section, we focused purely on developing the SQL/query for the requirements at hand. However, development does not stop at writing a SQL query that returns a bunch of rows.

It is important to expose these results in a digestible format, and the best way to do so is via visualizations – graphical representations of the results.

Databricks SQL supports a variety of visualizations. We'll discuss them in the following sections.

> **How Detailed Will We Get?**
>
> Visualizations provide a lot of levers for configuring and customizing the representation. We will not be going into explicit detail about each configuration. I am assuming that you will get a general sense of the configuration once you get hands-on with visualizations. The following discussions will get you hands-on up to that level. You can take your visualizations to the next level by playing with all the various configurations. At any point, if you feel lost, please refer to the official documentation at `https://docs.databricks.com/sql/user/visualizations/`.

Tables

Yes – tables are a form of visualization as well.

When building a SQL query, you use the `SELECT` statement to specify the data return format and the data columns to return, as well as the `ORDER BY` clause to specify the order of the columns and rows of data.

Databricks SQL presents these results by default in a *table* visualization, as shown in the following screenshot:

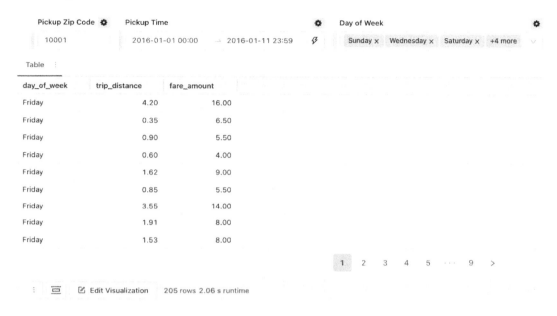

Figure 5.21 – Results visualized as a table

In the preceding screenshot, we can see the results of the SQL we developed for *Requirement 1*, visualized as a table.

Since this table is a visualization, we can now edit this visualization to reorder, hide, or format the data that was originally returned by the SQL.

To do so, we can click on the **Edit Visualization** button, as shown in the preceding screenshot. Doing so will open a visualization-specific pop-up that allows us to customize the visualization. In this case, the customization screen will look as follows:

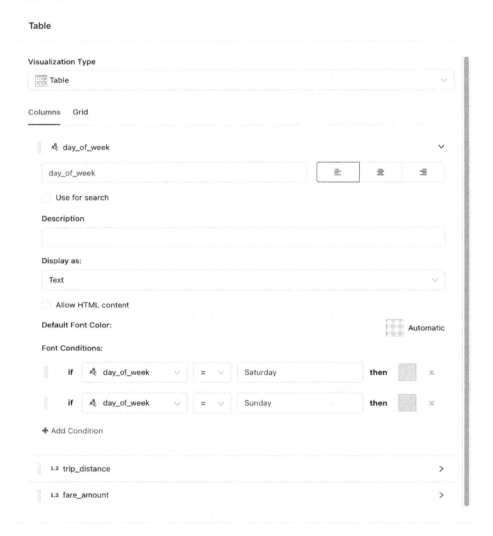

Figure 5.22 – Customizing the table visualization

Here, we apply a conditional color coding of rows based on the `day_of_week` column values (weekend versus weekday). Other possible customizations are as follows:

- Toggling the visibility of a column

- Formatting a numeric or temporal column, such as by limiting decimal places or using the ISO date format

- Conditional color coding of columns

It is important to highlight that Databricks SQL supports special data types:

- **Image**: Set the **Display as** option to **Image**. Databricks SQL will treat the cell value as a hyperlink to an image and render that image in the visualization.

- **Link**: Set the **Display as** option to **Link**. Databricks SQL will generate a clickable hyperlink based on a template, using the values returned in that row.

- **JSON**: Databricks SQL will pretty-print the JSON in the cell.

Charts

The next most popular visualization type is charts. In simple terms, these are any visualizations that use an *X*-axis and a *Y*-axis. Most of the charts are built on the same query, so you can switch between charts without changing the underlying data configurations. This way, you can easily find out which visualization conveys the meaning truthfully.

Returning to *Requirement 1*, we must create a fare trend analysis. This means we must visualize how trends vary with trip distances and how the day of the week affects it. If we were to visualize this on a chart, the *X*-axis would be the trip distance and the *Y*-axis would be the fare. The grouping criteria would be the day of the week. Let's add this visualization.

To add a new visualization, click on the **Add Visualization** button in the **results** pane. This will present a screen where we can select the type of visualization we want. Based on this selection, Databricks SQL will present the required configurations. On the right-hand side of this pop-up is the preview pane, which allows us to preview the chart based on the configurations; it updates in real time. We can create a scatterplot visualization like so:

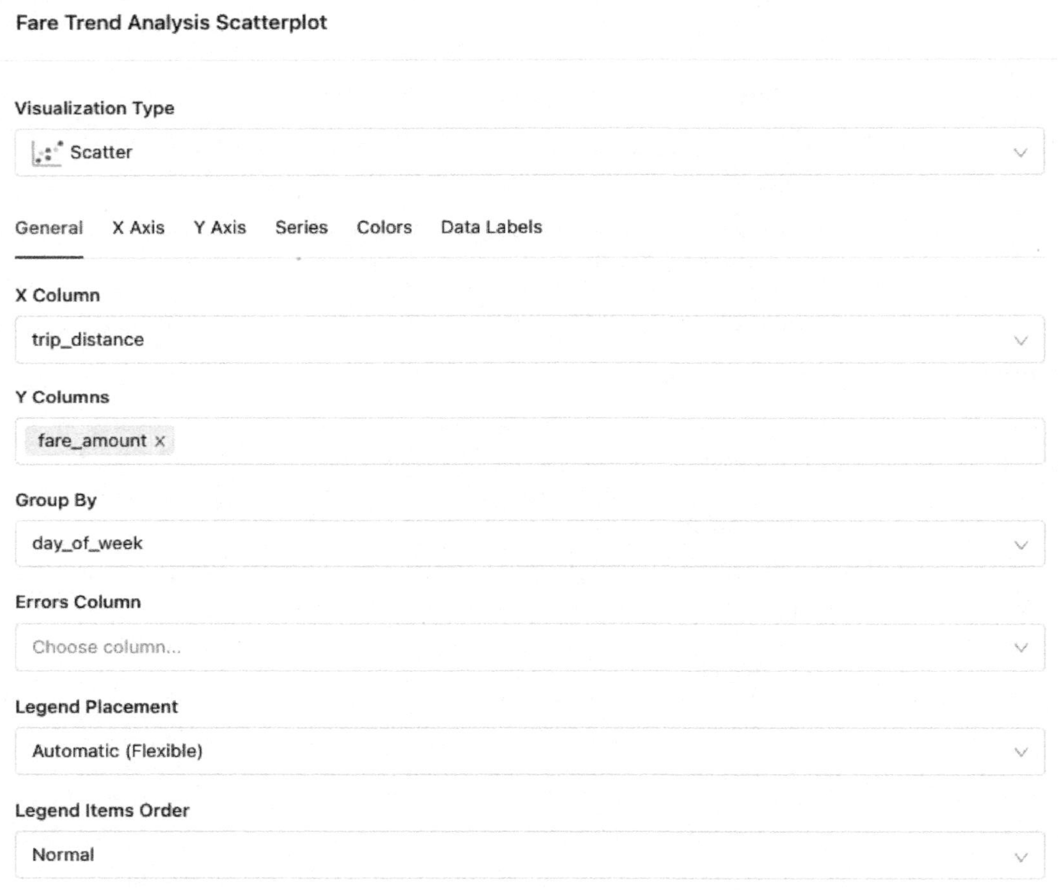

Fare Trend Analysis Scatterplot

Visualization Type

⌖ Scatter   ⌄

General   X Axis   Y Axis   Series   Colors   Data Labels

X Column

trip_distance   ⌄

Y Columns

fare_amount ×

Group By

day_of_week   ⌄

Errors Column

Choose column...   ⌄

Legend Placement

Automatic (Flexible)   ⌄

Legend Items Order

Normal   ⌄

Figure 5.23 – Creating a scatterplot

Saving this configuration creates a visualization and renders it based on the results returned, like so:

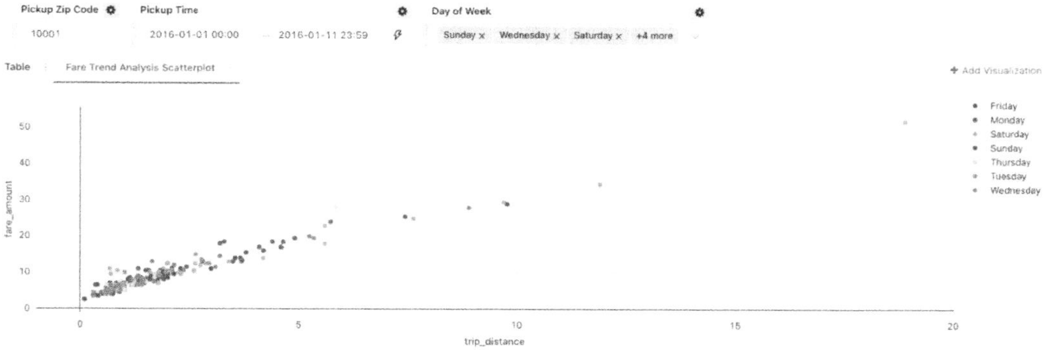

Figure 5.24 – The scatterplot has been rendered

Here, we can see how the relationship between trip distance and fare amount changes when the day of the week changes. This is also a perfect visualization for *Requirement 1* of our working example.

> **One Query, Multiple Visualizations**
>
> One query can be associated with multiple visualizations. This goes back to a query being a first-class citizen in Databricks SQL. Developers can create multiple visualizations based on the insight they want to deliver. Users of the query can choose which visualization to render. Users of the query can be actual users or developers, or they can be dashboards using the query to render a visualization. This enables a clear separation of responsibilities and removes any chance of data not being interpreted as the developer originally intended.

Now that we have a working example of a chart, we can introduce the primary concepts surrounding chart visualizations.

Grouping

As we saw from our example, **grouping** is used to create multiple traces for the same *X* and *Y* values – that is, it helps sort (x,y) tuples by certain (grouping) columns for a more succinct representation of data.

Stacking

Stacking *stacks* the Y-axis values on top of each other based on the grouping columns. Stacking can be applied with bar charts and area charts. In our example, for each (x,y) – that is, (trip distance, fare amount) – there would be seven stacks representing each day of the week. *Figure 5.25* shows a bar chart with stacking. Different colors in the stack represent different days of the week and the size of each color stack is proportional to how many instances of that (trip distance, fare amount) occurred during that day of the week. It is safe to say that this visualization is not even close to effective in terms of conveying the trend analysis. Our scatterplot was more on point:

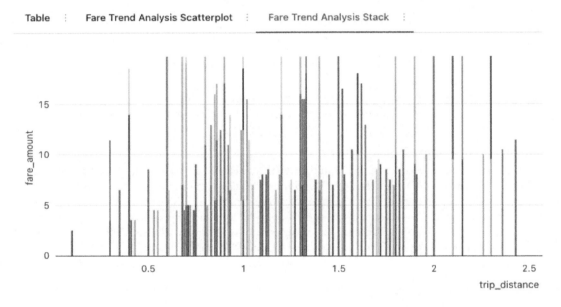

Figure 5.25 – Stacked bar chart for fare trend analysis

Error bars

Let's consider *Requirement 1* again. Our analysis is based on the premise of accurate trip distances. In the real world, trip distances are based on GPS readings. The GPS devices themselves have certain error margins and are dependent on the route and the GPS availability throughout the route. For example, GPS is inaccurate inside tunnels and among high-rise buildings in business districts. This means that our fare trend analysis should account for this error margin.

Our dataset does not contain this information, so we can fabricate our own for this discussion. I am using the following rule – 2% error for trips up to 2 miles, 5% error for trips between 3 and 10 miles, and 6% error for trips beyond 10 miles. For further simplicity, I am assuming that this percentage discrepancy in distance translates 1:1 into a percentage discrepancy in fare. The resulting table should look like this:

day_of_week	trip_distance	fare_amount	fare_error
Table : Fare Trend Analysis with Error			
Friday	0.60	5.00	0.10
Friday	1.91	8.00	0.16

Figure 5.26 – Fabricated error column

If we create a line chart with the error column configuration option set to `fare_error`, we will get the following visualization, which shows the degree of confidence at each data point with error bars:

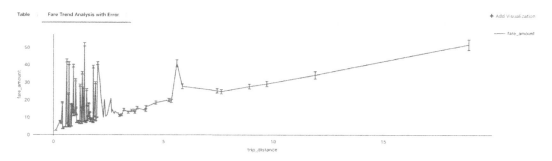

Figure 5.27 – Fare trend analysis with error bars

This concludes this discussion on charts. There are more chart visualizations apart from the scatterplot, stacked bar chart, and line chart, as follows:

- Area chart
- Pie chart
- Bubble chart
- Box chart
- Heatmap

I highly encourage you to create examples of these chart types using the same dataset while following the official documentation: `https://docs.databricks.com/sql/user/visualizations/charts.html`.

Specialized visualization types

Tables and charts typically suffice for most use cases. However, there can be times when more specialized visualizations are required. Databricks SQL provides the following specialized visualization types:

- Map visualization
- Cohort visualization
- Funnel visualization
- Pivot tables
- Sankey
- Sunburst
- Word cloud

We will discuss a few of these in the following sections. You are encouraged to follow the official documentation for the visualizations that we won't discuss here.

Map visualization

Of course, we must start with the most exciting of the lot. You can use map visualizations to display the results of a query on a geographic map. For example, you can show revenue by state or country on a map instead of using a vanilla table.

There are two map visualization styles, as follows:

- **Choropleth**: Choropleth allows you to work with geographic entities such as countries and states. At the time of writing, Choropleth supports visualizations at the country level, USA state level, and Japan prefecture level. Our New York Taxi dataset is not very well suited for this visualization. You can see this visualization in action by importing the Retail Revenue & Supply Chain Sample dashboard, which shows revenue by country on a world map (`https://docs.databricks.com/sql/get-started/sample-dashboards.html`). Detailed documentation is available at `https://docs.databricks.com/sql/user/visualizations/maps.html`.

- **Map Marker**: This visualization mode places markers at a specified latitude and longitude. These markers can be configured to provide certain information from the results, such as the number of taxi trips originating from this location.

Returning to our requirements, let's work on *Requirement 2* – that is, *A view of pickup volumes per hour*. We can build two visualizations for this requirement:

- A bar chart showing pickup volumes per hour for a pickup location
- A handy map visualization to show this pickup location on a map for context

There are many ways to construct the SQL query for these visualizations. The most logical would be to create two separate queries. The first query will perform a count aggregate by `pickup_zip` and `pickup_hour`. It would look like this:

```
SELECT
  pickup_zip, date_format(tpep_pickup_datetime, 'HH:00') AS
pickup_hour, count(*) AS `trip count`
FROM
  nyc_taxi.trips
WHERE
  tpep_pickup_datetime BETWEEN TIMESTAMP '{{ pickup_date.start
}}'
  AND TIMESTAMP '{{ pickup_date.end }}'
  AND pickup_zip IN ({{ pickup_zip }})
GROUP BY pickup_zip, pickup_hour
```

It will be straightforward to plot this bar chart as the aggregation has already been done by us. We just need to set the *X*-axis to *Pick up Hour* and the *Y*-axis to *Trip Count and Stack by Zip Code*. A map visualization can easily be created by joining the same data to the latitudes and longitudes of the ZIP codes.

However, I want to take this opportunity to showcase the powerful visualization-building capabilities of Databricks SQL.

Hence, I will start with a simple data collection query:

```
SELECT
  pickup_zip, date_format(tpep_pickup_datetime, 'HH:00') AS
`pickup_hour`, latitude, longitude
FROM
  nyc_taxi.trips
JOIN nyc_taxi.zip_codes
ON pickup_zip = zip_code
WHERE
  tpep_pickup_datetime BETWEEN TIMESTAMP '{{ pickup_date.start
}}'
  AND TIMESTAMP '{{ pickup_date.end }}'
  AND pickup_zip IN ({{ pickup_zip }})
```

The query is simple – it just gets `pickup_hour` and `pickup_zip` from each row that satisfies our query parameters – the `pickup_date` range and the `pickup_zip` codes.

You will notice that I am not doing any aggregation of any kind.

> **Note on Zip Code Coordinates**
>
> I have built a table that maps ZIP codes to their corresponding geographic coordinates – latitude and longitude. You can build this yourself by using the data from the US census. A quick Google search should get you going. I found the following GitHub Gist helpful: `https://gist.github.com/erichurst/7882666`. Save the raw version of the Gist on your desktop, use Databricks Data Explorer to upload this data file to a table, and then join it to the existing data.

Now, let's learn how to build two very different visualizations from this data.

Click on **Add Visualization** and select **Bar** under **Visualization Type**. As shown in the following screenshot, we can configure our *X*-axis to be `pickup_hour` from the results of the SQL query. More importantly, look at the *Y*-axis configuration – Databricks SQL allows me to apply a **Count** aggregation based on the `pickup_zip` grouping:

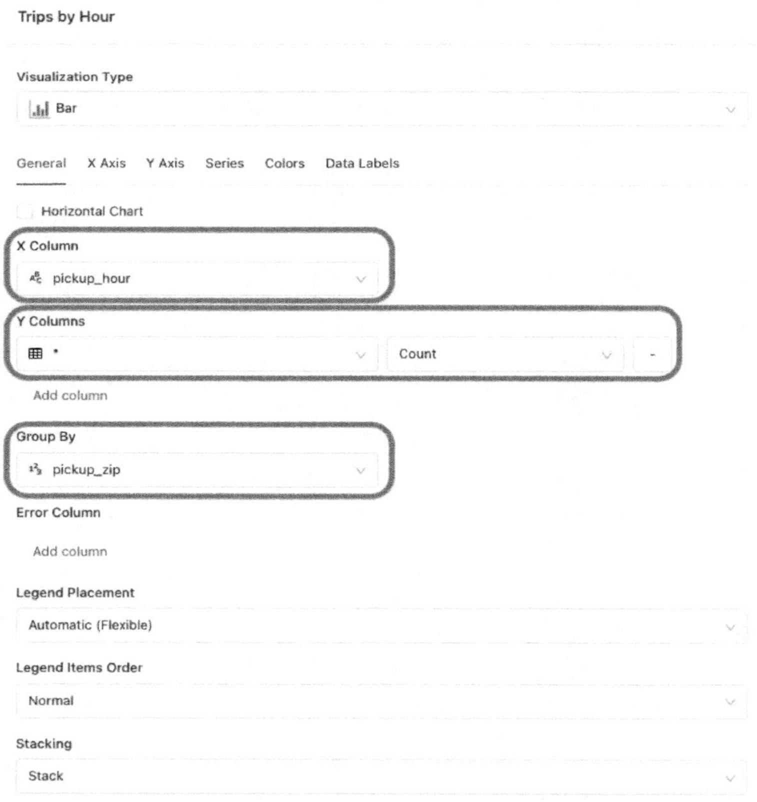

Figure 5.28 – Creating the pickup by hour trend

This is very powerful as it allows the developer of the query to expose correct interpretations of the data. The resulting visualization will look as follows:

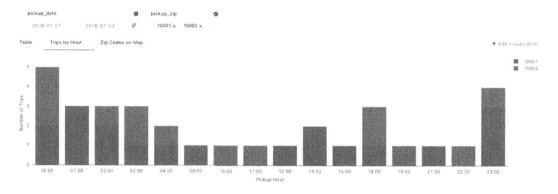

Figure 5.29 – Pickup hour trend distribution

Now, the same result set can also be used to create a visualization on the map. We will start by creating a **Map (Markers)** visualization and configuring the latitude and longitude columns from the result set, as shown here:

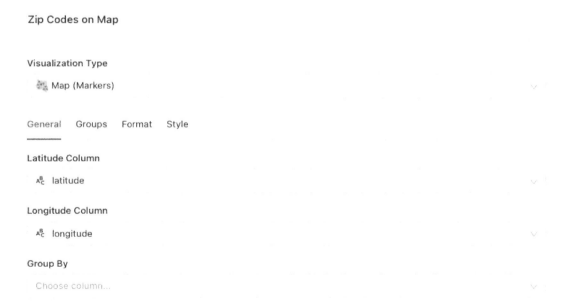

Figure 5.30 – Configuring the general settings for the Map (Markers) visualization

Optionally, we can configure a tooltip template that shows pertinent information if the markers on the map are clicked, as shown in the following screenshot. Here, we are configuring the map marker to show the ZIP code and pickup hour of the trip. You will also notice the use of the parameter format to refer to the columns in the result set. Bear in mind that these parameters are not the same as the query parameters:

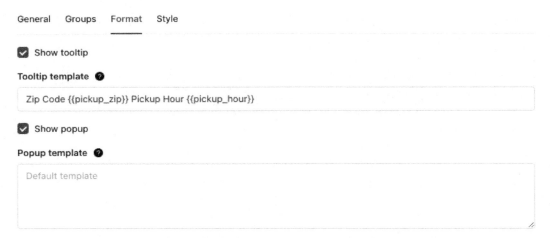

Figure 5.31 – Configuring the format settings for the Map (Markers) visualization

The preceding configurations result in the following map visualization:

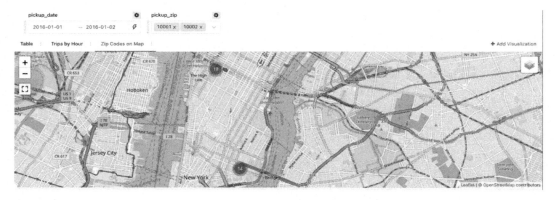

Figure 5.32 – Map visualization

In summary, it is ridiculously easy to use map visualizations in Databricks SQL.

Going back to our working example, the bar chart (*Figure 5.29*) and the map visualization (*Figure 5.32*) satisfy *Requirement 2*. If you look closely, *Requirement 3* is very similar. I will leave it up to you to construct the query and visualizations for the same.

Cohort analysis and visualization

Cohort analysis is useful when we want to measure or track a value across two different time series. Continuing with the Taxi example, we can define a cohort as users who signed up in a particular month – for example, January 2022. An example cohort analysis would have two time series:

- A month-on-month user signup time series.

- The activity level of each cohort (users who signed up in a month) across different months. For example, 100 users signed up in January but only 50 of those users booked a ride in January, 60 of those booked a ride in February, and so on. Similarly, 150 users signed up in February, and out of those 150, only 90 booked a ride in February; 110 booked a ride in March.

Cohort analysis and visualization will combine the two time series and present a visualization of user engagement.

Unfortunately, the NYC Taxi dataset does not contain user data, so performing cohort analysis on it will not be feasible. Due to this, we must fabricate some data. We will skip some steps and assume that the cohort analysis data is available. This fabricated cohort analysis works on monthly cohorts from January 2022 to June 2022. The following SQL snippet constructs this fabricated analysis:

```
CREATE TABLE cohort_analysis(
cohort_date DATE,
period INTEGER,
engaged_users INTEGER,
cohort_size DOUBLE
);
--Cohort Analysis From January to June
--In the month of January, 2022, out of the 35 people who
signed up in January, 33 showed activity
INSERT INTO cohort_analysis VALUES('2022-01-01', 0, 33, 35);
INSERT INTO cohort_analysis VALUES('2022-01-01', 1, 33, 35);
--In the month of March, 2022, out of the 35 people who signed
up in January, 25 showed activity
INSERT INTO cohort_analysis VALUES('2022-01-01', 2, 25, 35);
```

You are encouraged to fill out the rest of the cohort analysis values. Once done, configure a cohort visualization type, as shown in *Figure 5.33*.

Consider a sample row – that is, (`'2022-01-01'`, `2`, `33`, `35`). This sample row says *Out of the 35 people who signed up in January 2022, only 33 booked rides in March*. This means that we are talking about the engagement of users who signed up in January for rides in March – that is, 2 months after they signed up:

- **Date (Bucket)**: The cohort start date. In our example, one cohort represents the users that signed up in that month. This is 2022-01-01 in our sample row.

- **Stage**: This is the number of cohorts that have onboarded since this cohort (2022-01-01) started. This is 2 in our sample row.

- **Bucket Population Size**: This is the number of users in the cohort. In our sample, the 2022-01-01 cohort has 35 users.

- **Stage Value**: This is the number of users who booked rides in the stage (month). In our sample row, only 33 users from the 2022-01-01 cohort booked rides in stage 2 (March, or 2 months from January):

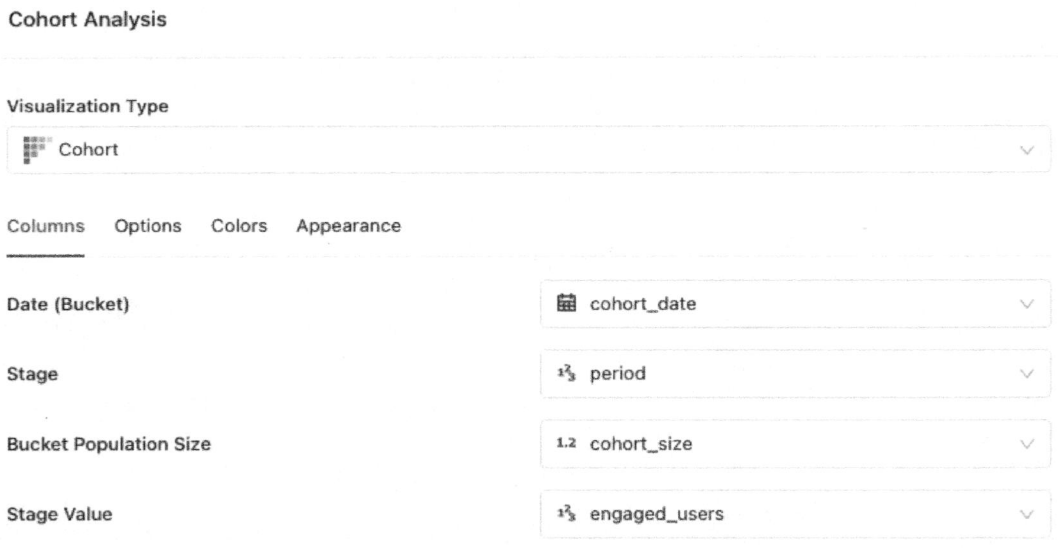

Cohort Analysis

Visualization Type

▦ Cohort	∨

Columns   Options   Colors   Appearance

Date (Bucket)	📅 cohort_date	∨
Stage	¹³ period	∨
Bucket Population Size	1.2 cohort_size	∨
Stage Value	¹³ engaged_users	∨

Figure 5.33 – Configuring a cohort analysis visualization

This configuration results in the following succinct visualization:

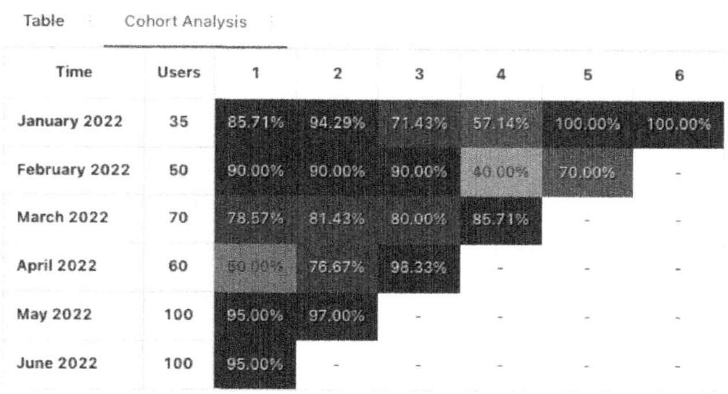

Figure 5.34 – Cohort analysis visualization for user engagement

> **Note**
>
> Databricks SQL only supports **Monthly**, **Weekly**, and **Daily** stages. This can be configured from the **Options** tab on the **Cohort Visualization** configuration page. The visualization in *Figure 5.34* uses **Monthly** stages.

Funnel visualization

Consider the cohort analysis that we did in the previous section. One of the things that stands out is that even though we have a lot of signups in every cohort, the signup is not translating into a booked taxi ride. For example, 35 people signed up in January, but only 33 booked a taxi ride. Now, you have been tasked with understanding why this is so.

Booking a taxi ride is a multi-step journey, starting from signup to profile creation, selecting a pickup location, selecting a destination, configuring a payment method, to finally making a booking. The users who are not active might be dropping off at any of these stages. These stages can be thought of as a funnel toward the final stage of making a booking. Performing funnel analysis and creating visualization will help you understand at which stage the user is dropping off. This will help the product team make decisions that can change this behavior.

Once again, we will fabricate some data. The fabricated data assumes that the funnel analysis for January has already been done:

```
CREATE TABLE funnel_analysis(
cohort DATE,
cohort_stage INT,
step STRING,
value INTEGER
```

```
);

INSERT INTO funnel_analysis VALUES('2020-01-01', 0,'Sign Up',
1000);
INSERT INTO funnel_analysis VALUES('2020-01-01', 0,'Create
Demographic Profile', 990);
INSERT INTO funnel_analysis VALUES('2020-01-01', 0,'Enter
Contact Details', 950);
INSERT INTO funnel_analysis VALUES('2020-01-01', 0,'Create
Avatar', 950);
INSERT INTO funnel_analysis VALUES('2020-01-01', 0,'Configure
Payment Method', 780);
INSERT INTO funnel_analysis VALUES('2020-01-01', 0,'Select
Pickup Location', 650);
INSERT INTO funnel_analysis VALUES('2020-01-01', 0,'Select
Destination Location', 650);
INSERT INTO funnel_analysis VALUES('2020-01-01', 0,'Select
Destination Location', 650);
INSERT INTO funnel_analysis VALUES('2020-01-01', 0,'Finalize
Booking', 630);
```

Configuring the funnel visualization is easy. As shown in the following screenshot, we must map the columns for the user journey step and the value – that is, the number of users who completed that step:

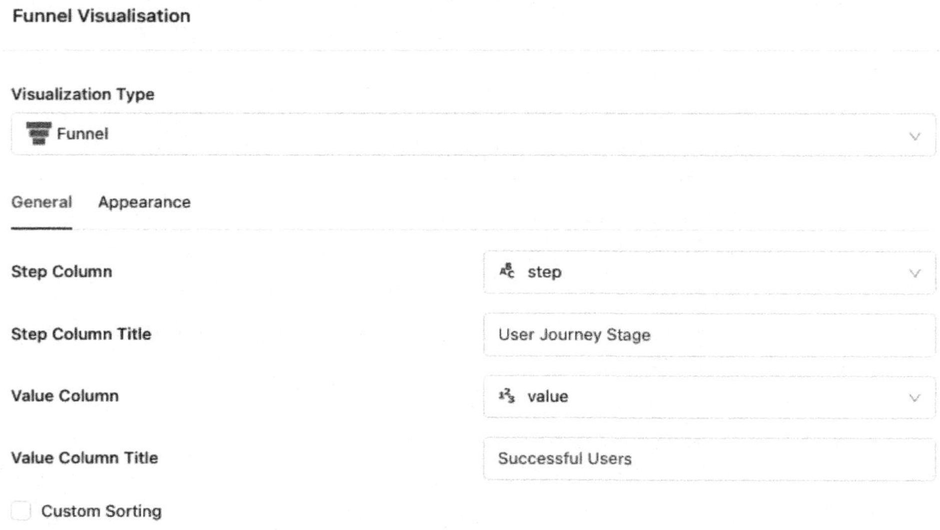

Figure 5.35 – Configuring the funnel analysis

This produces the following visualization:

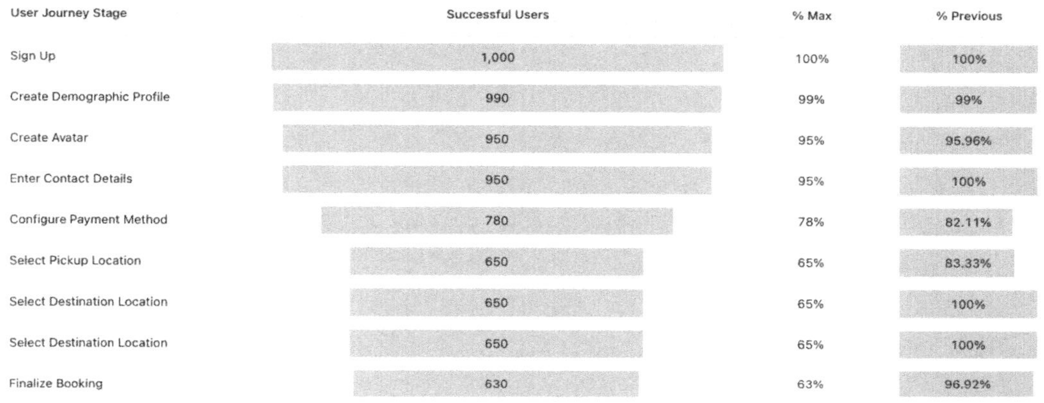

User Journey Stage	Successful Users	% Max	% Previous
Sign Up	1,000	100%	100%
Create Demographic Profile	990	99%	99%
Create Avatar	950	95%	95.96%
Enter Contact Details	950	95%	100%
Configure Payment Method	780	78%	82.11%
Select Pickup Location	650	65%	83.33%
Select Destination Location	650	65%	100%
Select Destination Location	650	65%	100%
Finalize Booking	630	63%	96.92%

Figure 5.36 – Funnel visualization of the user journey

In our example, we can see a clear inflection point in the payment configuration step. This means that the product team needs to simplify this step.

Pivot table visualization

The pivot table visualization allows you to create aggregated displays from an unaggregated query result. Consider *Requirement 4* – that is, *A route to revenue attribution*. Pivot tables will make easy work of this requirement. We will start by creating a query that returns unaggregated values of route and revenue – that is, `pickup_zip`, `dropoff_zip`, and `fare_amount`, where the date range is provided by the user as a query parameter:

```
SELECT pickup_zip, dropoff_zip, fare_amount
FROM nyc_taxi.trips
WHERE tpep_pickup_datetime BETWEEN "{{ pickup_time.start }}"
AND "{{ pickup_time.end }}"
```

Now, we can create a pivot table visualization that shows the total fare collected in the given time period for different routes. The pivot table visualization is a drag-and-drop builder. As shown in the following screenshot, the aggregation columns can be placed on the left. This aggregation can be selected from the drop-down menu. Here, the aggregation is **Sum** and is being used on `fare_amount`:

Figure 5.37 – Pivot table for route revenue attribution

This brings us to the end of this section on visualizations. We discussed some of the more generic (common) chart-based visualizations such as bar charts and scatterplots. We also discussed some of the more specialized visualization options, such as maps, cohorts, and funnels. Finally, we learned that a single query can be associated with multiple visualizations, allowing developers to create multiple interpretations of the same data.

Now that we have learned how to develop queries and visualizations, we have one more thing left to learn – how to bring them all together and present a dashboard for our end users.

Creating and publishing dashboards

Simply put, a dashboard is a presentation of various visualizations that provide context to your data and gives the observer of the dashboard actionable insights. For example, an operations team will look at the route-revenue visualization to decide the localities in which to place the taxis for maximum revenue.

We will learn about the various dashboarding features by bringing the queries and visualizations we have built in the preceding sections together.

Composing a dashboard

To create a new dashboard, simply open the **Dashboards** page and click **Create Dashboard**. Continuing with our working example, I am creating a new dashboard called **New York Taxi Operational Dashboard**.

The following screenshot shows the blank dashboard. We must associate a SQL Warehouse with the dashboard:

Figure 5.38 – Building a dashboard

A dashboard can have as many visualizations as you need. Click on the **Add Visualization** button to add a new visualization. In the following screenshot, I am adding the visualization for *Requirement 1*. Remember, a query is a first-class citizen. This is why, first, we select the query we built for this requirement – that is, the `Daily Fare Trends` query. Then, we select the pertinent visualization that we created for this query. Now, we can edit the query parameters. The default values are picked up from the last execution of the underlying query:

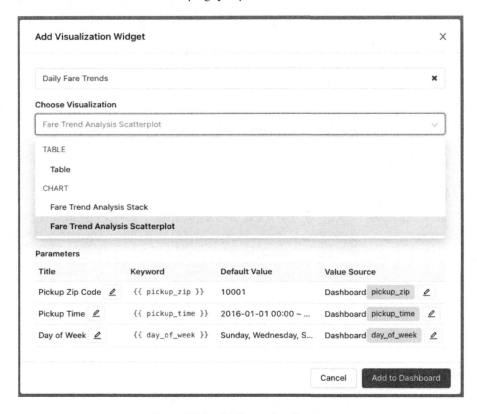

Figure 5.39 – Adding a visualization

It is important to focus on the **Value Source** column. This column allows us to configure the behavior of the query parameter. Clicking on the **Edit** button for any of the value sources opens a pop-up window, like so:

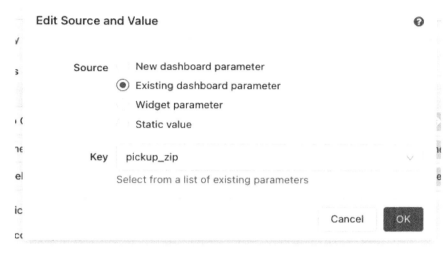

Figure 5.40 – The Edit Source and Value popup

There are four options to choose from:

- **New dashboard parameter**: This will place a new global parameter widget on top of the **Dashboards** page.

- **Existing dashboard parameter**: If the parameter key already exists (perhaps from configuring a different visualization), then that can be reused to avoid multiple global parameters for the same value.

- **Widget parameter**: If global parameters cannot be used for the visualization, then this option can be used to create a widget just for this visualization. This widget will be placed on the specific visualization tile instead of the top of the **Dashboards** page.

- **Static value**: If you do not wish to let the user change this parameter, use a static value.

> **Note**
>
> At this point, I have deliberately synced the query parameters for all the queries we have built so far. For example, I have changed the `pickup_time` parameters to a data and time range instead of a date range. Also, I have changed the `pickup_zip` parameter to be a query-based dropdown. You might be wondering why I didn't do that from the start – well, that is because I wanted to showcase different options as we go. Plus, it is a good exercise for you to revisit those queries and edit them for this synchronization.

Once we have placed all the visualizations, our shiny new operator dashboard will be ready, as shown here:

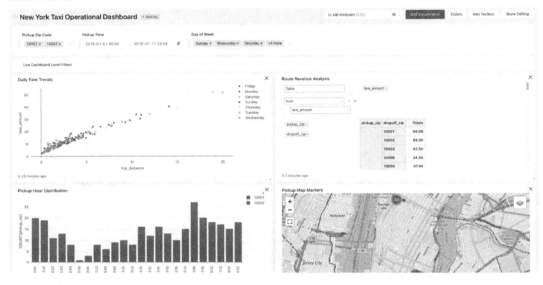

Figure 5.41 – NYC Taxi dashboard

As we can see, all the visualizations use global query parameters.

If your requirements call for user inputs for different visualizations, the visualizations can be edited accordingly. For example, a case can be made that the **Day of Week** parameter is relevant only to *Daily Fare Trends* and hence should be localized. We can edit this by clicking the context menu icon for the visualization, ⋮ .

Change the **Day of Week** parameter's **Value Source** to **Widget Parameter** from **Dashboard**, as shown here:

Parameters

Title	Keyword	Default Value	Value Source
Pickup Zip Code ✎	{{ pickup_zip }}	10001, 10002	Dashboard pickup_zip ✎
Pickup Time ✎	{{ pickup_time }}	2016-01-01 00:00 ~ ...	Dashboard pickup_time ✎
Day of Week ✎	{{ day_of_week }}	Sunday, Wednesday, S...	Widget parameter ✎

Figure 5.42 – NYC Taxi dashboard

Now, our dashboard presents the user with a specific choice of day of the week for the *Daily Fare Trends* visualization, as shown here:

Figure 5.43 – NYC Taxi dashboard with local parameters

Finally, dashboards allow you to change the layout of the visualizations and resize the visualization tiles with a simple drag and drop interface. When in edit mode, hovering over a visualization tile exposes a panning cursor, ✛. Once this cursor is exposed, you can drag the visualization around. The dashboard will automatically reconfigure the other visualizations relative to the movement. Similarly, hovering over the right-hand bottom corner of the visualization exposes a resizing icon, ⌟ . To use this feature, keep the left mouse button pressed down and resize the visualization.

Using the dashboard

Good job on compiling your dashboard! Make sure you click the **Done Editing** button to save your work. Now, there is one thing left to do: enable the intended audience of the dashboard to use the dashboard.

There are many ways to do so. Let's take a look at a few options.

Giving users access to the dashboard

One option is to give users access to the dashboard with **Can Run** permissions. To do so, click on the **Share** button for the dashboard. This will open a pop-up where you can configure which users or user groups have access to the dashboard, as shown here:

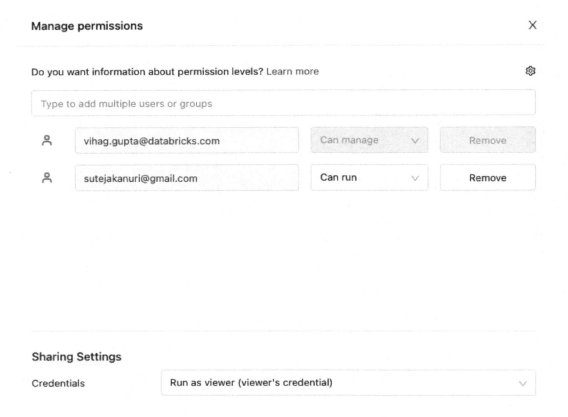

Figure 5.44 – Sharing the dashboard

In this example, we have shared the dashboard with Suteja. She only has permission to run it. If we had provided her with the **Can Edit** privilege, she would have been able to edit the dashboard and its visualizations.

> **Who Should Edit Dashboards?**
> Typically, you want to provide **Can Edit** privileges for fellow developers who are working on developing the dashboard. End users should only be able to view it.

Another significant configuration is **Sharing Settings**. Here, we are specifying that when Suteja runs the dashboard, her credentials will be used (**Run as viewer**). If Suteja does not have access to the underlying data source – the nyc_taxi database – the visualizations will fail. This is a great security feature as it can mitigate unwanted edge cases around permissions. The other option is **Run as owner**. This option is, again, good for allowing fellow developers to work on the dashboard.

Scheduling with subscribers

Another option is to refresh the dashboard on a schedule. Every scheduled run can then email a report of the dashboard in PDF format. To do so, click on the **Schedule** button. Configure the schedule to refresh the dashboard and configure the users (**Subscribers**) who will receive the reports, as shown here:

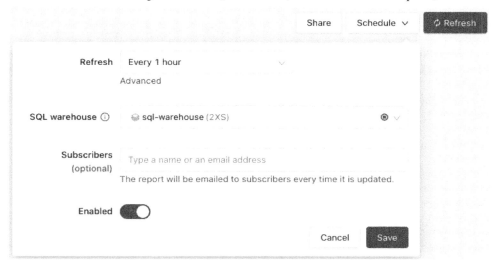

Figure 5.45 – Scheduling and sharing the dashboard with subscribers

The **Enabled** toggle button allows you to temporarily pause the scheduled refresh of the dashboard.

Other interactions with the dashboard

Users with access to the dashboard can download a PDF report of the dashboard manually. Click on the context icon, ⋮ , of the dashboard and click the **Download as PDF** option.

Users can also interact with individual visualizations. Every visualization tile exposes a menu so that you can download the results of the query powering the tile. Clicking the context icon for the visualization, ⋮ , provides options for downloading the results as a **comma-separated values** (**CSV**) file, a **tab-separated values** (**TSV**) file, or in **Excel** format. There is also a link to the original query for quick navigation.

Alerts

Sending refreshed dashboards is great, but actionable alerts are even better. It is possible that the users of the dashboard are only interested in seeing the dashboard when a particular metric on the dashboard has drifted away from acceptable ranges. Alerts are a great way to deliver on this.

Continuing with our working example, let's say that we want to have an alert if our earnings in the last hour have been significantly less than the historical earnings during that hour and day of the week.

> **DIY Please**
>
> We have not built a query that provides the analysis that we just described. Consider it an exercise to build it yourself.

It is important to note that an alert expects the underlying query to return a single row. Rather, it will only consider the first row of the returned results. This is logical. We want to configure an alert that will trigger based on some value deviating from a threshold. In our example, we want to know if the total fares earned in the last hour have deviated from the historical trend for that hour and that day of the week. This must be a single row.

To configure an alert, navigate to the **Alerts** page by clicking on 🔔:

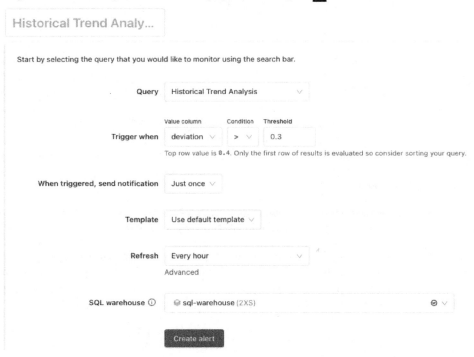

Figure 5.46 – Creating an alert

Here, we have configured a **Query** that performs a historical analysis. The query returns a column called **deviation** that represents a percentage of the deviation from historical fares for the hour and the day of the week. We have configured the alert to **Trigger when** the deviation is greater than 30%.

Other configurations can remain as their defaults or be configured.

The **When triggered, send notification** option configures the alerting behavior. You can configure it to send the alert **Just Once** or **Each Time** the alert is evaluated. A good in-between option is the **At Most** option. For example, you can configure the alert to send notifications **At Most** once **Every hour**. The *once* and *every hour* can be configured.

The notification itself can be customized by editing the template.

Finally, we can configure how often the alert should be evaluated or refreshed. In our case, it makes sense for it to be hourly since we are looking for deviations in fares hour by hour. Keep in mind that the refresh will require a SQL Warehouse to be turned on. It is recommended that you only configure alerts for desired notifications.

The alert will look as follows:

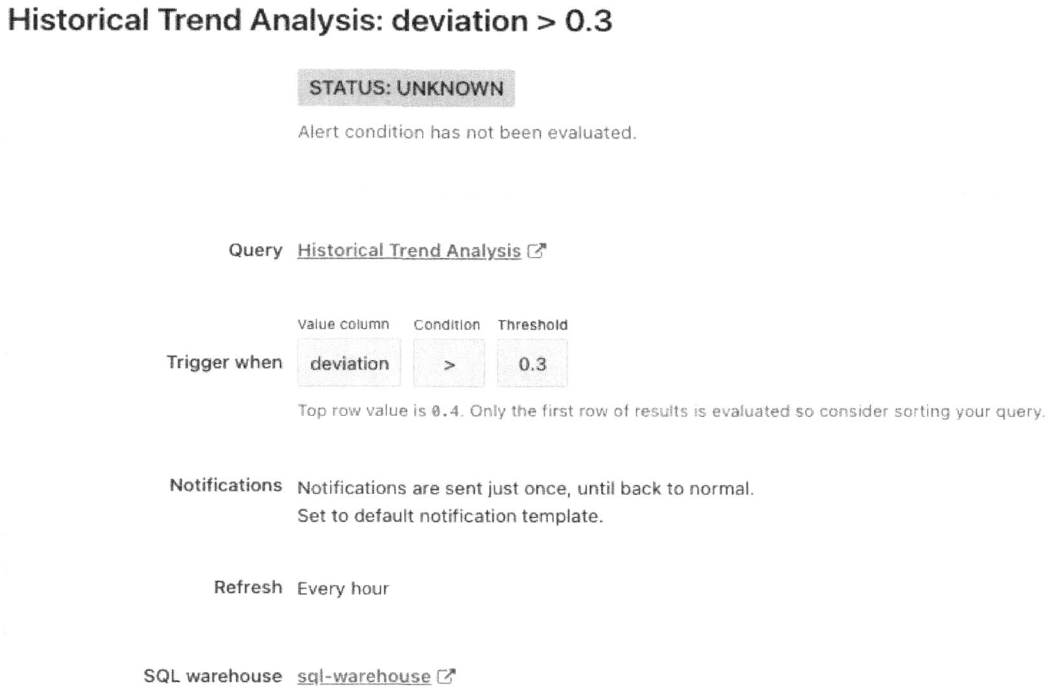

Historical Trend Analysis: deviation > 0.3

STATUS: UNKNOWN

Alert condition has not been evaluated.

Query   Historical Trend Analysis ⬀

	Value column	Condition	Threshold
Trigger when	deviation	>	0.3

Top row value is 0.4. Only the first row of results is evaluated so consider sorting your query.

Notifications   Notifications are sent just once, until back to normal.
Set to default notification template.

Refresh   Every hour

SQL warehouse   sql-warehouse ⬀

Figure 5.47 – Alert

By default, the alert notification is sent to the owner of the alert. We can add more destinations as required by clicking on the **Add** button (not visible in the screenshot).

It is important to note that only account administrators can configure destinations from the SQL Admin Console. However, once a destination has been configured, it is available to all users. Databricks SQL supports destinations such as emails, Slack, PagerDuty, and many more.

This concludes our discussion on workbench from a developer and user perspective. Now, let's learn how to administer and govern the queries, visualizations, and dashboards as a developer, as well as an administrator.

Administering and governing artifacts

Every query, visualization, and dashboard that we create is a crucial artifact. It should be protected from unauthorized consumption or sharing. On the other hand, artifacts should be shared securely so that others may build on existing work as well.

Hence, Databricks SQL provides a robust governance model for securing queries (and associated visualizations), dashboards, and alerts.

Administration by the artifact owner

The governance model is consistent across queries, dashboards, and alerts. All three of them have a **Share** button, similar to the one shown in the following screenshot:

Share

Figure 5.48 – The Share button

The **Share** button opens a pop-up where the owner of the query, dashboard, or alert can configure other users with **Can Edit** or **Can Run** privileges. Furthermore, the owner can configure the query or dashboard to run with the owner's credentials or the viewer's credentials. It is important to configure this carefully as it has security implications.

For example, a user with **Can Run** privileges may not have access to the underlying data sources for data security reasons. If the query or dashboard has been configured to run with the owner's privilege, then this user will be able to view the results and hence constitute a security breach. We saw this approach in *Figure 5.44*.

It is important to note that only the owner has the **Can Manage** privilege.

Sharing alerts has interesting dynamics. When sharing alerts, **Can Edit** or **Can Run** privileges can be granted. These privileges are self-explanatory. However, if a user receives **Can Run** privileges on the alert, they can still configure the alert to send them a notification when the alert is triggered. That said, they cannot edit the core conditions of the alert. Alerts run with the viewer's privilege, so if the viewer does not have privileges on the underlying data source, it will not execute.

Administration by the account administrator

Account administrators can also govern the artifacts. They have view permissions on all dashboards. They also have delete permissions on all dashboards.

This is by design. Consider the case where the owner of the artifact leaves the organization. In such a case, the account administrator can transfer ownership of the artifact to another resource.

That said, account administrators do not have **Can Edit** permissions on any artifact unless the owner explicitly grants such permissions.

> **Additional Context on Access Control**
>
> This discussion is enough to understand the access control model for queries, dashboards, and alerts. However, it is worth checking the official documentation, which provides a great tabular view of possible actions and required permissions. Check it out at `https://docs.databricks.com/sql/user/security/access-control/`.

Summary

In this chapter, we put on the lens of an end user of Databricks SQL – the business analyst or the data analyst – and learned about the features that enable end users to go through their daily workflows.

First, we learned how to build queries and visualizations and how to compose them into usable dashboards. After that, we learned how to put the dashboards to use with various sharing and alerting features. Finally, we learned how to administer and govern all these artifacts. We learned all this while navigating a hands-on example and compiled our very own operational dashboard.

In this chapter, we assumed that the required computation power is available to us to build and run queries and dashboards. In the next chapter, where we will cover SQL Warehouses, we will go behind the scenes and see how this computation power comes about and how to configure it for the best possible end user experience.

6

The SQL Warehouses

In this chapter, we will focus on the compute layer of the Lakehouse architecture. The compute layer in Databricks SQL is called the SQL Warehouse. We will learn how to create SQL Warehouses and configure them for the best possible user experience. We will also learn how the computation layer is instantiated on demand when a user executes a query.

The primary audience of this chapter is the Database administrators and Databricks workspace administrator personas. That said, Data analyst personas will also benefit from this chapter by learning how their queries are executed, how to avoid common pitfalls, and how to get the best possible performance.

In this chapter, we will cover the following topics:

- Understand the SQL Warehouse architecture
- Creating and configuring SQL Warehouses
- The art of SQL Warehouse sizing
- Organizing and governing SQL Warehouses
- Using Serverless SQL

Technical requirements

For this chapter, you will need the following:

- A basic understanding of the components of the cloud's **infrastructure as a service (IaaS)** for your cloud service provider of choice
- An understanding of the *The internals of cloud storage access* section of *Chapter 4, The Security Model*

Understanding the SQL Warehouse architecture

The official documentation for SQL Warehouses (`https://docs.databricks.com/sql/admin/sql-endpoints.html`) defines a SQL Warehouse as a computation resource that lets you run SQL commands on data objects within Databricks SQL.

In practice, this computation resource manifests as a logical/virtual grouping of one or more physical clusters. The physical clusters are Apache Spark clusters, as provisioned by Databricks.

A single physical cluster follows the core architecture of Apache Spark, as shown in the following diagram:

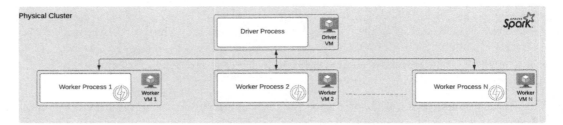

Figure 6.1 – Physical cluster topology

As shown in the preceding diagram, two distinct processes make a cluster:

- **Driver process**: Think of this process as the brain of the cluster. It is responsible for accepting users' queries, parsing them, planning them, and coordinating their distributed execution across the worker processes available in the cluster. The driver process runs on its own dedicated VM (or EC2 instance in AWS).

- **Worker processes**: Think of these processes as the muscle to the driver's brain. They are responsible for accepting tasks from the driver process, completing them, and returning the results. If you are familiar with the execution architecture of Apache Spark, you will note that the worker processes correspond to executors, which delegate work to smaller processing units called Tasks. The worker processes reside on their own dedicated VMs (or EC2 instances). However, since they are responsible for executing queries, they are spawned on VMs with higher CPU and RAM configurations. The number of worker VMs in a single physical cluster is fixed.

Should I learn Apache Spark?

You do not need to be an expert on Apache Spark to be able to work with Databricks SQL and SQL Warehouses. All you need to understand is that each physical cluster in the SQL Warehouse has one driver VM and multiple worker VMs. That said, a high-level conceptual overview will help you make better sense of the infrastructure requirements and performance tuning tasks. If you wish to deep dive into Apache Spark, follow the official guides: `https://spark.apache.org/docs/latest/cluster-overview.html`.

You will also notice a lightning-like icon on the worker processes. This represents the Photon engine. The open source Apache Spark system uses **Java Virtual Machine** (**JVM**)-based executors, which are not suited for high concurrency, interactive SQL workloads. Hence Databricks augments the JVM-based executors with a native C++-based engine called **Photon** that enables SQL workloads at high concurrency.

Do I Need to Know About Photon?

Not really. The presence of Photon is transparent. That said, Photon is an evolving engine and there are some nuances in how it handles certain SQL commands. These nuances are important for understanding the performance implications of certain edge workloads. We will discuss them further in *Chapter 9*, *The Photon Engine*.

Now that we have seen what a single physical cluster looks like, it is easy to visualize a SQL Warehouse, as follows:

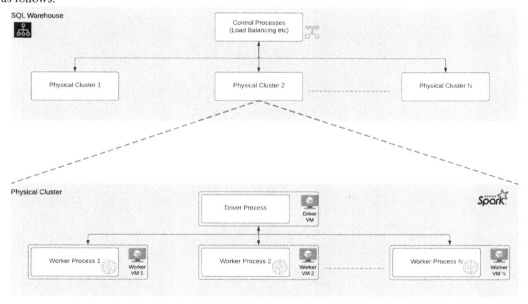

Figure 6.2 – SQL Warehouse topology

As shown in the preceding diagram, a single SQL Warehouse is composed of one or more physical clusters that receive user queries and execute them. The task of routing user queries to specific physical clusters is done by the control processes on the SQL Warehouse. The control processes are responsible for the following:

- Load-balancing queries onto existing physical clusters in the SQL Warehouse

- Maintaining user-session stickiness to a physical cluster to maximize the use of caching

- Autoscaling the number of physical clusters in the SQL Warehouse to accommodate for the current and predicted query workload

It is very important to highlight that all these processes are transparent. This heavy lifting is done for you in the background, albeit under the control limits that you specify.

Control limits can be specified while creating or updating SQL Warehouses, as we'll see in the next section.

Creating and configuring SQL Warehouses

In this section, we'll learn how to create or update SQL Warehouses. Specifically, we will learn about the configurations that are associated with SQL Warehouses. We will also learn what each configuration controls and how it contributes to the overall query experience. To begin, navigate to the **SQL Warehouses** page by clicking on the ⛃ icon.

Click on the **Create SQL Warehouse** button to bring up the creation pop-up, like so:

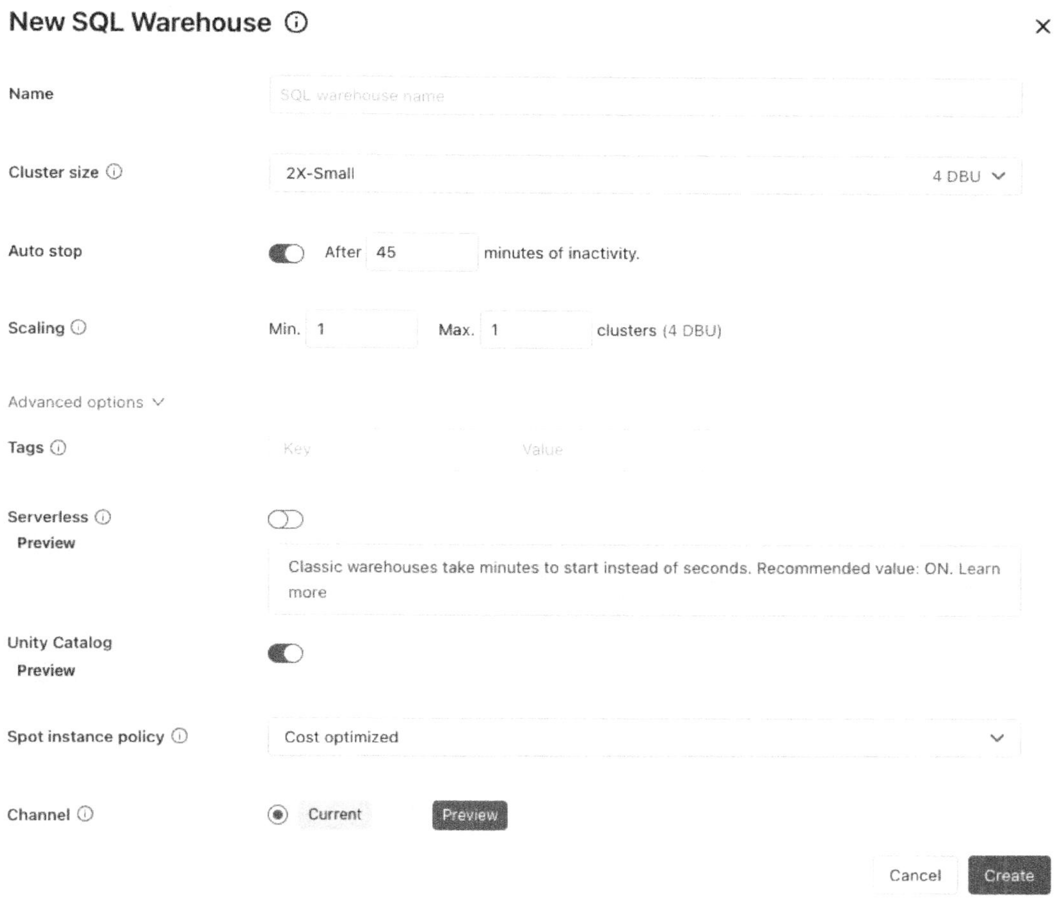

Figure 6.3 – New SQL Warehouse

As you can see, there are four primary decisions to make when creating a SQL Warehouse. Let's take a look.

Cluster size

When creating a SQL Warehouse, we must select its size. More accurately, we must select the size of the physical clusters that will constitute the SQL Warehouse. Refer to *Figure 6.2* to see how multiple physical clusters constitute a SQL Warehouse.

> **Note**
>
> Going forward, we will use the terms *SQL Warehouse size* and *cluster size* interchangeably.

Cluster sizes are represented as *T-shirt sizes* in Databricks SQL. Literally. You can choose from nine cluster T-shirt sizes, starting from **2X-Small** to **4X-Large**.

Great.

But wait – what are the measurements? How do I know which size fits me best?

The answer lies in the following fitting chart:

T-Shirt Size	Number of Workers
2X-Small	1
X-Small	2
Small	4
Medium	8
Large	16
X-Large	32
2X-Large	64
3X-Large	128
4X-Large	256

Each cluster is a collection of worker machines. Each T-shirt size represents the number of workers in the cluster and hence the available computing power in the cluster.

Again, you might be wondering, how much compute power does one worker represent? Each worker represents a computation resource of 8 vCPUs and 64 GB of RAM. At the time of writing, in Azure, this is the *standard_E8ds_v4* VM type. In AWS, this is the *i3.2xlarge* EC2 type. In GCP, this is the *n2-highmem-8* VM type.

Before running any SQL Warehouse, ensure that you have a large enough quota to support the number of required workers.

> **Note**
>
> The cluster size is proportional to the latency of an individual query (assuming that the query itself is not exceptionally bad in design). If individual queries are not completing fast enough, increase the cluster size.
>
> You can also think of the cluster size as the bandwidth for processing larger datasets. Larger cluster sizes have more CPUs and RAM and can accommodate more parallel data processing – if the query lends itself to parallelization.

Reiterating a crucial point, when creating and configuring SQL Warehouses, we can only select the T-shirt size. We cannot configure the instance types to be used. This is to keep things simple – the last thing you want to be doing is doing mental gymnastics with VM types, CPUs, and RAM counts.

At this point, you may again be thinking – knowing the number of workers in a T-shirt size is great, but how do I use that information?

Hold on to that thought – we will discuss that soon in the *The art of SQL Warehouse sizing* section.

Scaling

Scaling defines two things:

- The minimum number of physical clusters in the SQL Warehouse at any given time.
- The maximum number of physical clusters in the SQL Warehouse at any given time. The maximum number of physical clusters, per warehouse, at the time of writing, is 40.

SQL Warehouses have internal algorithms to bring the warehouses to the correct number of physical clusters, depending on the workloads. We will discuss the algorithm in the *Rules of query routing, queuing, and cluster autoscaling* section.

> **Note**
>
> The scaling configuration is proportional to the concurrency of queries that the SQL Warehouse will handle. If individual queries are queued for too long, you should increase the scaling range – that is, the maximum number of physical clusters in the warehouse.

Of course, there are more nuances when choosing the scaling range, as we will see in the *The art of SQL Warehouse sizing* section.

Spot instance policy

All the public clouds offer **spot instances** (by one name or other). Spot instances are unused compute resources in the cloud's data centers that the cloud provider offers at deeply discounted rates. You can read more about them at `https://aws.amazon.com/ec2/spot/` for AWS, `https://azure.microsoft.com/en-us/services/virtual-machines/spot/` for Azure, and `https://cloud.google.com/compute/docs/instances/preemptible` for GCP.

Using spot instances to build SQL Warehouses is an attractive proposition as it allows you to massively reduce the cost of running the SQL Warehouses. The only caveat is that spot instances can be reclaimed by the cloud provider with very short notice (for example, 2 minutes in AWS), which can undermine the stability of the SQL Warehouse.

Databricks SQL mitigates the problem of instability transparently. For example, if we choose the **Cost Optimized** policy, Databricks SQL will provision physical clusters whose target is to use spot instances for all workers, except one. Consider a *Large* T-shirt size cluster. The target would be to use 15 spot instance-based workers and one on-demand instance. This is to ensure that if a catastrophic event occurs, such as all spot instances being claimed back by the cloud provider, there is at least one worker still trying to clear the query backlog. However, the mitigation does not stop there. When a spot instance-based worker is reclaimed, it is immediately replaced by an on-demand worker to ensure continuity.

The Cost Optimized policy is great for workloads that can tolerate some SLA misses or for development workloads.

For production workloads, it is recommended to use the **Reliability Optimized** policy. This policy uses on-demand instances only and, as its name suggests, a more reliable, SLA-bound execution of workloads.

Auto Stop

The **Auto Stop** function, as its name suggests, terminates the SQL Warehouse (and the underlying physical clusters) after a configured period of inactivity. It is important to configure this correctly for a good user experience.

For example, if the auto stop time is too aggressive, the cluster will terminate after short periods of inactivity. Now, if a new query comes in, the SQL Warehouse needs to be brought up again, which, for a classic cluster, takes around 4 to 5 minutes. With an aggressive auto stop policy, there is an increased chance of new queries always having to wait for cluster startup, which is likely to result in a sub-optimal user experience.

> **Note**
> The use of Serverless SQL Warehouses mitigates this problem of startup and shutdown. We will learn more about them in the *Using Serverless SQL* section.

On the other hand, if the auto stop time is very lax, the cluster will remain idle and report poor levels of utilization, resulting in a bad return on investment.

Configuring auto stop is reasonably straightforward. The SQL Warehouse monitoring tools profile the workloads by time. This is a great tool to inform your auto-stop configuration. We will discuss this more in the *Monitoring the SQL Warehouse* section.

The rest of the configuration options are self-explanatory:

- **Tags**: These are key-value pairs of information that you can attach to the SQL Warehouse. These key-value pairs are propagated down to the VMs as well. This means you can monitor the usage and cost using these custom tags. Databricks SQL attaches some default tags to the SQL Warehouse, such as the Warehouse ID.

- **Channel**: Databricks SQL is evolving rapidly, and new features are introduced at a regular cadence. The **Preview channel** option allows you to run your workloads with the newer features ahead of them becoming generally available.

Now that we understand the various levers that we can adjust in a SQL Warehouse, let's learn how to configure them for the best possible user experience. In the next section, we will learn about the art of SQL Warehouse sizing.

The art of SQL Warehouse sizing

Warehouse sizing requires calibrating the cluster size and the scaling range. Simply put, we must configure the speed and concurrency with which the SQL Warehouse will process queries submitted by users.

That said, it is important to understand that speed and concurrency are not entirely independent metrics. For example, if you process your queries faster, then the overall throughput of queries will be higher and the amount of time a query spends in a queued state will be shorter. This will avoid having to scale the concurrency of the SQL Warehouse by increasing the cluster size.

So, let's start by understanding the mechanics of query routing, queuing, and cluster autoscaling.

Rules for query routing, queuing, and cluster autoscaling

The control processes in the SQL Warehouse follow a very simple decision tree for performing query routing, query queuing, and cluster autoscaling.

> **The 10-Query Rule**
>
> The core rule (at the time of writing) is that a single physical cluster in a SQL Warehouse can have, at most, 10 queries assigned to it. This is not configurable. This is to allow load balancing across the clusters in the warehouse and to avoid hotspotting within the warehouse.

Note the use of the word *assigned* instead of *running*. This is important and must be understood with case studies.

Case 1 – SQL Warehouse is not running

Consider a SQL Warehouse that is in a **stopped state** and has been configured to have a minimum of one (default) physical cluster(s). When users start submitting their queries, the SQL Warehouse will enter a **starting state**. However, the cluster(s) in the SQL Warehouse must be in the **running state** before any query can be executed. Hence, during this brief starting period, any queries that are submitted are **assigned** to the physical cluster and will be executed when the cluster (and hence the SQL Warehouse) is running.

Case 2 – SQL Warehouse is running

Similarly, consider that the same SQL Warehouse has entered the **running state** and has one physical cluster running and executing user queries. Consider that there are 10 queries already assigned to this cluster and that 10 more queries get submitted. The control process will decide to upscale the SQL Warehouse by adding more physical clusters in the SQL Warehouse. However, as in *Case 1 – SQL Warehouse is not running*, the new clusters will take some time to come into a **running state**, so they will have the queries **assigned** to them. As in *Case 1 – SQL Warehouse is not running*, they will be executed when the new cluster is running.

Hopefully, these case studies help you understand the nuance of **assigned** queries.

With this nuance clarified, let's discuss the rules for auto-upscaling.

Rules for upscaling

Databricks considers the following metrics to make upscaling decisions:

- T_C: Forecasted time to execute current running queries
- T_Q: Forecasted time to execute all queued queries
- T_I: Forecasted time to execute all incoming queries in the next 2 minutes

SQL Warehouses run an internal algorithm that considers the forecasted time to execute current running queries, all queued queries, and expected incoming queries. This algorithm can't be configured. For the sake of brevity, let's call this algorithm Festimate (T_C, T_Q, T_I).

These metrics come together, as shown in the following decision tree:

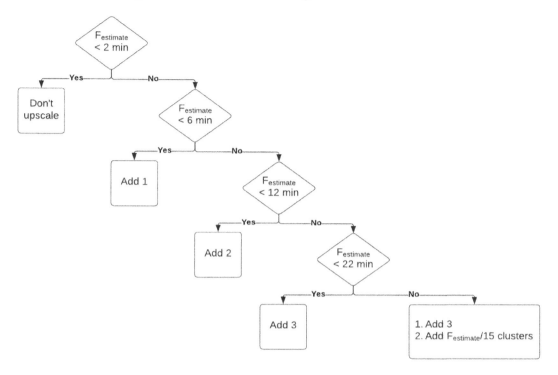

Figure 6.4 – Upscaling decision tree

The preceding decision tree shows the following rules:

- If all the clusters in the SQL Warehouse have 10 queries assigned to them and Festimate is less than 2 minutes, do not upscale.

- If all the clusters in the SQL Warehouse have 10 queries assigned to them and Festimate is between 2 and 6 minutes, add one cluster.

- If all the clusters in the SQL Warehouse have 10 queries assigned to them and Festimate is between 6 and 12 minutes, add two clusters.

- If all the clusters in the warehouse have 10 queries assigned to them and Festimate is between 12 and 22 minutes, add three clusters.

- If all the clusters in the warehouse have 10 queries assigned to them and Festimate is more than 22 minutes, add three clusters right away. Then, add one physical cluster for every additional 15 minutes of expected query load.

Finally, if any query remains queued for more than 5 minutes, upscaling is unconditionally triggered. Of course, the scaling has its lower and upper bounds as defined in the SQL Warehouse configuration.

Rules for downscaling

Downscaling decisions, by contrast, are simpler. If the current and forecasted workload is deemed low for the past 15 minutes, then downscaling the SQL Warehouse is initiated. Like the upscaling algorithm, the downscaling algorithm defines what constitutes a low workload and maintains enough capacity (number of clusters) to handle the next 15 minutes of the expected workload.

At this point, you must be thinking – the upscaling and downscaling rules seem to only consider the number of queries and their expected query completion time. How come they do not mention the computation power of individual physical clusters?

Excellent question – let's discuss this next.

Sizing the SQL Warehouse

To understand the art of sizing, let's start by discussing two very simple scenarios.

Scenario A – memory-bound workloads

There is a business table of 400 GB, and it is expected that there will be two concurrent users querying the whole table. Also, there might be other users querying subsets of the business table, but the size (total data scanned) of those queries is inconsequential.

In this case, we can see that the maximum memory usage at any given time will be 800 GB. Hence, we should choose the Large T-shirt size, which has 1,024 GB of RAM. This should be enough to accommodate for the required concurrency of 2.

This cluster size is 128 vCPUs since it has 16 workers and, as you may recall, each worker has 8 vCPUs. If the users feel that the queries are not executing fast enough, then we should increase the vCPU count. This can be done by selecting a higher T-shirt size. In this case, we should select the X-Large T-shirt size.

The workload suggests that the maximum query concurrency will rarely exceed 10, hence we can leave the scaling range to the default – no scaling.

Scenario B – CPU-bound workloads

Now, consider the scenario of CPU-bound workloads. There is a business table that's 40 GB in size, and it is expected that 10 people will be querying the whole table all the time.

In this case, we can see that the maximum memory usage will be 400 GB. Hence, we should choose the Medium T-shirt size, which has 512 GB of RAM. This should be enough to accommodate for the worst case of 10 concurrent queries, each scanning the full table.

This cluster has 64 vCPUs as well. If the users feel that the queries are not executing fast enough, then, as in the previous scenario, we should increase the T-shirt size.

The workload suggests that queries will come at a more interactive pace and that there is the possibility of getting more than 10 queries at the same time. Hence, we can start with a scaling range where there's a minimum of 1 and a maximum of 2 to accommodate for up to 20 concurrent queries.

These two scenarios are unapologetically simplified.

In the real world, this is not so simple:

- Users can submit queries at varying speeds based on the work they are doing. Hence, it is difficult to preempt the concurrency required.

- Queries often reference more than one table with varying filters and operations, leading to varying data scan volumes. Hence, it is difficult to preempt the amount of memory and vCPU required.

- SQL Warehouses are shared by multiple users running queries of different profiles. Hence, it is hard to establish a uniform query SLA for everyone without the risk of under or over-provisioning resources.

Does this mean that SQL Warehouse sizing is all about trial and error?

No. If you think about it, you do not need to pinpoint metrics about memory usage, vCPU count, and concurrency. You just need broad indicative signals on whether queries are being completed in a reasonable time. If not, is the reason that the queries are being executed slowly or excessive queuing? Thankfully, Databricks SQL has built-in instrumentation to get these signals. Now, let's discuss the different signals and how to inform our configurations with these signals.

Signal 1 – concurrency of queries

On the **SQL Warehouses** page, click on the SQL Warehouse you want to tune and navigate to the **Monitoring** tab. You should see a graph similar to the following:

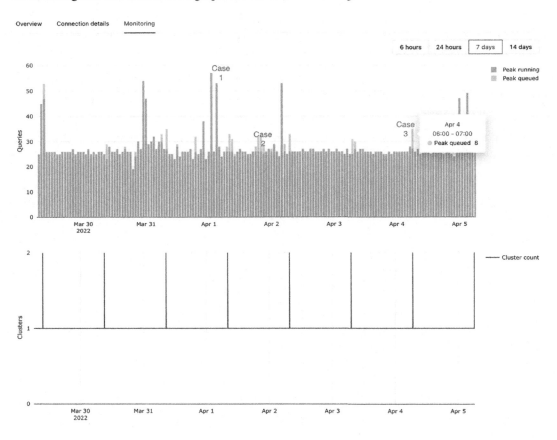

Figure 6.5 – Monitoring a SQL Warehouse

This is the monitoring graph of a medium-sized SQL Warehouse with a scaling range of 1 to 5 over 7 days. 7 days allows us to capture query concurrency patterns with a fair degree of accuracy. As we can see, whenever the number of concurrent queries shoots up significantly or there is significant queueing, the SQL Warehouse auto-scales and adds a new physical cluster to accommodate for the additional workloads. Keep in mind that each bar in the 7-day graph represents a time band of 1 hour. You can inspect the peak concurrency during that time band by hovering on the respective bar.

A closer inspection of the graph reveals three distinct cases, as denoted in the preceding screenshot.

Case 1

In this case, more than 60 queries are processed in 1 hour. There is no queuing, and there is no autoscaling event.

Case 2

In this case, more than 30 queries are queries processed in 1 hour. There is definite queuing, but this does not lead to an autoscaling event. If you recall the rules of autoscaling, this corresponds to the first rule, where all the clusters in the SQL Warehouse have 10 queries assigned to them and Festimate is less than 2 minutes, so no upscaling happens.

Case 3

In this case, more than 30 queries are processed in 1 hour. There is definite queuing, which leads to an autoscaling event. In this case, there are some longer-running queries and the queue buildup at a point in time is high. This leads to a forecasted time of completion of running and queued queries greater than 2 minutes, but less than 6 minutes. This corresponds to the second rule, so an upscaling event occurs, with one cluster being added to the SQL Warehouse.

These three cases show you how to interpret the concurrency requirements for the workloads running on this cluster.

In this setup, the scaling factor of the SQL Warehouse is well configured:

- There are few queuing events.
- Fewer queuing events means fewer upscaling events.
- The upscaling events are within the configured bounds.

This is not to say that upscaling is bad! It is a delicate line to thread. If there are fewer upscaling events, it just means that you forecasted the workload well. If you are unable to forecast the workload, leave it to autoscaling to figure out what is best.

Keep in mind that upscaling decisions anticipate expected incoming workloads. However, upscaling still requires time in the order of 3 to 4 minutes, which could potentially lead to long query times. If your SQL Warehouse is exhibiting frequent auto-upscaling events, you should re-evaluate the scaling minimum.

The following would have happened if the SQL Warehouse had been ill-configured:

- We would have seen frequent queuing events.
- The queuing events would lead to frequent upscaling events.
- The frequent upscaling events would have hit the scaling maximum.

So, to summarize, we can say the following:

- Initially, start with a wide band of scaling. Monitor the SQL Warehouse progressively to make corrections as required.

- If the cluster count is predictably higher than the configured minimum most of the time, consider increasing the minimum cluster count.

- If the cluster count is at the configured maximum most of the time, and there is noticeable queuing of queries, consider increasing the minimum and maximum cluster counts.

- If there is a consistent behavior of rapid upscaling and downscaling, consider increasing the minimum cluster count to avoid the wait for new clusters and query queuing.

- If there are no definite patterns to the autoscaling and there are a few stray events of hitting the maximum count with queuing, use your best judgment.

Use this guide to broadly read the concurrency indication signals. However, keep in mind that this is more art than science. Try not to get mired in the details of every single query execution. If the scaling limits are reasonably configured, the autoscaling algorithm will take care of catering to the workloads.

Signal 2 – execution speed of queries

The next signal is the execution speed of queries. This should be used in conjunction with the signals from the **Monitoring** tab.

For example, consider the monitoring signals in the following screenshot:

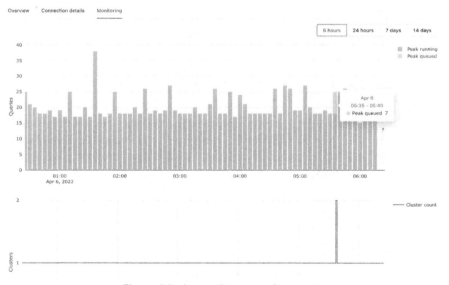

Figure 6.6 – Inspecting a queuing event

As we can see, on April 6, between 5:35 A.M. and 5:40 A.M., there was a big queuing event that triggered an autoscaling event. You, as an administrator, want to see if this could have been avoided with a bigger SQL Warehouse size, or whether this was a one-off case.

To do so, you can go to the **Query History** page and filter the queries on the SQL Warehouse during this time window, as shown in the following screenshot:

Figure 6.7 – Inspecting the query execution times

Closer inspection shows that there are indeed more than 10 queries running at a point in time, which warrants the upscaling event. Furthermore, we can see that the queries are taking inordinately long, so the upscaling event seems to be valid.

Now, depending on what we see here, if we decide that the queries are sufficiently well designed and yet running slow, we can decide to increase the T-shirt size of the SQL Warehouse. In this case, we can see that, at 5:38 A.M., there are a lot of long-running queries that are sufficiently well designed but take a lot of time to execute. If we increase the T-shirt size, these queries will finish faster and reduce the queueing.

On the other hand, if we see that the queries are poorly designed and the slow execution times are not a sustained event, we can brush this off as a one-off event.

> **What is a Well-Designed Query?**
>
> A well-designed query is a query that lends itself to parallel execution and avoids expensive operations such as cross joins as much as possible. You do not have to read the query to know if it is well designed. Clicking on a query in the **History** tab opens the query profiling tool, which provides a high-level view of what is happening in the query. You can read more about it at https://docs.databricks.com/sql/admin/query-profile.html.

Avoid the temptation to look at micro details. When looking at the query execution speeds, try to look at broad patterns and decide if increasing the T-shirt size is a valid strategy.

If you are struggling to find an initial size, use this very rough guide to start:

Workload	Size
10 GB / 1 – 10 million rows	S
100 GB / >10 million rows	M
250 GB / >100 million rows	L
500 GB / 1 billion rows	XL

If this is not possible, start with a medium-sized SQL Warehouse with scaling limits of 1 to 5.

That said, in either case, you should progressively monitor the SQL Warehouse signals to make corrections.

So, to summarize, we can say the following:

- If you see a lot of queuing in the **Monitoring** tab and corresponding slow queries in the **Query History** tab, consider increasing the SQL Warehouse's T-shirt size.

- Don't let cost be the only factor when it comes to cluster sizing. User experience is of equal importance. For example, for the same workload, a smaller SQL Warehouse will run for longer, while a larger SQL Warehouse will run for a shorter duration. The end cost will be the same. The user experience will be vastly different. It's possible that, for your workload patterns, it is not any more expensive to use a larger cluster for a workload than it is to use a smaller one. It's just faster.

This brings us to the end of our discussion on the art of SQL Warehouse sizing. Use the available signals, individually and together, to iterate over SQL Warehouse configurations.

Knowing how to configure a single SQL Warehouse is essential. However, it is only a part of the larger activity of organizing and assigning SQL Warehouses to various analysts. We will discuss this in the next section.

Organizing and governing SQL Warehouses

Organizations tend to have a sizeable number of data analysts working on various projects at the same time. Depending on the project, access to different data sources with varying data volumes will have to be accounted for. Depending on the staffing of the project, the number of concurrent users will also need to be accounted for. Depending on the sensitivity of the project, the access control to the work on the project will have to be accounted for. Finally, each project should be held accountable for the computation resources they incur.

The Databricks SQL platform is very flexible and accommodates all these considerations. Let's start by looking at how SQL Warehouses are distributed to various users or projects.

SQL Warehouse assignment strategy

There are no set rules on how SQL Warehouses should be assigned to users. Databricks certainly does not want to restrict assignment strategies either. There are two levels to the assignment strategy:

- Assigning users to workspaces.

- Assigning users in workspaces to SQL Warehouses in the workspace.

- When it comes to assigning users to workspaces, I recommend considering the Business Unit Subscription design pattern. If you want a refresher on what a Databricks workspace is, visit the official documentation: `https://docs.databricks.com/getting-started/concepts.html`.

Let's learn how to assign SQL Warehouses within the workspace.

Assignment criteria 1 – workload type

The first level of assignment should be on the lines of the type of the workload: production versus development.

Production workloads are scheduled workloads. A workload could be a Report, a Dashboard, or a Scheduled Query. A Report or a Dashboard can be composed of one or more queries.

Production workloads should be run on SQL Warehouses with the Reliability Optimized strategy. It is also recommended that production workloads run in a separate workspace dedicated to production workloads only – to reduce the possibility of human errors interfering with production workloads.

Development workloads, on the other hand, are more forgiving and flexible. They can be run on SQL Warehouses with the Cost Optimized strategy.

Assignment criteria 2 – sharing resources

The second level of assignment should be along the lines of resource sharing – should the workload be run on a dedicated SQL Warehouse or a shared SQL Warehouse?

Let's begin by talking about production workloads.

Dedicated SQL Warehouses mean that all the computation resources in the Warehouse will be used by the workload and guarantee the best possible performance for that one workload.

On the other hand, a shared SQL Warehouse will mean that the different workloads will be able to benefit from the caching of data that's triggered by each workload. This can help with the overall execution of all the workloads, not just one.

So, you must weigh the variables of the compute resources that are required, the shared data sources, and the workload SLAs to decide on the dedicated versus shared strategy.

Development workloads are usually executed on shared SQL Warehouses to maximize Warehouse utilization. There is the added benefit of caching data that's been triggered by various workloads to uplift the query performances in general. A case can always be made to have a single SQL Warehouse for a single user, but the administrative overhead that will build up if every user gets a dedicated SQL Warehouse should be kept in mind.

Assignment criteria 3 – projects and groups

Sharing SQL Warehouses is great, but there should be a method to this sharing. Ideally, users working on a particular project should share the same SQL Warehouses. A particular project can have multiple SQL Warehouses associated with it as well. The reasons for doing so can be varied – it could be that SQL Warehouses of different sizes are required for different developer groups in the project. It could also be that different developer groups need to work on different datasets. So, to maximize the benefits of caching, developer groups working on the same datasets use the same SQL Warehouse. This also enables easy chargeback processes. We will discuss this in more detail in the *Chargeback* section.

By now, it should be clear that there is no one correct assignment strategy. It depends on your organization's operating model. However, you can use the discussed assignment criteria to broadly consider how to assign users to SQL Warehouses.

Now that we have an idea of how to assign users to SQL Warehouses, the next question is, how do you enforce it? The answer lies in the access control feature of SQL Warehouses.

Access control in SQL Warehouses

Access control in SQL Warehouses is similar to the data security model we introduced in *Chapter 4, The Security Model*.

Like the data security model, there are four concepts:

- Users, groups, and service principals
- The SQL Warehouse is the securable object
- Privileges
- Operations

As with the data security model, users are granted certain privileges on the SQL Warehouse that allow them to conduct certain operations on or with the SQL Warehouse.

Now, let's discuss privileges and operations in more detail.

Privileges

There are three possible privilege levels:

- **No Permissions**: This privilege level means that the user cannot see the SQL Warehouse and cannot execute any queries on that SQL Warehouse. If a user has access to a report, dashboard, or a saved query that uses this SQL Warehouse, then the user will not be able to execute them and will have to use a SQL Warehouse that is available to them.

- **Can Use**: This privilege level means that the user can view the SQL Warehouse, start the SQL Warehouse, execute queries on it, and view their query history on it.

- **Can Manage**: This privilege level grants the user to view, use, and manage the SQL Warehouse. This is the highest level of privilege and allows for all possible operations on the SQL Warehouse.

Operations

Nine possible operations can be performed on a SQL Warehouse:

- View your queries on the Warehouse.
- View query details.
- View queries for all users on the Warehouse.
- View Warehouse details.
- Start Warehouse.
- Stop Warehouse.
- Delete Warehouse.
- Edit Warehouse.
- Modify permissions.

The **Can Manage** privilege allows you to perform all of these operations. The **Can Use** privilege allows you to view your queries, view the Warehouse's details, and start the Warehouse. Finally, the **No Permissions** privilege only allows you to view your queries.

Programming access control

Programming access control – that is, assigning a privilege to a SQL Warehouse for users and user groups – can easily be done via the UI:

- Navigate to the SQL Warehouse and click on the **Permissions** button to bring up the **Manage Permissions** UI, like so:

Figure 6.8 – The Manage Permissions UI

This UI shows the current permissions on the SQL Warehouse. The permissions for the owner of the SQL Warehouse – that is, the user that created the SQL Warehouse – can't be edited. Interestingly, however, the admins group can be restricted to the **Can use** privilege:

- To add a new permission, simply click on the search box to type or select the user that you want to give permissions to. The following screenshot illustrates this:

Figure 6.9 – Granting a new user privileges

The new user can be given the **Can use** or **Can manage** privilege:

- Permissions can be edited by clicking on the permissions dropdown for a user, as shown in the following screenshot:

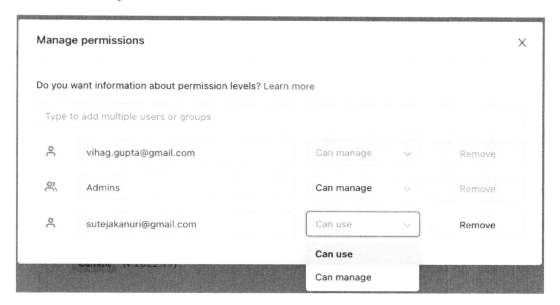

Figure 6.10 – Modifying a user's privileges

- Finally, permissions can also be revoked by simply clicking on the **Remove** button in the **Manage Permissions** UI.

As you can see, programming access control is very simple. Combined with a sound user group strategy, it is easy to scale the access control programming to cover all your analyst users.

Now that we have discussed strategies for assigning users to SQL Warehouses and how to enforce those strategies, let's discuss the final component of governance – chargeback.

Chargeback

Simply put, chargeback means accounting for how much cost (in $) was incurred by a particular user, group, or project. This is very important to keep teams accountable for the resources they are using, and to evaluate the return on investment on a project.

If we have a good user assignment strategy in place, chargeback boils down to the cost incurred by the SQL Warehouse(s) that the user, group, or project was using.

> **Databricks Pricing**
> To deep dive into Databricks pricing, head over to the official documentation: `https://databricks.com/product/pricing`.

In the Azure portal, you can head over to the Cost Analysis tool (`https://docs.microsoft.com/en-us/azure/cost-management-billing/costs/quick-acm-cost-analysis`) to view the costs. First, you must add two **Meter Categories** – **Virtual Machines** and **Azure Databricks** – and apply the **Tags** filter. Each SQL Warehouse gets a **Cluster ID** tag that uniquely identifies it. Filter on the *clusterid* tag that you wish to charge back on. The **Cluster ID** tag can be found in the SQL Warehouse **Overview** tab in the **Name** field. The cost analysis setup should look as follows:

Figure 6.11 – Setting up cost analysis

Once this has been set up, the cost analysis dashboard should populate the accumulated costs, like so:

Figure 6.12 – Accumulated cost

It should also populate breakdowns of the Databricks cost and the underlying VM cost, like so:

Figure 6.13 – Cost breakdown

If you are an AWS user, you might be expecting something similar in the Billing and Cost Management console. However, that is not the case. Databricks is a first-party service in Azure, so its billing is tightly integrated. We can see the Databricks billing in the cost analysis portal. Databricks is not a first-party service in AWS.

AWS users can see the Databricks spend on their Databricks account console, as documented here: `https://docs.databricks.com/administration-guide/account-settings-e2/usage.html`.

You will also notice that the console does not show the underlying VM costs. You must get those costs from the Billing and Cost Management console using cluster tags since they are propagated to the underlying VMs. You can read more about cluster tags and tag propagation here: `https://docs.databricks.com/administration-guide/account-settings/usage-detail-tags-aws.html`.

GCP users can see their spending on their account console, as documented here: `https://docs.gcp.databricks.com/administration-guide/account-settings-gcp/usage.html`.

In summary, a reliable chargeback is important, and reliability comes from having a sound user assignment strategy and strategy enforcement. Databricks SQL provides all the tools to implement this, and we discussed all the nuances in depth in this section.

Using Serverless SQL

It would be remiss not to introduce the Serverless SQL offering in Databricks SQL. SQL Warehouses – the classic SQL Warehouses that we have discussed so far – reside in your cloud account. That is, the workers of the warehouses are VMs in your cloud account. This has two implications:

- You incur the cost of Databricks and the cost of the VMs that Databricks uses to power the SQL Warehouses.
- You incur some latency in cluster cold starts and upscaling events.

Databricks SQL offers Serverless SQL to circumvent this. In Serverless SQL, the SQL Warehouses are provisioned in Databricks's account from a pool of pre-provisioned compute resources. This solves both the aforementioned implications:

- The cost of Databricks SQL Warehouses includes the VM costs, and you pay for only one line item
- Since Databricks uses a pool of pre-provisioned compute, no latency is incurred in cold starts, as well as when upscaling events

Apart from the location of the SQL Warehouse, everything else remains the same, as we discussed in the previous sections. However, this is a new implication of data security as the serverless SQL Warehouses are provisioned from a shared pool of compute resources. Serverless SQL uses a combination of network policies and security groups to isolate SQL Warehouses.

I haven't provided a detailed explanation of Serverless SQL as it is still a preview feature, and the product may change as it enters general availability. Perhaps a future revision of this book will contain a detailed exploration. You can read more about it here: `https://docs.databricks.com/serverless-compute/index.html`.

Summary

In this chapter, we put on the lens of a Database administrator and learned about SQL Warehouses in depth.

First, we learned how SQL Warehouses can be created, configured, and governed. We discussed the inner workings of SQL Warehouses so that we can configure them to get the best possible user experience. We discussed various strategies for assigning users to SQL Warehouses. Finally, we discussed how we can charge back users for their usage and create accountability.

SQL Warehouses are used within the Databricks SQL UI. However, they can also be leveraged from outside the Databricks environment with specialized BI tools.

In *Chapter 7, Using Business Intelligence Tools with Databricks SQL*, we will learn how to do this and elevate the analyst experience.

7
Using Business Intelligence Tools with Databricks SQL

Databricks SQL is a well-rounded, self-contained data analytics platform. It provides users such as analysts and data administrators with all the tools that are required for them to conduct their daily workflows. As we saw in the preceding chapters, pretty much everything can be done on Databricks SQL – exploratory data analysis, reports, dashboards, alerts, and more.

Despite all that, though, it is by no means a replacement for dedicated **Business Intelligence** (**BI**) tools such as Power BI, Tableau, Looker, or Qlik.

These BI tools can connect with Databricks SQL with simple, transparent mechanisms to query the data on the data lakehouse. In this chapter, we will focus on how to connect Databricks SQL to BI tools of your choice.

The primary audience of this chapter is analysts who want to use BI tools of their choice with Databricks SQL. The database administrator personas will also benefit from this chapter as it pertains to data access from outside the Databricks SQL platform.

In this chapter, we will cover the following topics:

- Connecting from validated BI tools
- Connecting from non-validated BI tools
- Connecting programmatically
- Databricks Partner Connect

Technical requirements

To understand this chapter, you must ensure the following:

- You must have gone through *Chapter 6, The SQL Warehouses*, before reading this chapter.
- You must have the BI tools that you intend to use, installed on your workstation.
- You must have the *Can Use* privilege on a SQL Warehouse.

Connecting from validated BI tools

Databricks SQL is an open platform, which means it supports integrations with all BI tools using open standards such as JDBC and ODBC. That said, there are certain BI tools and platforms that natively support connections to Databricks SQL. These are what we refer to as validated BI tools. In this section, we will learn how to connect validated BI tools to Databricks SQL. We will also learn what's meant by a connection to Databricks SQL.

> **Note**
> I will refer to business intelligence software as BI tools or BI platforms interchangeably in this chapter.

Databricks SQL supports validated integrations from various BI platforms. This list is constantly evolving and can be found at `https://docs.microsoft.com/en-us/azure/databricks/integrations/partners#--bi-and-visualization`.

How does a connection from an external BI tool to Databricks SQL work?

Recall from the previous chapters that Databricks SQL has three distinct layers:

- The data layer, which we covered in *Chapter 3, The Data Catalog*
- The compute layer, which we covered in *Chapter 6, The SQL Warehouses*
- The consumption layer, which we covered in *Chapter 5, The Workbench*

In those chapters, we learned how users submit queries from the workbench, and that the queries get executed on the SQL Warehouses. The data in the tables that's referred to in the queries is retrieved from the data layer.

When visualizing how connections from external BI platforms work, just imagine that you are replacing the default consumption layer – the workbench – with a workbench of your choice – that is, the BI platform.

When a BI tool is marked as *validated* by Databricks, you can expect the BI tool to have built-in driver connectors for Databricks and a *named* data source. For example, the following screenshot shows the named Databricks source on Tableau Desktop:

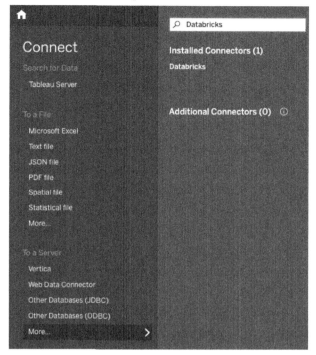

Figure 7.1 – Databricks connector in Tableau Desktop

Similarly, the following screenshot shows the named Databricks source in Power BI Desktop:

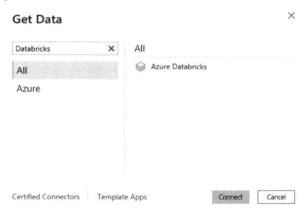

Figure 7.2 – Databricks connector in Power BI Desktop

Every validated BI tool will have a named Databricks connector and often, it will have the Databricks Driver Connector bundled in. There can be notable exceptions to the driver bundling. For example, Tableau Desktop requires that the driver connector be explicitly downloaded and installed before the Databricks connector is used. This does not mean that the integration is subpar – it is most likely a technicality of licensing and distributing the driver connector.

Moving on, making the connection is easy. Click on the Databricks data source to proceed to the required connection configuration. Let's use Tableau Desktop as an example:

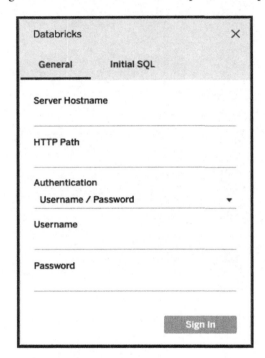

Figure 7.3 – Configuring a Databricks connector in Tableau Desktop

Tableau Desktop requires two sets of connection configurations – the details of the SQL Warehouse and the details of authenticating to the SQL Warehouse. Let's dive into these configurations.

SQL Warehouse details

The SQL Warehouse details identify the SQL Warehouse that will be used by this connection to execute user queries. The following SQL Warehouse details are required:

- **Server Hostname**: This identifies your Databricks workspace.
- **HTTP Path**: This identifies the SQL Warehouse within the Databricks workspace.

The **Server hostname** and **HTTP path** details can be obtained from the SQL Warehouse's **Connection Details** tab, as shown in the following screenshot:

Overview   Connection details   Monitoring

Server hostname	adb-28! ;01.1.azuredatabricks.net	🗗
Port	443	🗗
Protocol	https	🗗
HTTP path	/sql/1.0/endpoints/f2cb2b7ec319d5aa	🗗
JDBC URL	jdbc:spark://adb-28 ;01.1.azuredatabricks.net:443/default;transportMode=http;ssl=1;AuthMech=3;httpPath=/sql/1.0/endpoints/f2cb2b7ec319d5aa;	🗗

Figure 7.4 – Retrieving the connection details for a SQL Warehouse

Simply copy and paste the **Server hostname** and **HTTP path** details to the respective fields.

> **Note**
> Connections to Databricks SQL require that you know which SQL Warehouse you are assigned to use. The connections do not allow for a generic configuration that allows you to change the SQL Warehouse during an active session. Changing the SQL Warehouse will require you to reset the connection.

From a database administrator's perspective, you can see how users can only access the SQL Warehouses assigned to them. A user requires the Can Use privilege on a SQL Warehouse to be able to connect to it from an external BI tool. This means that the governance strategy for assigning users to SQL Warehouses, which we discussed in *Chapter 6, The SQL Warehouses*, in the *SQL Warehouse assignment strategy* section, is respected even when accessing Databricks SQL from external tools.

Authentication details

The next configuration is the authentication details. There are three possible authentication modes, as we will discuss now. Bear in mind that the way the three authentication modes are presented to you will differ across BI tools.

Databricks personal access token

A Databricks personal access token can be used to access Databricks SQL from external BI tools, as well as REST API functions. A personal access token is just an authentication mechanism to identify yourself to the Databricks SQL authentication and authorization mechanism.

Getting a personal access token is simple. Navigate to the **Personal access tokens** tab on the **User Settings** page and click on the **Generate new token** button, as shown in the following screenshot:

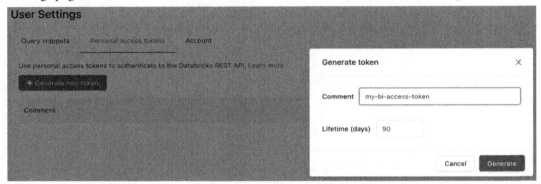

Figure 7.5 – Generating a personal access token

Optionally, you can configure the number of days this token will be valid. Ensure that you copy and save the generated token in a secure location since you will not be able to see it once you leave the page.

You can read more about personal access tokens and how to create them here: `https://docs.databricks.com/sql/user/security/personal-access-tokens.html`.

Databricks username and password

This is a self-explanatory authentication mechanism. Simply use the same username and password that you use to log into Databricks.

Azure Active Directory

If your organization enforces the use of Azure Active Directory authentication, use this option. Different tools may have different flows for this. For example, in Tableau Desktop, you will be prompted for the authentication endpoint, while in Power BI, you will be automatically navigated to your organization's login.

From a database administrator's perspective, you should note that the choice of authentication mechanism should be in line with your organization's security policies. For example, if the policies disallow the usage of personal access tokens, the administrator can disable the usage of personal access tokens in the workspace. This way users don't get a chance to create a personal token, instead they will have to use the other authentication mechanisms. Further, it is important to note that all three mechanisms authenticate that a user is indeed a valid member of this installation of Databricks SQL. This means that the security model that's implemented in this installation, as we discussed in *Chapter 4, The Security Model*, is respected even when accessing Databricks SQL from external tools.

To complete the authentication configuration, select the applicable authentication mechanism and key in the details. Once all the configurations have been completed and you have clicked the **Sign In** button, the connection will be attempted. If you are authorized to use the SQL Warehouse, and your authentication credentials are correct, you will be signed in.

> **Note**
> It is important to note that the **Sign In** activity will power on the SQL Warehouse if it is not already running.

And that's it! The data lakehouse data catalog should be visible in the BI tool. If you are following this example with Tableau, you should see a catalog similar to the following:

Figure 7.6 – Exploring the airlines database from Tableau Desktop

Now, you can start querying!

> **Note**
>
> One important thing to keep in mind is that each BI tool will have nuances on how to work with the data. For example, Power BI has two modes – Direct Query and Import Mode. Consult the official documentation based on your BI tool for details at `https://docs.databricks.com/integrations/partners.html#bi-and-visualization`.

And that's it. It is that simple to connect to Databricks SQL from validated BI tools. Now, let's turn our attention to non-validated BI tools and, subsequently, programmatic access.

Connecting from non-validated BI tools

There are plenty of popular SQL database tools that are not (yet) validated – that is, they do not have a named Databricks connector. In this section, we will learn how to connect these non-validated BI tools to Databricks SQL using Databricks JDBC and ODBC drivers.

Non-validated BI tools do not come with bundled driver connectors and may or may not support all three authentication mechanisms supported by validated BI tools. However, Databricks SQL Warehouses support JDBC and ODBC connections. We can leverage these connections to connect from non-validated tools. Full documentation on JDBC and ODBC connections is available at `https://docs.databricks.com/integrations/bi/jdbc-odbc-bi.html`. They are straightforward and do not warrant detailed unpacking.

There are three steps:

1. Download the JDBC or ODBC driver as applicable.
2. Install the driver in the BI/SQL database tool.
3. Configure the SQL Warehouse connection.

Let's take the example of SQLWorkbench/J (`https://www.sql-workbench.eu/`), a popular, DBMS-independent, cross-platform SQL query tool.

Step 1 – download the driver

Download the latest JDBC driver from `https://docs.microsoft.com/en-us/azure/databricks/integrations/bi/jdbc-odbc-bi#download-the-jdbc-driver`. Unzip the file to extract the JAR file.

Step 2 – install the driver

In SQLWorkbench/J, navigate to **File | Connect Window | Manage Drivers**. Provide an appropriate name. I have named it Databricks SQL JDBC Driver. Finally, point it to the JAR file that we extracted in *Step 1 – download the driver*, as shown in the following screenshot:

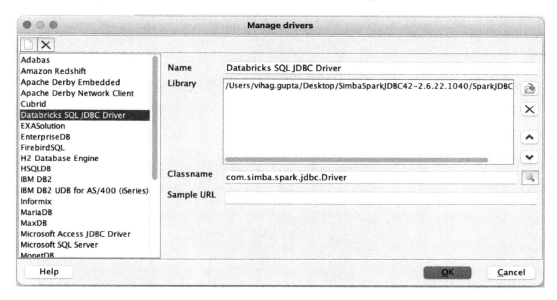

Figure 7.7 – Installing the JDBC driver

As you can see, I have configured the driver to use the JAR file of the driver. The **Classname** area should be automatically populated.

Step 3 – configure the SQL Warehouse connection

In the **Connect** window, create a new connection profile. As shown in the following screenshot, configure it to use the new driver we installed. In the **URL** field, copy and paste the JDBC URL from *Figure 7.4*. Finally, in the **Username** and **Password** fields, key in the username and password that you use to log into Databricks SQL. You can also use personal access tokens instead of your username and password. To use them, set **Username** to "token" and paste your personal access token in the **Password** field.

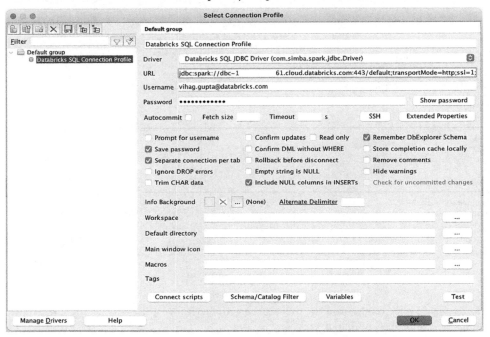

Figure 7.8 – Creating a connection to Databricks SQL from SQLWorkbench/J

Now, you can test the connection and save the connection profile. If you have the *Can Use* privilege on the SQL Warehouse and you have provided the correct authentication credentials, the connection will be successful, and you will be able to explore the data on the data lakehouse. The following screenshot shows how we can explore the airlines database that we created in the preceding chapters:

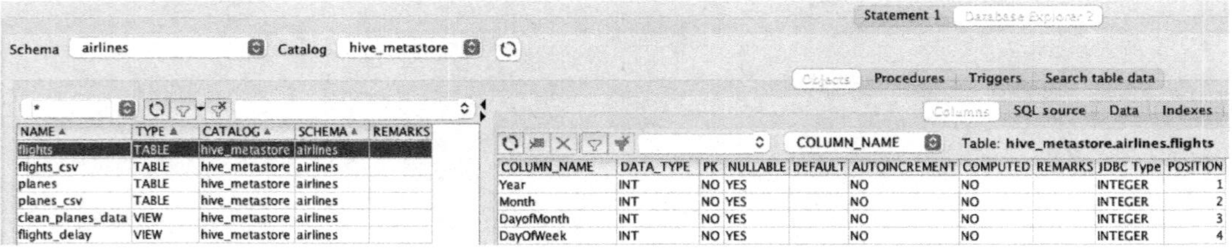

Figure 7.9 – Exploring the airlines database in SQLWorkbench/J

And that's it! With a few extra manual steps, you can connect your BI tool of choice to your instance of Databricks SQL. You can even perform these steps in a validated BI tool that has a named Databricks connector. Try it out!

Connecting programmatically

While we are discussing JDBC and ODBC Driver Connectors, we must make an honorable mention of a very important use case. This use case is how application programs access the data on the data lakehouse via Databricks SQL. For example, consider the dashboard that we compiled in *Figure 5.41* in *Chapter 5*, *The Workbench*. The taxi company may build a desktop or a web application that renders this dashboard. To do so, the application must issue SQL queries to the tables via a connection to Databricks SQL. These applications can be programmed in any of the modern languages, such as Java, Python, and Scala, to name a few, using their constructs for working with JDBC and ODBC drivers.

> **Note**
>
> A note of caution: Databricks SQL and the data lakehouse are not a replacement for your relational database management systems or online transactional processing systems.

Application programmers are not the intended audience for this book; however, Databricks SQL can hold use for them. Hence, I am going to conclude this section by providing a link to the official documentation for using JDBC and ODBC drivers with Databricks SQL: `https://docs.databricks.com/dev-tools/python-sql-connector.html`.

Databricks Partner Connect

The steps that we employed to connect to validated tools in the *Connecting from validated BI tools* section are simple and clear. However, they were still manual steps that required copying and pasting. The steps are simple and clear, but the user experience is not – that is, having to juggle between the SQL Warehouse overview page and the BI tool. Databricks Partner Connect is a tool that aims to improve this experience. Let's learn how.

To access Databricks Partner Connect, follow these steps:

1. Click on the 🔡 icon to bring up the Partner Connect landing page. Navigate to the **BI and Visualization** section, as shown in the following screenshot:

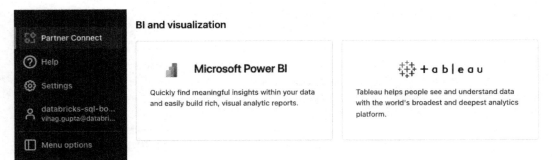

Figure 7.10 – The Partner Connect landing page

2. Click on the tile representing your BI tool. It will download a connection file to your desktop. The connection file is specific to the BI tool. For example, a Tableau data source `.tds` file (`https://help.tableau.com/current/pro/desktop/en-us/environ_filesandfolders.htm`) is downloaded for Tableau and a Power BI data source `.pbids` file (`https://docs.microsoft.com/en-us/power-bi/connect-data/desktop-data-sources#using-pbids-files-to-get-data`) is downloaded for Microsoft Power BI. Let's continue with our example of Tableau Desktop. Clicking on the Tableau tile prompts the download, like so:

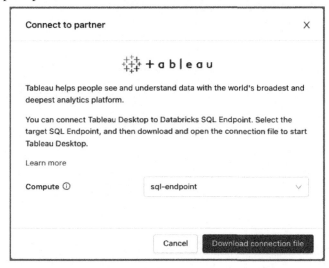

Figure 7.11 – Downloading the Tableau .tds connection file

3. Double-click on the downloaded `.tds` connection file. It will open Tableau Desktop and ask you for your credentials, as shown in the following screenshot:

Figure 7.12 – Connecting with the .tds file

4. Key your personal access token in the **Password** field and start exploring. If you need to change the authentication mechanism, click the **Edit Connection** button to choose the relevant one.

And that's it! All you must do is key in your credentials. Contrast this to the other mechanisms where we had to manually figure out the SQL Warehouse details. Partner connect makes the experience seamless. From an administration perspective, it simplifies and secures the connection process – instead of users searching for and choosing SQL Warehouses, administrators can download the connection files on behalf of the users and share them with them.

The internals of a data source file

If you are curious, you can open the `.tds` file with any text editor. It will show that the SQL Warehouse connection information has been compiled for you into a format understood by the BI tool. In this case, this is an XML file, as shown in the following screenshot:

```
● ● ●                        databricks-sql-endpoint.tds ∨
<!-- build 20211.21.0511.0935                              -->
<datasource
    formatted-name='federated.hLXHZ9pCtYGAM5VZ1456ga5FrNJO'
    inline='true'
    version='21.3'
    xmlns:user='http://www.tableausoftware.com/xml/user'>
  <connection class='federated'>
    <named-connections>
      <named-connection
          caption='dbc-19      ≥61.cloud.databricks.com'
          name='databricks.ja8o2cacI6fQ25xuVUPeDjEhZsIq'>
        <connection
            authentication='auth-pass'
            authentication-type=''
            class='databricks'
            dbname='/sql/1.0/endpoints/5028b812e371355a'
            odbc-connect-string-extras=''
            one-time-sql=''
            schema=''
            tableName=''
            server='dbc-19          61.cloud.databricks.com'
            username='token'>
          <connection-customization class='databricks' enabled='false' version='21.3'>
            <vendor name='databricks' />
            <driver name='databricks' />
          </connection-customization>
        </connection>
      </named-connection>
    </named-connections>
  </connection>
</datasource>
```

Figure 7.13 – Inspecting the .tds file

As you can see, the `connection` construct instructs Tableau to consider this a Databricks data source by setting the class field to Databricks. A Databricks connection will require the server hostname and HTTP path values for the SQL Warehouse. Hence, they are applied to the `server` and `dbname` fields, respectively. Finally, the authentication is set to personal access tokens by default, as seen in the `authentication` field. Tableau understands the `datasource` construct and creates a connection to Databricks.

The data source file for each BI tool is different. If you are working with a different data source file, you will likely see a different format. For example, the Power BI `.pbids` file represents the connection information in JSON format.

That said, you don't need to know what is inside the data source file to be able to use it. Just double-click and start exploring!

Summary

In this short but very important chapter, we learned how we can connect our preferred BI tools to Databricks SQL and query the data on the data lakehouse.

First, we learned about the various connection configurations that must be made. Then, we learned about the differences between validated and non-validated BI tool integrations. Finally, we learned about the Databricks Partner Connect feature, which simplifies the process of connecting our preferred BI tool with Databricks SQL.

Now, you should have a working understanding of Databricks SQL from an end user perspective, as well as an administrator's perspective. You should be good to start working with Databricks SQL. Now, we will turn our attention to the core technology enablers that power Databricks SQL.

In the next chapter, *Chapter 8, The Delta Lake*, we will unpack the internals of the storage layer of the lakehouse and focus on the Delta Lake storage format. We will learn how it enables Data Warehouse-like performance on the data lake.

Part 2: Internals of Databricks SQL

This part focuses on the internals of Databricks SQL. It unpacks the concepts and workings of the revolutionary technologies that enable business intelligence and data warehousing in a data lakehouse!

This part comprises the following chapters:

- *Chapter 8, The Delta Lake*
- *Chapter 9, The Photon Engine*
- *Chapter 10, Warehouse on the Lakehouse*

8
The Delta Lake

Up until this chapter, we were singularly focused on enabling you to use Databricks SQL. Now that we have accomplished that, let's investigate the technologies that enable Databricks SQL to run your data warehousing workloads on what seems to be a data lake.

In this chapter, we will focus on the primary storage format of the Databricks Lakehouse —**Delta Lake**. Why should you care? You should care because, unlike other cloud data warehouses, the Databricks Lakehouse stores data in open storage formats such as Delta Lake, Parquet, **Optimized Row Columnar (ORC)**, **comma-separated values (CSV)**, and so on, instead of proprietary formats.

We will begin by understanding the challenges posed by using other storage formats, how they affect the **business intelligence (BI)** experience on traditional data lakes, and how the Delta Lake format addresses them. Then, we will learn about the performance boosters available with Delta Lake in Databricks.

The primary audience of this chapter is data engineers, data administrators, and data modelers who will be collectively responsible for ingesting the data into the Lakehouse in the most optimal data layout for the best BI experience.

In this chapter about Delta Lake, we will learn about the following topics:

- Fundamentals of the Delta Lake storage format
- Built-in performance-boosting features of Delta Lake
- Configurable performance-boosting features of Delta Lake

Technical requirements

To make the most of this chapter, you must ensure the following:

- You have access to a working Databricks SQL workspace to execute the examples.
- You have knowledge of data engineering pipelines for data lakes with Apache Spark.

- You have knowledge of the execution model of Apache Spark.

- You have access to the GitHub repository for the book, available at the following link:

`https://github.com/PacktPublishing/Business-Intelligence-with-Databricks-SQL-Analytics`.

Fundamentals of the Delta Lake storage format

In this section, we will learn about the Delta Lake storage format and its core objectives. To do so, we will first detour into the realm of data engineering, which will provide the context for the core objectives. Finally, we will see how the Delta Lake format achieves the core objectives and simplifies the data engineering process.

Delta Lake (`https://delta.io/`) is an open source storage format that enables an organization's data engineering teams to build the Lakehouse (see *Chapter 1, Introduction to Databricks*). Delta Lake aims to bring the following data warehousing characteristics to your data lake:

- Reliability

- Simplicity

- Performance

- Governance

To understand why this is a big deal, we must understand how data engineering on data lakes is currently done, how it affects BI users, and why these characteristics are the holy grail for data engineering teams.

Data engineering before Delta Lake

Data engineering on a data lake is the process of collecting data from various data sources—internal or external—converting them into usable information, and storing them on the lake for data scientists and business analysts to interpret.

On the one hand, data engineers must read and wrangle data from a wide variety of data sources. Data sources can range from transactional systems of records such as relational databases to application logs, click streams and event streams, files, and extracts from **application programming interface** (**API**) calls. Each data source produces data in a different volume and different velocity. The semantics of the data could be different as well—for example, the source system might allow updates and deletes to existing data. In this case, the updates and deletes must also be efficiently reflected onto the data lake.

On the other hand, data engineers must write the wrangled data and information onto cloud object stores that are not filesystems and do not support any notion of transactions or random file access.

Combined, the reading and writing steps create multiple challenges that data engineers must solve. Let's broadly categorize the workflow steps that data engineers take, and the challenges associated with them.

Extracting and writing data

Data sources such as databases constantly get new records inserted and existing records updated or deleted. Other data sources, such as log files, event streams, and so on, only get new records. Hence, the data engineering pipelines must be able to extract, insert, update, and delete events in the source systems and replicate them in the data lake. There are two challenges involved here, as follows:

- **Append-only file formats**

  Popular data lake file formats such as Apache Parquet or Apache ORC are **append-only** file formats. This means that once a file is written in one of these formats, it cannot be modified. Any modification to any record within the file requires reading the file into memory, applying the changes in memory, deleting the physical file, and finally writing a new file in its place.

  Hence, while appending new records (`INSERT` events) is supported by creating a new file for new records, updating or deleting records requires custom tooling and separate data pipelines to be built by the data engineers.

- **Object stores**

  Data lakes are built on cloud object stores such as **Amazon Simple Storage Service** (**Amazon S3**), **Azure Data Lake Storage** (**ADLS**), or **Google Cloud Platform Google Cloud Storage** (**GCP GCS**). However, they are not filesystems, hence they do not provide any transactional guarantees or random lookup capabilities on the objects stored in them—the objects being the files that we are writing.

  This causes a lot of problems, as noted here:

  - Consider the scenario where a particular transaction is writing multiple files and the write fails midway. Depending on the reason for failure, the files that have already been written may or may not be deleted. This will leave the data lake in an inconsistent, possibly corrupt, state. This is the problem of **atomicity**. To counter this, data engineers must create customized tooling to clean up the failed write and roll back any changes.

  - Consider the scenario where a user tries to read data while a data pipeline is writing to the same dataset. Typically, during a read, the reader lists all the available files and then scans them to compute the results. Now, if the data pipeline is performing appends (insert events) and is in the process of writing the files, it is likely that the user will also read the partial outputs of ongoing events. Similarly, if the data pipeline is performing updates or deletes, it is likely that the user will try to read a file that was deleted as part of the update or delete. In either case, the user will likely get incorrect results. This is the problem of **isolation**. To counter this, data engineers must run pipelines when no one is using those tables or create methods that hide new files as they are being written.

- Consider the scenario where there is a multistep data pipeline currently executing and an outage then happens. When the system comes back online, which step should the reprocessing start from? This is the problem of **durability**. To counter this, data engineers must create custom tooling to record the state of the data after each step so that rollback or partial rerun can be achieved.

- Consider the scenario where multiple data streams are writing into a single table. It is important that each write should build on the transactions committed on the data in the past so that no data is lost. This is the requirement of **consistency**. To counter this, data engineers must write different streams to different tables before reconciling them into a single table as a batch operation.

- As a thought exercise, consider how you would perform updates and deletes. Cloud object stores do not support random-access reads in files, nor do they support any index of which file contains which ranges of data. This will make it very hard for you to pinpoint which data files are relevant for the update or delete. This leads to rewriting data at a partition level, or worse, at the table level.

Optimizing the data layout

An important aspect of writing data to a data lake is the data layout. As we saw in the previous section, cloud object stores and append-only file formats prohibit the random lookup of data. Further, traditional indexes are not very efficient or widely available on data lakes.

This means that data engineers must organize the data in such a way that readers of the data (query engines) can reduce the number of files being scanned. This is crucial for efficient querying of the data.

> **Why Are Traditional Indexes Not Popular?**
>
> A. The volume and velocity of the data. Updating indices is a computationally expensive task. Traditional indexes will not scale well with big data.
>
> B. The immutability of the files. Any update or delete will delete existing data files. This means the full index will have to be recomputed every time.
>
> C. The decoupling of compute and storage. Indexing works best when designed with the query engine in mind. On a data lake, this is difficult with a wide variety of query engines.

Apart from using columnar or binary file formats to minimize the **input/output** (**I/O**), there are four methods usually employed by data engineers to optimize the layout. Let's discuss these in the following subsections.

Partitioning

A partition is a subset of rows in a table that share the same value for a predefined set of columns. For example, consider the following **Structured Query Language (SQL)** table definition:

```
CREATE TABLE museum_visitors(
    name STRING,
    id_type STRING,
    id_number STRING,
    country STRING
) PARTITIONED BY (date DATE)
```

In this case, when records are written into the table—that is, files are written into the folder hosting the table data—the records will be arranged into subdirectories. Each subdirectory will be representing museum visitors for a date associated with that subdirectory—for example, s3://museum_visitors/date=2022-04-16 or s3://museum_visitors/date=2022-04-17. Now, when a user queries the museum visitors for April 16, 2022, the query engine will only read the files in the subdirectory for this date, hence skipping data that is not relevant to the query and thus improving query runtime.

Now, there is an obvious flaw in this mechanism. Data engineers must know the query patterns beforehand to create the correct partitioning scheme. Further, any query that does not use partition filters will end up with a full table scan. Hence, defining the perfect partition scheme is nearly impossible.

Clustering

Clustering is a complementary method to partitioning. It helps reduce the number of files scanned within a partition. Clustering groups together all data that shares the same value for a predefined column. For example, consider the following SQL table definition:

```
CREATE TABLE museum_visitors(
    name STRING,
    id_type STRING,
    id_number STRING,
    country STRING
) USING PARQUET PARTITIONED BY (date DATE) CLUSTERED BY
(country) INTO 5 BUCKETS LOCATION 's3://museum_visitors/';
```

In this case, within the directory for each date, the visitors for each country are grouped together. Hence, when a user queries for visitors from Singapore on April 16, 2022, the query engine will scan only the relevant files in the partition for the date April 16, 2022.

> **Note**
>
> If you are executing the preceding code snippet in the Databricks SQL workbench, ensure that your SQL warehouse is configured with an instance profile that has access to the S3 location. Likewise, if you are using Azure, the SQL warehouse should have access to the ADLS location. See *Chapter 4, The Security Model,* for a refresher on how to configure this access. Finally, if you are using Unity Catalog, use external locations and storage credentials to work with cloud storage locations.

As with the partitioning method, there are obvious flaws in this mechanism as well. Data engineers must know the query patterns beforehand to create the correct partitioning and clustering scheme. Further, any query that does not use partition and clustering filters will end up with a full table scan. Hence, defining the perfect partition and clustering scheme is nearly impossible.

Statistics collections

Another method employed by data engineers is to collect statistics on all the files on the data lake. An example of a statistic is the minimum and maximum value of an integer column in a particular file. If the query engine has this information, it will avoid scanning all files that do not contain the required integer value. For example, consider the `flights` table that we introduced in *Chapter 4, The Security Model.* We believe that most of the queries against this table filter on the `year` and `tailnum` columns. Hence, the following `ANALYZE` command can be used to selectively compute statistics for these columns:

```
ANALYZE TABLE flights COMPUTE STATISTICS FOR COLUMNS year,
tailnum
```

There are significant challenges with these statistics, though. First, collecting statistics is an expensive operation that must be run separately after every write. Second, the effectiveness of statistics is dependent on the query engine understanding those statistics. Hence, data engineers should selectively choose which tables to run statistics collections on. This is less than ideal.

Optimal file sizes

Query engines on data lakes work best if the individual files that make up a table are of consistent size and within an optimal size range. However, this is very hard to achieve as the amount of data extracted from a source per extraction might not be as high as to create data files of optimal sizes. This is exacerbated even more in streaming scenarios.

To counter this, data engineers often run compaction pipelines that combine the files written on the lake into optimal-sized files. For example, consider the following Python code:

```
spark.read.parquet('/path/to/data/partition').
repartiton(<repartition_count>).write.mode('overwrite').
parquet('/path/to/data/partition')
```

In this case, the code will do the following:

1. Read the data partition that contains data files of suboptimal file sizes.

2. Compute the total size of the data files.

3. Compute the optimal file count as repartition count = (total size)/(desired optimal file size).

4. Repartition the data accordingly and overwrite the partition.

Obviously, this is not optimal as it must be run when no one is using the table, and utmost care should be taken to avoid any corruption or loss of data.

Synchronizing data warehouses

The discussion in the previous two sections highlights the fact that due to the limitations of data layout optimizations, the data will never be accessible with the performance required for interactive querying. Therefore, a common approach was to selectively ship data on the data lake to data warehouses to support the querying requirements of BI users.

This creates a whole new set of challenges for data engineers as they must create and manage pipelines that synchronize data in the warehouse with data in the lake. Any mistake in the synchronization will cast doubts on the reliability of the data in either system. It also creates two copies of the same data in two different systems with different governance mechanisms. This also creates a challenge of synchronizing governance and access control across disparate systems.

The Delta Lake storage format

The discussion in the previous section should help you appreciate why I said that the quad of reliability, simplicity, performance, and governance is so hard to achieve.

The Delta Lake storage format aims to achieve this quad and solve the challenges discussed in the previous section.

The Delta Lake storage format builds on the goodness of Apache Parquet. The core innovation of Delta Lake is the introduction of a transaction log to accompany Parquet data in the table. A transaction log is the linear, immutable record of all modifications against a table. Modifications are inserts, updates, and deletes performed on a table. For all intents and purposes, if a modification is not recorded on the transaction log, it did not happen. The transaction log also stores statistics about each file that was written as part of the respective modification.

So, how does a transaction log work, and what does it look like?

> **Note**
>
> In this section, we will deep dive into file layouts of tables by executing Python commands. Hence, we must switch to the **Data Science & Engineering** persona view and create a notebook for us to execute our commands.

When we create a table with Delta Lake, the table's transaction log is automatically created. The transaction log is hosted in the `_delta_log` subdirectory of the table location.

To see the workings of the transaction log, let's consider the example of museum visitors from the previous section and perform the following steps:

1. Inspect the storage location of the `museum_visitors` table before any data is written to it. You can see this presented in the following screenshot. Since we did not specify a storage format when creating the table, Databricks created the table in Delta Lake format, which is the default storage format:

Figure 8.1 – The transaction log for a table

As you can see in *Figure 8.1*, we have not inserted any records into the table yet. Hence, there are no data files present yet. However, if you inspect the `_delta_log` folder, you will find a `00000.json` transaction log file that has captured a `CREATE TABLE` event. You can use the `dbutils.fs.head()` command to inspect the contents of the log file.

2. Now, make a modification by inserting a record into the table, as follows:

```
INSERT INTO museum_visitors VALUES('Vihag Gupta', 'Passport',
'Z123456', 'India', date '2022-04-16')
```

Running the `display` command from *Figure 8.1* will now show the data file containing this record, as shown in the following screenshot. The exact name of the file will be different for you, so let's call this file `file-1`:

	path	name
1	dbfs:/user/hive/warehouse/museum_visitors/_delta_log/	_delta_log/
2	dbfs:/user/hive/warehouse/museum_visitors/part-00000-4aed5189-7c97-4321-a5f3-638c8ab06f4f-c000.snappy.parquet	part-00000-4aed5189-7c97-4321-a5f3-638c8ab06f4f-c000.snappy.parquet

Figure 8.2 – Data files after first insert

An inspection of the `_delta_log` folder will also reveal a second transaction log, `00001.json`, which records the `INSERT` statement that we just executed. Use the `dbutils.fs.head()` command to inspect the contents of the log file. You will see details of the insert activity recorded, including the minimum and maximum value of columns.

3. Next, let's insert another record, like so:

```
INSERT INTO museum_visitors VALUES('Suteja Kanuri', 'Passport',
'A123456', 'India', date '2022-04-16')
```

There will now be two data files making up the current state of the table, as shown in the following screenshot. Let's abbreviate the new file as `file-2`:

	path	name
1	dbfs:/user/hive/warehouse/museum_visitors/_delta_log/	_delta_log/
2	dbfs:/user/hive/warehouse/museum_visitors/part-00000-4aed5189-7c97-4321-a5f3-638c8ab06f4f-c000.snappy.parquet	part-00000-4aed5189-7c97-4321-a5f3-638c8ab06f4f-c000.snappy.parquet
3	dbfs:/user/hive/warehouse/museum_visitors/part-00000-ef5c3319-14aa-422f-8115-e0790a4d42cb-c000.snappy.parquet	part-00000-ef5c3319-14aa-422f-8115-e0790a4d42cb-c000.snappy.parquet

Figure 8.3 – Data files after second insert

At this point, any reader attempting to query the `museum_visitors` table will first consult the transaction logs and conclude that it must read `file-1` and `file-2` to get the latest records in the table.

4. Finally, let's modify our visit record by updating the **identifier (ID)** number, like so:

```
UPDATE museum_visitors SET id_number = 'Z567890' WHERE id_
number = 'Z123456'
```

As we learned earlier, Parquet files are immutable, hence a new file must be created with the updated record. Inspecting the table path will show the new file, which will abbreviate as `file-3`. You can see an illustration of this in the following screenshot:

	path	name
1	dbfs:/user/hive/warehouse/museum_visitors/_delta_log/	_delta_log/
2	dbfs:/user/hive/warehouse/museum_visitors/part-00000-4aed5189-7c97-4321-a5f3-638c8ab06f4f-c000.snappy.parquet	part-00000-4aed5189-7c97-4321-a5f3-638c8ab06f4f-c000.snappy.parquet
3	dbfs:/user/hive/warehouse/museum_visitors/part-00000-6d68fdab-a5bd-429d-a6de-5fcd428c0b7b-c000.snappy.parquet	part-00000-6d68fdab-a5bd-429d-a6de-5fcd428c0b7b-c000.snappy.parquet
4	dbfs:/user/hive/warehouse/museum_visitors/part-00000-ef5c3319-14aa-422f-8115-e0790a4d42cb-c000.snappy.parquet	part-00000-ef5c3319-14aa-422f-8115-e0790a4d42cb-c000.snappy.parquet

Figure 8.4 – Data files after record update

At this point, any reader attempting to query the `museum_visitors` table will, first, consult the transaction logs and conclude that it must read `file-2` and `file-3` only to get the latest records in the table. `file-1` now contains an outdated record that is no longer included in the latest version of the dataset, and hence it must not be read.

And so, all modification events—that is, the addition of new files and the marking of old files as obsolete—are captured in the transaction log.

> **Down in the Weeds**
> For an in-depth discussion of the Delta Lake storage format and its associated protocols, I highly recommend that you read the whitepaper published by the authors of Delta Lake at `https://docs.delta.io/latest/delta-resources.html`.

In the next section, we will see how the Delta Lake storage format, with this simple atomic activity of capturing transactions as immutable logs, allows Delta Lake to solve all the challenges we discussed in the previous section and hence deliver on the quad of goals.

Data engineering after Delta Lake

Using the Delta Lake storage format is very simple. Simply create a destination table with the Delta format. In Databricks, the default format is Delta, but you can make it explicit, like so:

```
CREATE TABLE museum_visitors(
  name STRING,
  id_type STRING,
  id_number STRING,
  country STRING,
  `date` DATE
) USING delta
```

Any modification to this table—inserts, updates, or deletes—will automatically use the **atomicity, consistency, isolation, and durability (ACID)** capabilities available with the Delta format. Further, the table will automatically inherit the out-of-the-box performance-boosting features available in the Delta format.

Let's now look at how data engineering problems are solved with Delta Lake.

Extracting and writing data

Delta continues to use the Apache Parquet file format and cloud object stores for the data file format and data file storage, respectively. It cannot change the immutability of Parquet files, nor can it convert cloud object stores into filesystems with transactional guarantees or random lookup capabilities.

What it does is abstract the heavy lifting of the workarounds we discussed in the previous section behind simple INSERT, UPDATE, and DELETE statements. This abstraction ensures that these modifications are optimized for performance and correctness so that you do not have to engineer them.

We will go through case studies that show the simplification of extraction and writing data in *Chapter 11, SQL Commands Part-1*. However, as a quick demonstration, consider the following SQL command:

```
MERGE INTO user_details target USING (
   select id, name, email, zip, operation, rec_update_time
   from (SELECT *, ROW_NUMBER() OVER (PARTITION BY id ORDER BY
rec_update_time DESC) as rank from user_details_cdc)
   where rank = 1
) as source
ON source.id = target.id
WHEN MATCHED AND source.operation = 'DELETE' THEN DELETE
WHEN MATCHED AND source.operation = 'UPDATE' THEN UPDATE SET *
WHEN NOT MATCHED AND source.operation = 'INSERT' THEN INSERT *
```

In this example, user_details_cdc is a table in which each row represents a modification event (insert, update, or delete) that has occurred in the source data system. Using the rank() and row_number() functions, we get the latest operation for a given user ID. Based on the type of modification, which is captured in the operation column, we instruct the command to replicate the modification on our table in the Lakehouse. If the operation type is INSERT, then the command inserts the data as a new record in the user_details table. If the operation type is UPDATE, then the command updates the corresponding record in the user_details table (as identified by the id column). Similarly, a DELETE event results in the deletion of the corresponding record.

This should suffice to show how Delta Lake simplifies extracting and writing data using SQL primitives. This is just not possible with other file formats.

Solving append-only file formats

When presented with UPDATE, DELETE, or MERGE commands, Delta Lake simply recomputes a new data file with the required modifications and saves it to the object store. Any reader of the file simply consults the transaction log of Delta Lake and reads only the files that represent the current state of the table. We saw this in action in *Figure 8.4*.

You might be wondering how this operation is optimized. Does Delta Lake rewrite the entire dataset or just file(s) with UPDATE or DELETE targets? The answer is simple—the transaction log. The transaction log records the minimum and maximum values of columns in each file. By consulting the transaction log, Delta Lake can pinpoint which files contain records that are targeted by the command. Delta Lake then proceeds to rewrite the affected files.

Solving object store limitations

Simplifying writes to the data lake solves one half of the challenges associated with extracting and writing data. Without transactional guarantees, even with the ability to perform updates and deletes, data engineers will have to run commands in sequence to not corrupt an ongoing command. Let's revisit the transactional scenarios to learn how Delta Lake solves them, as follows:

- **Atomicity**: Whenever a modification happens, be it inserts, updates, or deletes, the writing process creates and executes a transaction. Upon successful completion of all steps of the transaction, the transaction is recorded as a commit in the transaction log. If any step fails, the transaction will not be recorded as a commit in the transaction log. This ensures that readers will always see a consistent state of the data, and data engineers do not have code-expensive rollback and rerun pipelines.

- **Isolation**: Whenever a transaction is in progress (which means it is computing new data files), it is not visible as a committed transaction. So, any reader who is reading data from the table while a write is happening will not see the partial results of the write. This is because prior to the read, the reader would have consulted the transaction log and got a list of data files in the latest committed version. This list will not contain uncommitted data files from the ongoing write. This enables data engineers to run data through the pipelines as it arrives, instead of waiting for consumption on the table to stop. Seasoned engineers will understand that isolation guarantees can come at a compromise of performance. Delta Lake provides two levels of isolation: **WriteSerializable** (default) and **Serializable**. For a deep dive, head over to https://docs.databricks.com/delta/optimizations/isolation-level.html.

- **Consistency**: Whenever there are two competing writes—that is, two writes submitted at the exact same time—the write processes should not leave the lake in an inconsistent state. Delta Lake uses **optimistic concurrency control** (https://docs.databricks.com/delta/concurrency-control.html) to avoid this. With optimistic concurrency control, a new transaction works in three stages. First, it consults the transaction log of a table to identify which files need to be modified. This is the read phase. Second, the operations of the transaction are executed in isolation and the results are staged in new files. This is the write phase. Finally, before the staged changes are committed to the table, Delta Lake checks whether the staged changes conflict with other concurrent transactions. An example of a conflict would be a transaction inserting data into a partition while a concurrent transaction is deleting data from the same partition. An example of a non-conflict would be two transactions inserting data into the same partition. If there are no conflicts, all the staged changes are committed. If there are conflicts, the write operation is failed. If the semantics allow for it, it will be retried automatically. This enables transactions on Delta Lake, which in turn allows robust data engineering—for example, it enables writing batch and stream data into the same table at the same time. Another application is the ability to correct data on the fly while new data is being streamed in without halting the entire data pipeline.

- **Durability**: Transactions, once committed, are durable as they are on the cloud storage and inherit cloud storage durability guarantees. This means that even if multistep pipelines fail midway, the last known transaction enables selective reprocessing of the pipeline.

As you can see, Delta Lake allows data engineers to bring the data to the data lakehouse for consumption with *reliable* and *simple* data pipelines.

However, as we saw in the data engineering challenges, another big component is preparing the data for optimal consumption—that is, the performance of user queries. Let's look at how Delta Lake enables data warehouse-like query performance by optimizing the storage layer while avoiding proprietary file formats.

Built-in performance-boosting features of Delta Lake

Delta Lake provides built-in performance boosters that complement the data layout strategies that we discussed in the *Optimizing the data layout* section. If there is a well-working data layout strategy in place, performance is accelerated further. If the data layout strategy is lacking or limited due to a wide variety of query-filtering patterns on the data, then the boosters make sure that performance is still improved by reducing unnecessary I/O. Let's learn about these performance boosters.

Automatic statistics collection

The first, and arguably the most important, performance booster is automatic **statistics collection** (**stats collection** for short), which enables a process called **data skipping**. Stats collection is an automatic process on Delta Lake. For every data file written, the stats collection process computes the minimum and maximum values for the columns present in the file.

By default, stats collection will be done on the first 32 columns of a table.

How does this help? Let's see an example here:

1. Consider a table representing a chess board. Each record in the table represents the coordinates of the cell and its current occupant. The table definition is shown here:

```
CREATE TABLE chess_cells(x INT, y INT, occupant STRING);
```

2. Since there are only three columns, stats will be collected for all three columns. For this demonstration, let's ensure that stats are not collected for the y and occupant columns by executing the following command:

```
ALTER TABLE chess_cells SET TBLPROPERTIES ('delta.
dataSkippingNumIndexedCols' = '1');
```

Next, let's insert some data so that we can see stats collection in action. Please note that this will have to be run in a notebook in the **Data Science & Engineering** persona. The code is illustrated in the following snippet:

```
val schema = StructType( Array(
            StructField(" x" , IntegerType,true),
            StructField(" y" , IntegerType,true),
            StructField(" occupant" , StringType,true)
        ))

val rowData1= Seq(
            Row(1,1," white_queens_rook" ),
            Row(1,2," white_queens_knight" ),
            Row(1,3," white_queens_bishop" ),
            Row(1,4," white_queen" ),
            )
var df1 = spark.createDataFrame(rowData1,schema).coalesce(1)
df1.write.format(" delta" ).mode(" append" ).saveAsTable("
chess_cells" )
```

By executing the preceding code, we are inserting four records at a time, which ensures there are four records in each file. Since this is a chess board representation, the total number of records should be 64, and the total number of files across which these 64 files are spread should be 16 (64/4).

Note

The source code in the preceding snippet is Scala code. It also represents only four cells. You are encouraged to extend this code to cover all 64 cells. If you are feeling lazy, you can refer to the book's GitHub repository for the full code.

3. You can verify the file count by executing the following line of code:

```
dbutils.fs.ls('dbfs:/user/hive/warehouse/chess_cells/')
```

4. Now, we have the data ready. Let's execute a query that uses the y column as a filter, as shown in the following screenshot:

```
1   %sql
2   SELECT * FROM chess_cells WHERE y=4;
```

▼ (2) Spark Jobs

    ▶ Job 91   View (Stages: 1/1)
    ▶ Job 92   View (Stages: 1/1)

Figure 8.5 – SQL query without stats collection

5. Click on the **View** link on the latest Spark job. This will open the Spark **user interface** (**UI**), where you can click on the link titled **Associated SQL Query** to bring up the following query-plan visualization UI:

Details for Query 94   ◉ Download screen as png

Submitted Time: 2022/04/19 07:59:20
Duration: 90 ms
Succeeded Jobs: 91 92

☑ Expand all the details in the query plan visualization

Figure 8.6 – SQL query without stats collection (continued)

6. We are interested in the **Scan** phase. Expand the `details` tab and navigate to the rows pertaining to the number of files, as shown in the following screenshot:

number of files pruned	0
number of files read	16

Figure 8.7 – Number of files scanned with no stats

As we can see the whole table, all files in the table were scanned to find records where y = 4. However, we know that only 8 of 16 files contain records where y = 4.

If we re-execute the preceding steps, without disabling the stats collection for the y column, we will see the following information in the details of the **Scan** phase:

number of files pruned	8
number of files read	8

Figure 8.8 – Number of files scanned with stats

As we can see, the number of files is just 8 now. This is a 50% reduction in I/O without any partitioning or clustering involved!

This is the magic of automatic stats collection. It allows the query engine to smartly read only the files that are required to serve the query. Statistics are captured when transactions are committed. The captured statistics are stored in the transaction log. Since statistics are captured at the transaction level (and not at the table or partition level), the operation is relatively inexpensive. Also, since statistics are tagged with transaction logs, reverting back changes or new modifications does not require full table statistics recollection. This makes the process optimized and scalable.

If tables are partitioned, stats collection complements the partitioning scheme. For example, when a query has filters belonging to both partitioning and non-partitioning columns, the query engine can skip (prune) irrelevant partitions and check statistics only in the relevant partitions.

Finally, as a best practice, avoid running stats collection on string columns as they are very expensive and might not give enough **return on investment** (**ROI**). To avoid running stats collection on strings, make sure that string columns are at the end of the table and the `delta.dataSkippingNumIndexedCols` configuration is less than the index of the first string column.

In summary, the query engine's optimization component uses information on the minimum and maximum values of columns within any file to determine whether the file should be read.

Next, we will discuss the performance booster that optimizes the file sizes themselves to maximize the distributed processing capabilities of Delta Engine.

Automatic Compaction and Optimized Writes

Data engineers can opt in for Automatic Compaction and Optimized Writes for the tables on the data lakehouse. When enabled, these two properties ensure that the writes to a table generate optimal-sized files. Here, optimal refers to optimal query processing speeds and minimum computation resource waste.

To see the effects of Automatic Compaction and Optimized Writes, we need a bigger dataset. Thankfully, we created one such dataset—airlines, in *Chapter 4, The Security Model*, in the *The security model in practice* section:

1. Consider the flights table. The flights table was generated without any Automatic Compaction and Optimized Writes. If we execute the dbutils.fs.ls() command on the flights table location, you will see precisely 99 data files.

2. Now, let's change the table definition to enable Automatic Compaction and Optimized Writes with the following statement:

```
CREATE TABLE flights USING DELTA TBLPROPERTIES (delta.
autoOptimize.optimizeWrite = true, delta.autoOptimize.
autoCompact = true) AS SELECT * FROM flights_csv;
```

Executing the dbutils.fs.ls() command will reveal that only 19 data files were generated.

3. At this point, I encourage you to execute this very simple query against the two variations of the tables:

```
SELECT Month, Origin, count(*) as TotalFlights
FROM flights_optimized
WHERE DayOfWeek = 1
GROUP BY Month, Origin
ORDER BY TotalFlights DESC
LIMIT 20;
```

You will notice a very drastic increase in query performance when this query is run on the table with Optimized Writes. In my case, on a 2XS-size SQL warehouse, a *cold query* ran in 3.6 seconds on the table with Optimized Writes versus 7 seconds on the table without Optimized Writes.

How did this drastic increase in performance happen? What did the automatic Optimized Writes do?

Optimized Writes works at two levels, as outlined here:

- **Automatic Optimized Writes**: Right before the write stage, the optimized write dynamically changes the dataframe's partition sizes, either increasing them or decreasing them to reach a target file size—128 **megabytes (MB)** by default.

- **Automatic Compaction**: After the write is completed, existing files in the table directory are checked. If there is an opportunity to merge newly created files with existing files in pursuit of the target file size, then a merge is performed. For example, even after an optimized write, it is likely that there is not enough data to reach the target file size. In this case, during the next write, new files will be merged with older ones to create files closer to the target.

Automatic Compaction and Optimized Writes are both enabled on our `flights` table, and hence we can see that individual files with sizes closer to the target are created.

Since the data files are of optimal size, the query engine can optimally distribute the work across the workers of the SQL warehouse and achieve enhanced performance.

This concludes our discussion on the performance-enhancing effects of optimized writes. For a detailed commentary on when and how to use Automatic Compaction and Optimized Writes in your data engineering pipelines, see the official documentation at `https://docs.databricks.com/delta/optimizations/auto-optimize.html`.

Automatic caching

With Databricks SQL, you get **Delta caching** out of the box. Very simply, whenever a query first executes against data it has not encountered since the warehouse started, it retrieves files from the cloud object storage. This retrieval is limited by the speed of the network over which the retrieval happens. To avoid this, Databricks SQL uses Delta caching, which simply caches any new file retrieved from the cloud object storage as part of any query onto the SQL warehouse's local **solid-state drives (SSDs)** in an optimized format. The next time a query executes that needs access to the same file, it simply reads the optimized file from the local SSD, which will always be faster than reading over the network.

Delta caching ensures the freshness of the cache. This is attributable to the transaction log. If a file in the Delta cache is marked as invalid in the transaction log, the file can be immediately evicted.

Let's see this in action. Recall our chess example from the previous section. Proceed as follows:

1. First, let's execute a cold query—that is, the first query after the SQL warehouse is started. This will ensure that there are no entries in the cache. The following statement should suffice:

```
SELECT * FROM chess_cells WHERE occupant LIKE '%kings%'
```

2. If we navigate to the **Query History** page and click on the entry corresponding to this execution, it will bring up the **Query Profile** view. We are interested in the **IO** section, which will show that no data was read from the cache. The **Query Profile** view should look like this:

IO

Rows returned	**6**
Rows read	**64**
Bytes read	**17.62** KB
Bytes read from cache	**0** %
Bytes written	**0** bytes

Figure 8.9 – Query with no cache hits

3. Next, execute another command that references the same table, but with a different filter predicate. The following statement should suffice:

```
SELECT * FROM chess_cells WHERE occupant LIKE '%queens%'
```

We will see that the files are read directly from the cache:

IO

Rows returned	**6**
Rows read	**64**
Bytes read	**2.70** KB
Bytes read from cache	**100** %
Bytes written	**0** bytes

Figure 8.10 – Query with cache hits

The usage of the cache is reflected in the query performance as well. On a 2XS-size SQL warehouse, the cold query took 3 seconds, and the subsequent query took merely 620 milliseconds!

As an exercise, I encourage you to update the table and see its effect on cache hits— does the query use stale data or fresh data? If it uses fresh data, how is this reflected in the cache I/O details?

As we have seen through this section, Delta Lake boosts the performance of queries with the smart use of transaction logs and out-of-the-box enhancements.

That's not all, though—Delta Lake has some more features that can be strategically configured to accelerate the performance of queries even further. Let's learn more about them in the next section.

Configurable performance-boosting features of Delta Lake

Delta Lake in Databricks has features that allow you to accelerate query performance further based on your knowledge of specific query patterns. Let's learn about them here.

Z-ordering

Automatic stats collection is a great performance accelerator. However, it is effective only when the **minimum-maximum** (**min-max**) ranges of the query filter column(s) in each data file are narrow and optimally overlapping across data files. What does this mean?

Consider a high-cardinality column such as the `TailNum` column in our `flights` table, which has a cardinality of 13150. The tail number is like a registration number for airplanes. Consider a short-haul flight that does many round trips a day. This means that the tail number of this flight will be present across a lot of time bands and hence across a lot of data files. So, if we try to query the `flights` table with a selective filter on `TailNum`, it will not be able to effectively skip irrelevant data files. For example, run the following query:

```
SELECT * FROM flights WHERE tailnum = 'N641DL'
```

During the execution of this query, 29 of 99 files are pruned (skipped)—that is, 70% of the dataset is read.

Now, imagine having multiple such columns in your dataset that are not natural partitioning columns but are frequently filtered on (together)—for example, `Distance` and `CRSElapsedTime`.

The effectiveness of the automatic stats collection will be further reduced as there are no guarantees that the min-max ranges of these columns will coincide in the same data files—meaning files will not be skipped effectively.

Let's unpack this with an example. The distance and elapsed time are correlated. The tail number is sort of correlated as there might be many tail numbers with similar distance and elapsed time values. However, it is very likely that records for such tail numbers will be spread across multiple data files. So, a query with predicates such as `where distance between` or `where crselapsedtime between` will have to scan through a lot of files. What if we could reorder the data such that records with similar values of `distance` and `crselapsedtime` are in the same data files? This would drastically improve the performance of queries with the preceding predicates.

This is where ZORDER comes in. ZORDER rearranges the data in such a way that the statistics for the columns in question are useful. ZORDER makes statistics great again.

ZORDER is an optimization technique akin to multidimensional clustering. It optimizes the number of data files and ensures that related information across the required dimensions—columns—is collocated on the same data file. Let's look at this super-simplified diagram:

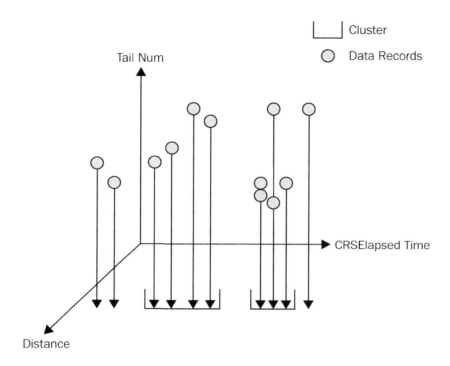

Figure 8.11 – The concept behind ZORDER

In *Figure 8.11*, we are assuming that we perform a ZORDER operation on three columns—TailNum, CRSElapsedTime, and Distance. ZORDER will map current records and the respective data files onto the **three-dimensional** (**3D**) space based on the values of the three columns. This mapping is then projected onto a single dimension, as illustrated in the preceding diagram. This projection reveals clusters of records that are related along these three dimensions. Using this technique, records that are now found to have related and similar values for the three dimensions can be clubbed together—in short, multidimensional clustering.

Of course, in practice, things are not so simple, and the simple act of projection itself requires complex algorithms. Databricks uses the Hilbert curve, a space-filling curve algorithm, to implement ZORDER.

Since the clusters will have closely related information, the probability that a filter across the dimensions will be served by the data in this cluster is increased. This makes the statistics on these files for these columns effective again.

Continuing our example, we will run ZORDER on TailNum like so:

```
OPTIMIZE flights ZORDER BY talinum
```

ZORDER rewrites the records to represent the clusters and optimize the layout. It also uses this opportunity to compact the files to ideal file sizes. Now, instead of 99 data files, the table is represented by five data files that respect the ZORDER. Running the same query as before, we will see that only one of the five data files is read to execute the query—that is, only 25% of the data files are read. This is a 45% improvement in data skipping. Keep in mind that we are looking at data-skipping effectiveness as our metric.

> **ZORDER by Default**
>
> ZORDER is not automatic. You must run an OPTIMIZE command whenever ZORDER is required. To find out more about this, read https://docs.databricks.com/delta/optimizations/file-mgmt.html#optimize-faq.

At this point, I must point out two things, as follows:

- My explanation of ZORDER is overly simplistic and will probably offend mathematicians all over.
- I am cutting corners in the ZORDER example by not applying traditional partition layouts with columns such as year and month before applying the ZORDER operation.

This is because of the following:

- Implementation of space-filling curve algorithms is an involved mathematical concept that Databricks has applied onto the Delta Lake filesystem. We are not interested in the math of it or the implementation of it. We are interested in the benefits of it.
- Showing ZORDER effectiveness at scale and along multiple dimensions requires a large dataset. Performing this experiment at scale will prove too costly to you.

Hence, I humbly redirect you to this blog by Databricks: https://databricks.com/blog/2018/07/31/processing-petabytes-of-data-in-seconds-with-databricks-delta.html.

This blog does the following:

- It explains how ZORDER works.
- It shows the effects of ZORDER at scale with proper instrumentation to showcase the benefits of ZORDER.

So, in summary, ZORDER allows you to optimize a dataset to handle queries with filters beyond what traditional partitions and stats collections can optimize for. It does so by applying a multidimensional clustering mechanism called **Z-order** curves to collocate related information on the same data file. This creates narrow min-max ranges that are non-overlapping and delivers the best possible file skipping.

Finally, before leaving this topic, I will say two things about not abusing the powers of ZORDER, as follows:

- The effectiveness of ZORDER reduces with the number of dimensions—this should be apparent in the diagram in *Figure 8.11*. Too many dimensions will reduce the size of clusters to the point where there is no effective data locality, and hence data skipping won't be effective. Four columns are a good upper limit.

- ZORDER depends on statistics collections. Hence, it inherits the limitation that statistics collections on long strings will be expensive. Try not to apply ZORDER on long strings.

Bloom filter indexes

You must have noticed by now that we have been working with purely numeric columns. We even ended the previous discussion with a warning on long strings. So, how does Delta Lake help improve queries that require arbitrary string searches?

The answer is Bloom filter indexes.

Bloom filters aim at improving data skipping or file pruning for columns that are not well suited for automatic stats collection. Bloom filters create index files for every data file in the table. The index is consulted by the data-skipping algorithm during query time. The index provides one of the two data points in either of the following cases:

- Whether the searched string is 100% not present in the file

- Whether there is a probability that the searched string is in the file, and what the probability is that this is a false alarm

The data-skipping algorithm uses the data point and decides whether to read the file.

At this point, ideally, I would walk you through a practical example that shows how this Bloom filter index improves the performance. But this time, I leave it up to you to try it out.

Here are a few hints for you with regards to testing Bloom filter indexes:

- First, ensure that you disable stats collection on the column you are planning to create the index on. This will help you observe a Bloom filter in isolation.

- Second, the syntax to create the index looks like this:

```
CREATE BLOOMFILTER INDEX
ON TABLE flights
FOR COLUMNS(TailNum OPTIONS (fpp=0.1, numItems=20000))
```

Fair warning, though—TailNum is not a good candidate for observing the benefits of Bloom filter indexes.

- Third, use data-skipping metrics such as *files pruned* or *parquet groups read* to measure improvement. Query execution time can be misleading as it depends on the load on the SQL warehouse and query result caching.

- Finally, if you're feeling really lazy, head over to the official documentation. They have an excellent notebook that walks you through the effects of Bloom filters with relevant examples: https://docs.databricks.com/delta/optimizations/bloom-filters.html#notebook.

CACHE SELECT

Last, but not least, we have explicit data caching. Automatic Delta caching caches tables read during actual queries submitted by users. However, automatic Delta caching still faces the cold-start problem where the first query on any table will have to do the dual tasks of fetching data files from the cloud object store and populating the local Delta cache while executing the user query. This leads to slower first queries. By running an explicit CACHE SELECT statement, we can cache certain datasets beforehand and avoid cold-start problems. A practical use case would be caching data from various tables before a long-running report or dashboard. Another could be caching data for interactive reports or dashboards so that users get instantaneous responses.

Using CACHE SELECT is easy. For example, if we had to cache the flights table, we would execute the following line of code:

```
CACHE SELECT * FROM airlines.flights
```

Any query on the flights table will read data from the cache.

A pro tip: CACHE SELECT statements are a great way to schedule an automatic start of SQL warehouses before the workday begins—that way, the SQL warehouse startup time and cold-query latency are avoided in one go.

This brings us to the end of the discussion on configurable performance boosters in Delta Lake, and the end of the chapter as well.

Summary

In this chapter, we deviated from our usual personas of data analysts and database administrators. Instead, we put on the hat of data engineers who are responsible for delivering data to analysts and administrators. Data engineers are wholly responsible for optimizing the data layout on the Lakehouse so that data analysts get the best possible query experience.

That said, we saw how the inputs of data analysts will be integral to getting the data layout correct. Inputs on query-filtering patterns, ordering of data columns, and frequency of optimizations are required for data engineers to make the best decisions.

In this chapter, we learned how Delta Lake is the storage layer for Databricks SQL. We learned how it provides the best out-of-the-box query experience. We also learned about additional features in Delta Lake that can elevate query performance even more. Finally, we discussed the internal workings of Delta Lake and how it enables all the features that Delta Lake provides.

In the next chapter, we will look at the accompanying compute layer in Databricks SQL.

9
The Photon Engine

In this chapter, we will turn our attention back to SQL Warehouses. This time, however, we will focus on the query engine running on SQL Warehouses. The query engine is known as Photon Engine. We will begin by learning about Photon Engine and its place in the Apache Spark framework. Going ahead, we will understand the core engineering philosophy of Photon Engine. Finally, we will go through its limitations and the roadmap to overcome them.

I do want to highlight that you don't need to learn the details of Photon Engine to work with Databricks SQL. This chapter is intended for those who are interested in how Databricks SQL achieves record-beating query performances on the Lakehouse setup with open source storage formats.

In this chapter, we will cover the following topics:

- Understanding Photon Engine
- Understanding vectorization
- Discussing the Photon product roadmap

Technical requirements

Before reading this chapter, you must ensure the following:

- You have access to a working Databricks SQL workspace to execute the examples
- You understand the execution model of Apache Spark
- You are familiar with data structures such as trees and matrices

Understanding Photon Engine

In this section, we will learn about Photon Engine. We will begin by understanding its place in the Databricks SQL ecosystem. Then, we will get a bit more technical and see how Databricks SQL uses Photon Engine with Apache Spark to provide the speed and concurrency that it proclaims to have.

What is Photon?

Photon (https://databricks.com/product/photon) is a **vectorized** query engine that is written in C++ that can leverage the data and instruction-level parallelism available in modern-day CPUs.

Photon is 100% compatible with Apache Spark APIs. This means you do not have to learn any new language or programming paradigm or rewrite your code to be able to leverage Photon.

The mission of Photon is simple: eliminate the need for data warehouses by providing the same or better performance than data warehouses while querying data in open file formats over cheap, elastic cloud storage.

It is the compute complement to the Delta Lake file format we discussed in *Chapter 8, The Delta Lake*. Delta Lake aims to optimize the data layout and data retrieval process. Photon Engine, which is optimized for Delta Lake, in turn, aims to make quick work of the user queries on the retrieved data with speeds expected by BI users.

Photon is the query engine built into SQL Warehouses and incurs no additional cost apart from the regular Databricks SQL pricing. However, you can also use Photon in Databricks data engineering and data science clusters by clicking on the Photon checkbox when selecting the Databricks runtime version of your cluster. Since a discussion of data engineering and data science clusters is outside the scope of this book, I will point you to https://docs.databricks.com/runtime/photon.html for reference as well as the following screenshot, which shows that enabling Photon is a matter of switching on a checkbox. Bear in mind that Photon on data engineering and data science clusters incurs additional costs. See https://databricks.com/product/pricing for more details:

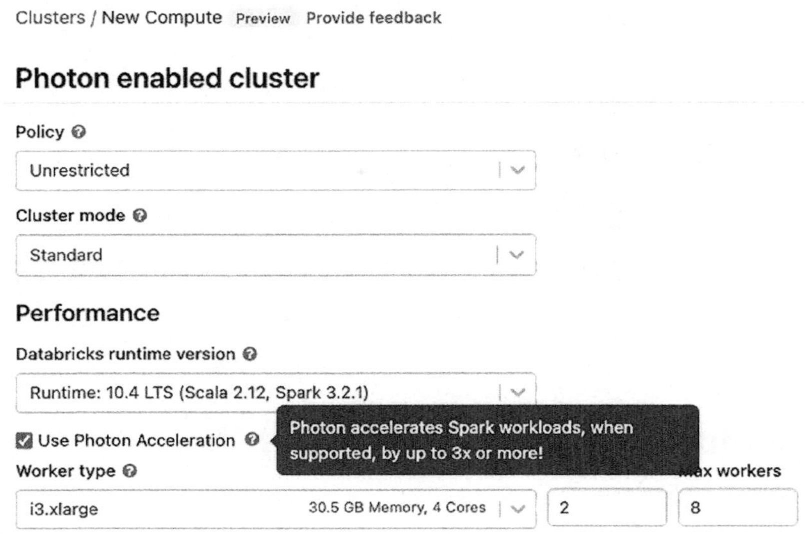

Figure 9.1 – Enabling Photon in data science and data engineering clusters

Before we continue, I must tell you that Photon is one of the ingredients of the secret sauce that makes Databricks SQL as performant as data warehouses while operating on the decoupled compute and storage architecture of data lakes. I cannot give away the secret sauce. The content in this chapter is based on what is publicly known about Photon Engine from documentation and public talks. I aim to simplify and explain the concept of vectorization and how Photon leverages it within the Apache Spark execution model.

Let's begin our deep dive into Photon with a quick discussion of the Apache Spark execution model.

The Apache Spark execution model

In this section, we will briefly learn about the journey of a query from submission to execution as it happens in Apache Spark.

The following diagram represents the first step where the user query is converted into machine-readable code, ready for execution:

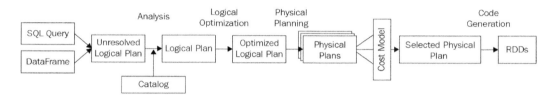

Figure 9.2 – Phases of the Catalyst optimizer

This step is the responsibility of the **Catalyst optimizer**. At its core, Catalyst is a general library for representing trees and manipulating them.

> **Why Trees?**
> The tree data structure is a popular and powerful way to represent a user query – SQL or otherwise.

The Catalyst tree transformation framework is used in four phases. Let's take a look.

Analysis

When a query is submitted, it is nothing but text. When this text enters Catalyst, it is converted into an **unresolved logical plan**. It is a simple tree representation of the query.

At this stage, we do not know anything about the attributes in the query. In the analysis phase, the tables are validated, and the data types of direct and composite attributes are resolved. This is done by consulting the schema metadata in the data catalog.

For example, consider the airlines dataset we built earlier in this book. Let's say we were to write the SQL query:

```
SELECT tailNum, Year+1 as y FROM flights
```

The analysis phase will consult the data catalog to resolve the existence of the table flights in the database being used in the current session and record that this table is in fact `airlines.flights`. Then, it will resolve the `tailNum` and `y` columns. It will resolve `tailNum` as a string column in the `airlines.flights` table. Finally, it will resolve that `y` is an integer since it is calculated as an integer literal being added to the `y` integer column – `year`.

At the end of the analysis phase, we get a **logical plan** that has annotated the simple tree with information about the tables and columns being represented by various nodes in the trees.

Logical optimizations

In this phase, a standard set of rule-based optimizations is applied to the logical plan. In essence, it will look for operators that can be rewritten in known optimal ways.

For example, consider the following SQL query:

```
SELECT tailNum FROM flights WHERE tailNum LIKE 'ND%'
```

In this case, the logical optimization phase will see that it has the rule to replace the inefficient `LIKE` operator with a more efficient `String.startsWith("ND")` implementation.

At the end of the logical optimizations phase, the **logical plan** from the analysis phase is transformed into an **optimized logical plan** using known, standard plan optimization techniques. Examples of such techniques include Boolean expression simplification, predicate pushdown, projection pruning, and more.

Physical planning

In this phase, the **optimized logical plan** is converted into multiple candidate physical plans. A **physical plan** is generated from a logical plan by replacing the operators in the logical plan with matching operations in the Spark execution engine.

For example, consider the following SQL query:

```
SELECT f.FlightNum, f.tailNum, p.manufacturer, p.model FROM
flights f LEFT OUTER JOIN planes p ON f.tailNum = p.tailNum
```

When this query enters the physical planning phase, multiple physical plans will be computed. For this query, the different plans will be based on the JOIN operator implementation. In Spark, it could be a broadcast join, sort merge join, or a shuffle hash join. The physical planning process will use cost models to decide the best join implementation. In this case, if you observed the query stages in the Query UI, the physical plan with broadcast joins was chosen.

At the end of the physical planning stage, the logical plan from the logical optimization phase is converted into a viable, optimal **physical plan** that is ready for execution.

Code generation

This is the final phase of query optimization. In this phase, bytecode (`https://en.wikipedia.org/wiki/Java_bytecode`) is generated for the physical plan based on what was selected from the physical planning phase. Notably, during the bytecode generation phase, the code generation operation fuses multiple operations in a **stage** to produce an optimized operation. This fusion eliminates the virtual function calls and limits the data exchanges to inter-stage shuffles only. This results in the overall execution being sped up. This process is called **WholeStateCodeGen**.

> **Note**
> The purpose of this chapter is to discuss the Spark execution components in a simplified manner so that we can contrast the changes when Photon is introduced. For an in-depth discussion on these components, for example, how `WholeStateCodeGen` works with **Just-in-Time (JIT)** compilation, please refer to the official Apache Spark documentation.

Execution

Finally, the specialized code generated by the compiler must be executed. The Spark code that was submitted (the SQL query, in this case) is called a **job**. A job contains multiple **stages**. To execute a stage, multiple **tasks** are spawned. Each task runs the same code – that is, the code that was generated in the code generation phase. However, each task runs the code on a subset of the data, which makes it the smallest unit of parallel execution. Each task is run within a construct called the **executor**, which provides the task with physical resources such as CPU cores and RAM to execute the code.

Consider the following SQL query:

```
SELECT f.FlightNum, f.TailNum, p.manufacturer, p.model FROM
flights f LEFT OUTER JOIN planes p WHERE f.FlightNum between
1460 and 1470;
```

When the code generation happens for this query, it will fuse the filter and broadcast loop instead of having them as separate operators. You can visit the Spark UI for the query to observe this:

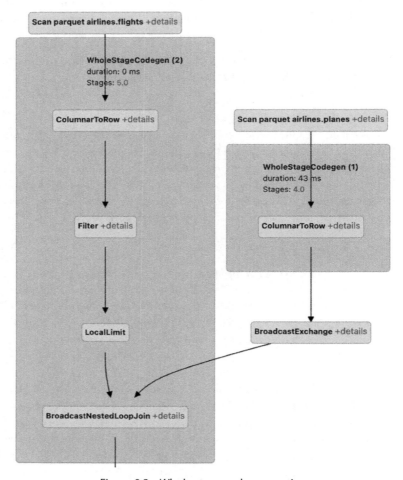

Figure 9.3 – Whole stage code generation

As you can see, the query has two stages, both of which are code-generated.

Now, let's talk about Photon and its place in the Apache Spark execution model. We can think of Photon as replacing the steps that start from the code generation phase:

- Instead of the whole state code generation of Java bytecode, Photon creates C++-based **vectorized** native engine implementations.

- During the execution of tasks, Photon provides native executors instead of the traditional JVM-based ones to run the native engine implementations.

The following diagram should help make this clear:

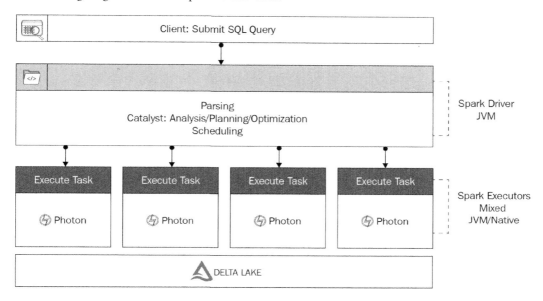

Figure 9.4 – Photon's place in the Spark execution model

So, what is vectorization? Why does Photon use it instead of the tried and tested Spark code generation? Let's dive in!

Understanding vectorization

To understand Photon, we must understand the different query execution philosophies. There are three popular query execution models. We will learn about them now. To keep it simple, let's learn about them with a non-data example.

Consider the simple task of increasing the brightness of a photograph. This task will involve increasing the brightness of every single pixel in the photograph. Modern cameras can easily capture photographs with pixel counts in millions. Let's also assume that our processor can handle eight parallel tasks at a time.

Finally, let's assume three functions will help with this task:

```
function getPixelRGB(PixelAddress): PixelRGB
function addBrightness(PixelRGB, BrightnessFactor): PixelRGB
function setPixelRGB(PixelAddress, PixelRGB)
```

There are three ways that the controller can be programmed to do this function.

Volcano model

In this model, we increase the brightness of the photograph one pixel at a time. A pseudocode implementation will look like this:

```
for pixel in pixels:
  pixelRGB_current = getPixelRGB(pixel)
  pixelRGB_new = addBrightness(pixelRGB_current, 1)
  setPixelRGB(pixelAddress, pixelRGB_new)
```

In this implementation, we loop over all the available pixels and execute the three functions to increase the brightness of each pixel, one at a time. There are glaring flaws in this implementation:

- At each step, the executing process must evaluate the next function to be called and call the function. Further function calls will require data objects to be created and then passed as parameters or returned as results. This is wasteful.
- The steps can't be chained together by the processor either as function evaluation must happen with every iteration. This is suboptimal.

Previously, we mentioned that our processor can handle eight parallel tasks. So, one redemption is that we can assign each processor a unique range of pixels to work on. However, that still does not remove the actual issue that each processor is spending more time on interpreting the steps rather than executing the simple task of adding 1 to the brightness.

Code generation

In this model, we still increase the brightness of the photograph one pixel at a time, but we depend on the processor to fuse the three functions into one "generated" function. Consider the following pseudocode implementation:

```
for pixel in pixels:
increasePixelBrightness(pixel, 1)
```

In this implementation, we still loop over all the available pixels, but we "fuse" the different steps into one function. This addresses a major flaw of the *volcano model* – that is, there is just one function call and no intermediate data objects are created. There is an input as well as an output. The processing of each pixel will be much faster now.

This can be combined with the parallel capabilities of the processor. Each processor will be able to complete its range of pixels much faster. That said, the processing is still done one pixel at a time, which is still slow.

This is the same code generation philosophy that Apache Spark uses as part of the Catalyst optimizer. Multiple tasks running across the various workers in the cluster execute the generated code against their assigned range of data. This is the key to the speed of execution in Apache Spark.

Vectorization

This model solves the pixel-at-a-time problem. Consider the following pseudocode implementation:

```
for pixel_batch in pixels:
  pixelRGB_current = getPixelRGB(pixel_batch)
  pixelRGB_new = addBrightness(pixelRGB_current, 1)
  setPixelRGB(pixelAddress, pixelRGB_new)
```

In this implementation, we return to the simple, clean, modular functions of the *volcano model*. However, instead of processing a pixel at a time, we modify the functions to work with a batch of pixels. A batch is represented as an **array** or **1D matrix** or a **vector**. So, the first function will obtain the RGB values for a vector of pixels. Similarly, the second function receives a vector of RGB values and adds 1 to all of them. Finally, the third function receives the vector of new RGB values and sets them onto the respective pixels.

The implementation still requires the next function to be evaluated, but because we are processing batches of one pixel at a time, the number of evaluations is dramatically reduced.

This is the core philosophy of Photon as a vectorized query engine.

Let's get a bit more technical here. Vectorization works best when we work on one column at a time, with a simple operation. Hence, in the vectorized implementation, we returned to using modular functions. These functions take one vector (column) at a time and apply a simple operation to it. Today's CPUs provide specialized processing powers for vector processing. For example, consider the `addBrightness()` function. It could be implemented as `pixelRGB_current[:]+1`, meaning a matrix operation where each element has 1 added to it. The vector processing capabilities allow CPUs to add 1 to each element in the array in parallel instead of looping over the array. Even if we implement it as a loop over the array elements, the loop will be "unrolled" into a vector operation since it applies a simple operation on one column.

> **Note**
>
> There is much more to implementations of query execution models than my overly simplistic explanations of the three models. I just wanted to convey the core philosophy. Feel free to deep-dive into these topics outside of this book.

Now that we understand the core concept of vectorization, let's look at vectorization from a query processing lens. Let's return to our beloved airlines dataset with the following SQL query:

```
SELECT Year, TailNum, SUM(Distance)
FROM airlines.flights
WHERE ArrDelay+DepDelay > 0
GROUP BY Year, TailNum
```

There are three operators in action here:

- **Scan** the `flights` table in the `airlines` database.
- **Filter** out records that are on time or before time.
- **Aggregate** the total distance covered by each flight in a year with delays.

We can visualize these as follows:

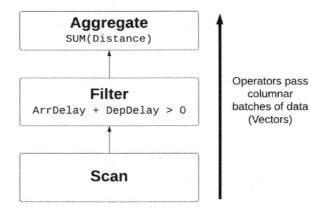

Figure 9.5 – Flow of operators in the query

Let's examine the **Filter** operation shown in the preceding diagram. The following diagram shows the evaluation tree of the **Filter** operation:

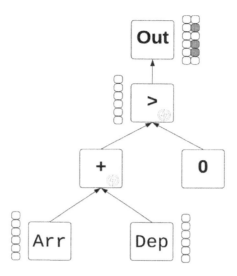

Figure 9.6 – Evaluation tree of the Filter operation

As we can see, Photon focuses on executing simple operations on columnar batches of data. Photon provides vectorized implementations of such operations. In this case, the addition operator (+) and the greater than operator (>) are Photon-vectorized implementations or kernels.

Let's zoom in on the addition kernel. The kernel accepts the vectors of data of two columns – ArrDelay and DepDelay. The kernel uses CPU-level data parallelism to execute the operation. This is called **Single Instruction Multiple Data (SIMD)** in the hardware world – that is, the ability to execute an instruction against multiple data entries in a truly parallel fashion.

Consider a modern multi-core CPU. Each core has an independent SIMD execution unit. The kernel will get the core to hold the two vectors on its on-chip memory and the SIMD execution unit will simultaneously apply the addition operation to the data elements in the two vectors in one CPU cycle. Now, the bigger the CPU register, the higher the number of data elements that will be processed in one CPU cycle!

Furthermore, because the kernel processes a single instruction, there can be CPU-level data pipelining. With every cycle, the core can process the vector in memory while simultaneously fetching the next batch of data (from RAM) to be loaded into its memory. This eliminates the wastage of CPU cycles.

Finally, Photon optimizes the data representation. In *Figure 9.6*, there's a second vector of data next to the *Out* stage. This is Photon's way of representing the data that was filtered out. Instead of recreating the whole dataset of filtered values (which could be hundreds of columns), it just adds a marker vector that denotes which rows are active after the filter. This avoids unnecessary intermediate data object (re)creation. It enables better memory management and eliminates CPU cycle wastage.

All these optimizations are possible due to the native implementation of Photon in C++. This is in stark contrast with the execution of tasks in the traditional Apache Spark execution, where the tasks are cocooned inside a **Java Virtual Machine** (**JVM**) and do not have access to CPU instruction set level optimizations. This is what makes Photon so fast.

Let's look at side-by-side comparisons of traditional code-generated DAGs versus Photon vectorized DAGs for our example query:

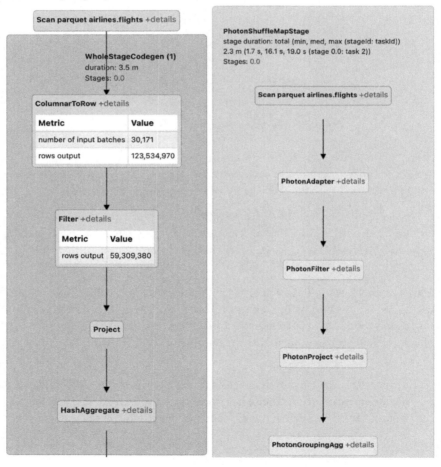

Figure 9.7 – Comparison of stage 1

Here, we are looking at *stage 1* of the query, which scans the data, performs the necessary filtering, and performs local aggregation. The left-hand side shows the traditional Apache Spark code-generated stage. The right-hand side shows the same stage in Photon. Though it is not apparent, traditional Spark has fused the filter, project, and local aggregate operators. Photon does not do so since it does not use `WholeStageCodeGen`:

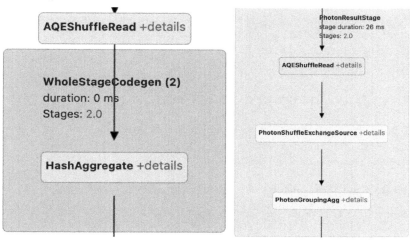

Figure 9.8 – Comparison of stage 2

Here, we are looking at *stage 2* of the query, which receives all the local aggregates and combines them into the final global aggregate. Once again, though it is not apparent, traditional Spark has fused the filter, project, and local aggregate operators.

Now, let's zoom out a bit. Consider a medium T-shirt-size SQL Warehouse in a Databricks on AWS setup. It has eight workers of the `i3.2xlarge` EC2 instance type. Each `i3.2xlarge` EC2 instance has 8 CPUs with 4 CPU cores each – that is, 32 cores. For the sake of this discussion, let's assume that each core supports SIMD. Now, when a query is executed, Spark will schedule tasks and these tasks will be executed by Photon, as shown in *Figure 9.3*. If the query uses the whole cluster, we can assume that 32 x 8 = 256 Photon tasks are executing. Each is executing on one core. Each task also gets a partition of data to work on. As we saw previously, each Photon task will further use CPU-level data parallelism to execute the operation on its data partition, hence achieving the maximum possible speed.

Compare this to the JVM-based task execution. Each task is still executed on a core, but the task executes the operation one row at a time. This does not make use of CPU-level data parallelism or instruction-level parallelism, which avoids idle CPU cycles.

Hence, Photon is fast. In Databricks SQL, Photon is combined with Delta Lake, which reduces the amount of data to be processed using techniques such as data skipping, caching, and indexing. This is where the data warehouse-beating performance of Databricks SQL comes from.

With this, I hope you understand the concept behind Photon. Of course, there are more nuances to implementing a vectorized engine, but hopefully, this discussion has enabled you to think about how operators can be vectorized and how they make Photon so fast.

> **Hey, Why Don't You Explain the Aggregate Operator?**
> I am going to leave that to you. Talking about the aggregate operator will open the rabbit hole of discussing hash aggregation algorithms and data structures. If you are so inclined, you can refer to the sources mentioned in the *Further reading* section at the end of this chapter.

Discussing the Photon product roadmap

Photon is a brand-new query engine. As we saw in the previous section, it must implement vectorized kernels for all operations that are possible in Apache Spark. At the time of writing, there are still a few operations that are not available with Photon:

- Photon Scan and Write operators work with Delta and Parquet files only
- Window and Sort operations are not yet supported
- User-defined functions are not yet supported
- Spark Structured Streaming is not yet supported

Work is in progress on all of these and I recommend that you visit `https://docs.databricks.com/runtime/photon.html#limitations` for the latest status.

That said, does this mean that you cannot use Window and Sort operations with Databricks SQL or that you cannot use your own user-defined functions in Databricks SQL?

You can! Recall *Figure 9.3*. It shows that the tasks scheduled by Spark are executed by Photon or JVM-Core as applicable. If an operation is not supported by Photon yet, that operation is scheduled on JVM-Core. This is transparent to the user, but it can be seen on the Spark UI. Let's quickly see this in action. Consider the following SQL query:

```
SELECT
  TailNum,
  flightNum,
  DepTime,
  DayOfMonth,
  RANK() OVER (
    PARTITION BY DayOfMonth,
    TailNum
    ORDER BY
```

```
      DepTime ASC
   ) AS rank
FROM
   airlines.flights
where
   year = 2004
   and month = 12;
```

This query is ranking the flights that have been made by a particular aircraft by the aircraft's departure time. In the Query UI, you will see the distinction between the Photon executed stages and the non-Photon stages. The following snippets from the full UI should help you understand this:

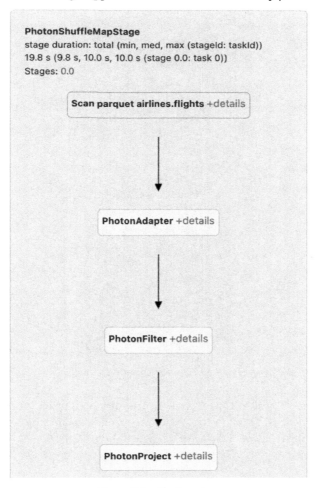

Figure 9.9 – Photon stage

The preceding diagram shows the **directed acyclic graph** (**DAG**) portion of the query that is executed by Photon. We can see that Photon is performing the Scanning and Filter operations.

As per the query, the scanned and filtered rows must now be sorted and ranked. Both functions are not supported by Photon yet, so the DAG clearly shows them being executed with traditional Spark JVM-Cores:

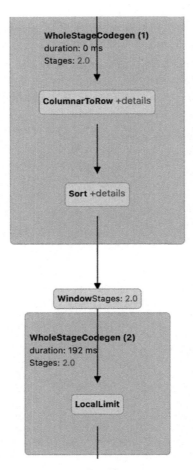

Figure 9.10 – Non-Photon stages

The preceding diagram shows that Spark used non-Photon execution for the Sort and Window operations. This is marked using yellow for Photon stages and blue for non-Photon stages. Another telltale sign is the **WholeStageCodegen** tag in the non-Photon stages.

> **Using Photon for Data Engineering**
>
> You might be thinking, if it is so fast, why not use Photon for data engineering and data science workloads as well? The answer is that you absolutely should! Just bear in mind that Photon is not free in data engineering and data science clusters. However, it is free in Databricks SQL.

This brings us to the end of our discussion on Photon. Hopefully, you have a better understanding of the core concept behind Photon and why it is so fast.

Summary

In this chapter, we dove headfirst into Photon Engine. We discussed the standard Apache Spark execution model and what has made Apache Spark so fast. Then, we discussed the prevalent query engine design models and why the vectorization model was chosen to replace the code generation design of Apache Spark. We learned about the core concept of vectorization and how it enables Photon to be as fast as it is. Finally, we discussed what Photon can and cannot do now and what its known feature roadmap is.

Before we end this chapter, I will provide you with one final reminder – the aim of this chapter is only to give you a conceptual idea of how Photon works and why is it so fast. All the concepts have been simplified for better understanding. To deep dive into the nuances, follow the content in the section Further Reading.

With that, we have a complete understanding of the Databricks SQL toolset and its storage and computation technologies. In the next chapter, we will discuss the concept of the data warehouse and how to translate our understanding of various data warehousing components into the data lakehouse.

Further reading

I have used publicly available information sources for this chapter, without which this chapter would not have been possible. I wish to acknowledge them here:

- A talk by Alex Behm at the *Data and AI Summit*: `https://databricks.com/session_eu20/photon-technical-deep-dive-how-to-think-vectorized`

- White paper on Photon submitted at SIGMOD-2022: `https://cs.stanford.edu/people/matei/papers/2022/sigmod_photon.pdf`

- Master's thesis by Giorgi Kikolashvili at the University of Amsterdam – *On the design of a JVM-based vectorized Spark query engine*: `https://homepages.cwi.nl/~boncz/msc/2019-GiorgiKikolashvili.pdf`

If you are interested in deep -diving further into Photon, then use these resources.

Warehouse on the Lakehouse

Traditional data warehousing implementations are comprised of different components such as a staging area, operational data store, enterprise data warehouse, and data marts. Depending on the implementation of the system, these components may or may not be transparent to the user. One of the biggest mental leaps you must take when adopting the Lakehouse is how to translate these components to the Lakehouse.

In this chapter, we will learn how to design and implement these components on the Lakehouse using Delta Lake features and ETL design patterns of the Lakehouse.

In this chapter, we will cover the following topics:

- Organizing data on the Lakehouse
- Implementing data modeling techniques

The primary audience of this chapter is database administrators and data engineers who will be responsible for designing and implementing the data models corresponding to the different architectural components.

Technical requirements

To make the most of this chapter, you must ensure the following:

- You know about data modeling techniques such as Kimball, Inmon, Data Vault, and others.
- You have read *Chapter 8, The Delta Lake*, and *Chapter 9, The Photon Engine*, of this book.

Organizing data on the Lakehouse

In this section, we will discuss the architectural components of a traditional data warehousing infrastructure/system and how these components can be designed and implemented on the Lakehouse. This is particularly interesting because, as we learned in *Chapter 8, The Delta Lake*, there is a single data layer on the Lakehouse known as Delta Lake. It does not have purpose-built database-like components that can be used for data warehousing components such as the operational data store or data marts.

Let's start with a brief overview of the components of a generic data warehousing system implementation.

Components of a warehouse system

The following diagram shows the various components of a generic data warehouse system:

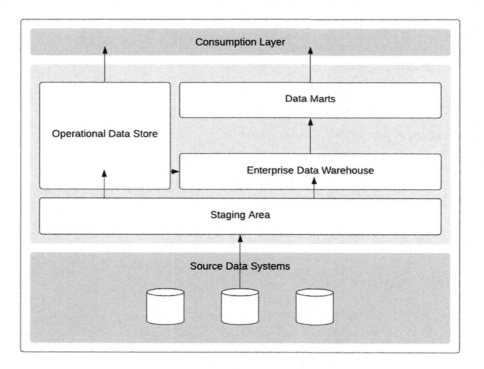

Figure 10.1 – Data warehouse infrastructure components

The data that is captured from source data systems enters the data warehousing system at the **staging area**. The data in the staging area is free of any form of processing and is a faithful as-is replica of the data in the source system.

The data in the staging area is continuously moved to the **operational data store** (**ODS**). Depending on the capability of the implementation, this process may or may not be real time in nature. Due to the continuous data influx, the ODS is a snapshot of data from source systems, optionally consolidated into a more sophisticated representation, and supports tactical business intelligence.

The data in the ODS is moved to the **enterprise data warehouse** (**EDW**) at a fixed schedule. The ODS can contain multiple changes to the same data entity that may have occurred throughout the day. When the ODS data is moved to the EDW, only the latest state of the data entity is moved. This is done through processes such as de-duplication, merging, consolidating, and cleaning records in the ODS. The data in this layer is still non-aggregated and at a line-item level.

It is also possible that the data in the staging area is directly processed into the EDW component. This scenario is likely when there is no visible need for an ODS for tactical business intelligence.

The ODS and EDW systems are usually a **third normal form** representation of data, based on the design of the source systems and any domain-specific data model being used in the enterprise.

Finally, the data in the EDW is moved to the **data marts**. Data marts represent summarized and aggregated data, perhaps in a dimensional data model. These data marts can be department or project-specific and are used for analysis and reporting from the consumption layer, which could be an array of business intelligence tools and suites.

Depending on the implementation of the system, these components may have different names – they may even have more intermediate components. The components may use dedicated, specialized software and hardware stacks as well. What remains the same is the journey of the data as it transforms from a raw representation, to a refined and cleaned representation, to an enriched, aggregated, and summarized representation.

The Databricks Lakehouse allows you to build this journey for the data as well. Let's learn how.

The Medallion architecture

In the Lakehouse architecture, the storage and compute layers are decoupled. That is, the Lakehouse has a single storage layer that stores data in Delta format and has a single compute layer represented by SQL Warehouses (see *Chapter 6, The SQL Warehouses*) running Photon Engine.

What this means is that on the Lakehouse, the staging, ODS, EDW, and data marts are simply collections (schemas) of Delta tables residing on cloud storage. Each collection conforms to the data quality characteristics and data modeling techniques appropriate to the component it represents.

From a Databricks lens, the journey of the data through these layers is called the Medallion architecture (`https://databricks.com/glossary/medallion-architecture`). In the Medallion architecture, the first data layer, also known as the **bronze layer**, is an as-is replica of the source data systems. The data that's captured from the source data systems enters the Lakehouse at the bronze layer. In an ideal setting, the replica of the source data systems in the bronze layer will be Delta tables. However, the **change data capture** (**CDC**) system in your setting may not support writing data in Delta format, in which case you can have an intermediate step in the bronze layer that converts the data into Delta format. The following diagram should make this clearer:

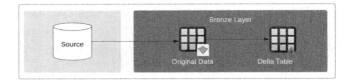

Figure 10.2 – The bronze layer

Converting the data into Delta format in the bronze layer is especially useful if you intend to perform near real-time reporting on the data. Delta format, as we saw in *Chapter 8, The Delta Lake*, comes with many features that will ensure optimal reporting performance. Databricks provides a mechanism called the **Autoloader** (`https://docs.databricks.com/ingestion/auto-loader/index.html`) that can automatically sense the arrival of new data in the original capture format table and process it into the bronze delta table.

The bronze layer can be equated to the **staging area** component. This is because the bronze layer data model is a faithful as-is replica of the source systems where data continually flows in. This makes it a reliable archive of all data. Any reprocessing of data can use data in this layer instead of querying source systems. Using Delta tables at this layer will ensure optimal near real-time reporting performance.

The data in the bronze layer is de-duplicated, cleaned, consolidated, and merged into a third normal form such as a data model or a domain-specific logical model. This is the **silver layer** of the Medallion architecture, and it can be equated to a combination of the **ODS** and **EDW** components. The bronze layer data is continually streamed into the ODS representation. Next, all enterprise-level business rules and transformations are applied to the ODS representation to create the EDW representation. The EDW is the key enabler of self-service analytics, reporting, and advanced analytics.

The following diagram should make this clearer:

Figure 10.3 – The silver layer

This flow is made possible by the Delta Lake format. Delta Lake tables can inherently behave as streaming data sources. Delta tables can be configured to continually emit what is called a **change data feed**, which essentially represents events such as inserts, updates, and deletes in the table. This means the following:

- The changes in the bronze/staging layer can be streamed into the silver/ODS representation, enabling the freshest snapshot of operational data for tactical business intelligence.

- The change in the silver/ODS layer can be streamed or batch-processed into the silver/EDW representation, as per business requirements.

We will see examples of change data feeds in action in *Chapter 11, SQL Commands – Part 1.*

> **Note**
>
> This is a good time to mention the fact that the bronze, silver, and gold layers are design patterns that reflect the progressive refinement of the structure, quality, and performance of the dataset. They are not enforceable entities. I am only drawing analogies of data warehouse components to these layers for ease of understanding. You can call them whatever you like.

Finally, the silver/EDW representation is summarized, aggregated, and modeled into data marts or dimensional models based on individual project requirements. These tables are referred to as the **gold layer** in the Medallion architecture. This layer can be equated to the data marts component. The following diagram should make this clearer:

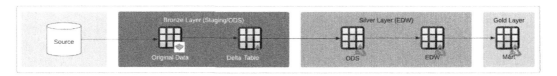

Figure 10.4 – The gold layer

As with the silver layer tables, the gold layer tables can be created in batch mode or streaming or near-real-time mode, as per the business requirements.

Bringing this all together, we can superimpose the Medallion architecture on the generic data warehouse system architecture to show how the Lakehouse can be used to build a warehouse:

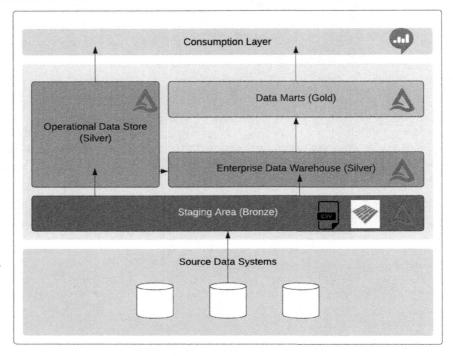

Figure 10.5 – The warehouse on the Lakehouse

With this, it should be clear how a warehouse can be architected on the Lakehouse and how your existing understanding of warehousing infrastructure can be ported over to the Lakehouse architecture. Once you have grasped this component mapping, all that remains is to define your data models as per the warehouse component or Medallion layer with standard DDL commands. The compute layer – that is, the SQL Warehouse running Photon Engine – will allow users to query all these components on demand, hence behaving as traditional warehouse systems.

In the next section, we will learn about the considerations when implementing the layers and how to use the performance-optimizing features of Delta Lake for an optimal setup.

Implementing data modeling techniques

In this section, we will look at the layers of the Medallion architecture. We will discuss the design considerations for the layers, possible data modeling techniques to employ, and how to apply Delta Lake features.

Consider the airlines dataset example that we have been working on throughout this book. Let's extend that example here to visualize how the various layers can be brought to life on the Lakehouse.

The bronze layer

As we discussed in the previous section, the bronze layer is an as-is replica of source systems and hence the data models will follow that of source systems. Also, the bronze layer tables should ideally be in Delta format for optimal near-real-time query experience and data versioning.

A typical airlines system will contain source systems for functions such as booking, ticketing, check-in, flights, loyalty, and more. Each source system will contain a host of tables.

Consider the following diagram:

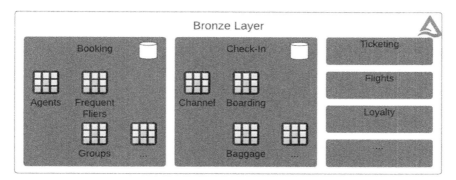

Figure 10.6 – The bronze layer of the airlines dataset

This is a replica of the source systems in the bronze layer. For example, the booking system will contain tables for agents, operating and marketing flights, class, frequent fliers, seat details, special requests, group bookings, and more. Similarly, the check-in system will contain tables for carriers, check-in channels, agents, segments, boarding status, baggage status, and more.

The silver layer

The silver layer is very active since it is receiving and processing data constantly. This means that speed and agility in ingesting data are prime requirements. While speed can be considered a function of the processing engine and the computing power, a case can also be made that the data model that the data is being written into will also affect the speed of ingestion.

From this perspective, a write-performant data modeling technique such as **Data Vault** (https://en.wikipedia.org/wiki/Data_vault_modeling) is a good candidate for the tables in the silver layer. Let's see why.

Data Vault defines three key entities:

- **Hubs**: These represent core business entities. They will have a natural key that identifies them.

- **Links**: These are entities that represent the relationship between two or more hubs. They just contain the join keys to the hubs.

- **Satellites**: These are entities that represent additional attributes of hubs or links.

The clean separation of business entities from relationship to entities means that ETL processes will be simple as there won't be any complex preprocessing before records are written. Also, new entities can easily be added without the need to touch existing entities or processes. This means it delivers on both the speed and agility requirements of the silver layer.

Data Vaults require a staging zone, which is a natural fit for the bronze layer of the Medallion architecture. Furthermore, Data Vaults have a **raw vault**. The raw vault receives the staging zone data in the hub, link, and satellite entities. The business rules are then applied to the raw data vault to generate the **business vault**. When combined, the raw and business vaults make up the silver layer.

Let's return to our airlines example. Consider the following diagram:

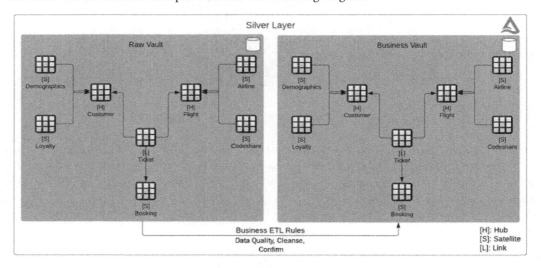

Figure 10.7 – The silver layer of the airlines dataset

In this **entity-relationship** (ER) diagram, we can see how a sample silver layer can be built. There is a raw vault that is built from data in our bronze layer.

When building the raw vault from the data in the bronze layer, we can build it in scheduled batch mode or a streaming fashion. This is one of the defining reasons why the Lakehouse is an excellent platform to build your warehouse on – the ability to process ETL data as fast as possible and make it consumable.

Here, we can see two hubs – **Customer** and **Flight**. They are connected by a link – **Ticket**. The hubs and links are also augmented by satellite tables, which contain descriptors for the hubs and links, respectively.

There is also a business vault that has been built by applying business rules for data quality and other transformations.

> **Note**
>
> This is not to say that Data Vault is the only viable data modeling technique for the silver layer. Consider your requirements to make an informed decision on the data modeling technique to use. A case can be made that if we have a mutable file format such as Delta Lake, do we need the Data Vault pattern?

Finally, ensure that the implementation makes the most of Delta Lake. Here are some basic guidelines:

- Z-Order the join keys of the hubs, links, and satellites.

- Resist the urge for fine-grained partitions for naturally small tables such as satellite tables.

- If there are current-flag columns for changing dimensions, consider adding Bloom filter indexes to them. Keep in mind that Bloom filters can slow down the write processes, so use them with caution.

The gold layer

The **gold layer** needs to be read optimized to be able to deliver the best possible experience to the BI practitioners. This translates to a more denormalized data organization that reduces the need for expensive join operations. Hence, dimensional modeling techniques such as the Star schema (https://en.wikipedia.org/wiki/Star_schema) are the best candidates for tables in this layer.

The Star schema is a very well-known technique. Since Star schemas are denormalized, the requirement to perform joins (which are computationally expensive) is reduced. It also lends itself to faster aggregations. That is – the design of the Star schema itself lends to great performance, regardless of the computing platform.

Let's return to our airlines example. Consider the following diagram:

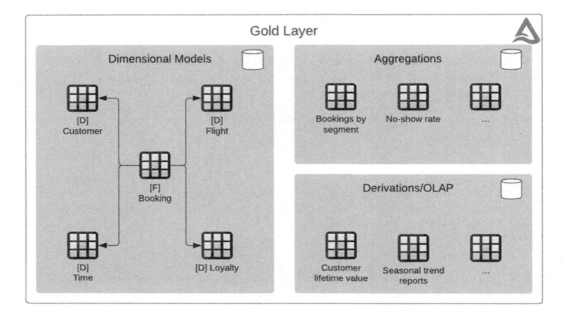

Figure 10.8 – The gold layer of the airlines dataset

In this ER diagram, we can see how a gold layer can be built. There is a dimensional model for flight bookings that is derived from the business vault of the silver layer. There are also aggregations built on top of this dimensional model. We can also have some derivations such as seasonal trend reports and customer lifetime value built from the dimensional model.

With Databricks SQL, we can use certain techniques to further improve the performance of queries on the gold layer. Here are some basic guidelines:

- Create Z-Orders on your fact tables. Limit the Z-Ordering columns to the top four columns that are used in query predicates. In practice, this might involve limiting the foreign keys to the largest dimension tables.

- Create Z-Orders on your dimension key fields. In practice, this might be a surrogate key. Limit the Z-Ordering columns to the top four columns that are used in query predicates.

- Use the materialized views capability to create gold layer tables that can reflect near real time updates

- Run periodic `ANALYZE` processes on the tables involved in complex joins. The `ANALYZE` command will be discussed in detail in *Chapter 12, SQL Commands – Part 2*.

This brings us to the end of our discussion on implementing a data warehouse architecture on the Lakehouse.

> **Note**
>
> Please bear in mind that the discussion of Data Vault or dimensional data modeling techniques in different layers is not prescriptive. Consider your requirements and choose the data modeling technique that suits them.

Hopefully, by now, you have a firm understanding of how you can implement warehousing components, the necessary architecture, and the processes with ease on the Lakehouse.

Summary

In this chapter, we learned about the general components of a data warehousing system and how those components can be implemented in the Databricks Lakehouse with the Medallion architecture. We also learned about the best practices for implementing popular data modeling techniques on the Lakehouse.

This brings us to the end of *Part 2* of this book, which focused on the core technology enablers of Databricks SQL. In the next chapter, which also marks the beginning of *Part 3* of this book, we will discuss the SQL commands that are available in Databricks SQL, starting with commands that allow us to manipulate and work with our data.

Part 3: Databricks SQL Commands

This part focuses on the SQL commands available in Databricks SQL. It introduces Databricks SQL-specific commands that enable advanced usage patterns in a data lakehouse. This part is not intended to be a complete SQL reference.

This part comprises the following chapters:

- *Chapter 11, SQL Commands – Part 1*
- *Chapter 12, SQL Commands – Part 2*

11
SQL Commands – Part 1

Databricks SQL supports ANSI SQL and all standard SQL commands are available and applicable. It also exposes additional commands for Lakehouse-specific capabilities. In this chapter, we will focus on these Lakehouse-specific SQL commands and learn their practical usage with scenario-based examples. We will start by exploring the commands for the **data definition language** (**DDL**). Then, we will explore commands for the data manipulation language. Finally, we will learn about functions that handle semi-structured data and unlock advanced data manipulation.

In this chapter, we will cover the following topics:

- Working with data definition language commands
- Working with data manipulation language commands
- Working with the built-in functions in Databricks SQL

> **Note**
>
> This chapter is not intended as a complete SQL command reference. We will cover the practical usage of SQL commands that are specific to Databricks SQL and Lakehouse. The rest of the standard SQL commands can be studied at `https://docs.databricks.com/sql/language-manual/`.

Technical requirements

To complete this chapter, you must ensure the following:

- Familiarity or experience with SQL and writing SQL queries
- You have reviewed the official general reference (`https://docs.databricks.com/sql/language-manual/#general-reference`)

Working with data definition language commands

In this section, we will learn about data definition commands that are specific to Databricks SQL and Lakehouse. Specifically, we will focus on commands that allow administrators to manage data catalogs, cloud storage locations, and Delta Sharing.

Databricks SQL supports the common data definition commands such as the following:

- CREATE/ALTER/DROP database/schema
- CREATE/ALTER/DROP/TRUNCATE table
- CREATE/ALTER/DROP view

These are standard commands in the database and data warehouse world. They have the same semantics in Databricks SQL and do not require detailed unpacking. However, as we learned in *Chapter 3, The Data Catalog*, Databricks SQL encapsulates database objects in a new type of object called the catalog. Let's learn how to create catalog objects and work with them.

DDL for catalogs

Databricks SQL supports a three-level namespace, with the catalog being the highest-level namespace. As a reminder, a catalog is a securable object that is used to organize your data assets. Also, creating new catalogs is only supported if you are using the Unity Catalog.

Creating catalogs

A catalog can be created with the following command:

```
CREATE CATALOG [ IF NOT EXISTS ] catalog_name [ COMMENT comment
]
```

For example, we can create a catalog called `airlines_dev_catalog` as follows:

```
CREATE CATALOG airlines_dev_catalog
```

This command only has two customizations:

- IF NOT EXISTS: This is a common clause and specifies that if the catalog exists, do not try to create the catalog. Applying this clause ensures that the command exits gracefully if the catalog already exists instead of throwing an error.
- COMMENT: This is a clause that specifies a comment for the catalog. The comment is free-form text and can be used to supply important contextual metadata about the catalog.

Altering catalogs

An existing catalog can be altered with the following command:

```
ALTER CATALOG [ catalog_name ] OWNER TO principal
```

In contrast to other data objects such as tables and views, the only alteration that is possible on catalogs is the change of ownership. `principal` represents a user, user group, or service principal, as discussed in *Chapter 4, The Security Model*.

Dropping catalogs

Finally, an existing catalog can be deleted or dropped using the following command:

```
DROP CATALOG [ IF EXISTS ] catalog_name [ RESTRICT | CASCADE ]
```

This command has two customizations:

- CASCADE: Like dropping or deleting databases, dropping a catalog is not allowed if the catalog is not empty. If you wish to override this behavior, you can specify the clause. The RESTRICT clause is the opposite of the CASCADE clause and will cause the command to error out if there are databases in the catalog.

- IF EXISTS: If you wish for the command to exit gracefully if the catalog does not exist, specify the IF EXISTS clause.

Finally, bear in mind that a catalog can only be created, altered, and dropped by metastore administrators (`https://docs.databricks.com/data-governance/unity-catalog/key-concepts.html`).

DDL for external locations

In *Chapter 4, The Security Model*, we learned how Unity Catalog allows you to manage cloud storage locations. It does so by exposing two new objects:

- **External Location**: A data object that represents a cloud storage location

- **Security Credential**: A data object that represents the security credential to access the storage location

This is a very powerful capability as it allows database administrators to program access to cloud storage locations with universal SQL commands and semantics instead of cloud-specific IAM constructs. For the end users, it means easy, self-service access to data files available on the cloud storage if that data has not been cataloged as a relational table.

> **Note**
>
> The power of the external location construct is most applicable for data engineers and data scientists who require direct access to certain locations. An example would be to access non-relational data that cannot be cataloged as a relational table. Databricks recommends giving users access to the location object rather than the security credential object.

Now, let's learn how to create the external location objects and work with them.

Creating external locations

An external location can be created with the following command:

```
CREATE EXTERNAL LOCATION [IF NOT EXISTS] location_name URL url
WITH STORAGE CREDENTIAL credential_name [COMMENT comment]
```

Before we talk about the configurations of this command, we must talk about the other data object referred to in the command syntax: STORAGE CREDENTIAL.

To create an external location, we must specify the cloud credentials that can be used to access this location. In AWS, this will be an IAM role, while in Azure, this will be an Azure Service Principal.

At the time of writing, the storage credential cannot be created with SQL. The DBA must run a Databricks command-line utility (https://docs.databricks.com/dev-tools/cli/index.html) to create a storage credential; for example:

```
databricks unity-catalog create-storage-credential --json '{
"name ": "airlines_cred ", "azure_service_principal ": {
"directory_id ": "dir-id ", "application_id ": "app-id ",
"client_secret ": "secret "}}'
```

Here, the Azure service principal will hold the necessary privileges that allow access to the required location on Azure Data Lake Storage.

> **Note**
>
> If you are using Databricks on AWS, you will use S3 locations and IAM policies. Similarly, with Databricks on GCP, you will use GCS buckets and service accounts.

Now that the storage credential has been sorted, let's look at the CREATE command concerning the example we introduced in *Chapter 4, The Security Model*, in the *Going beyond Read Access – part 1* section:

- LOCATION: This is the identifier or name that you must give to the external location object; for example, airlines_loc.

- URL: This is the absolute path of the cloud storage location that the external location object refers to; for example, `abfss://dbsql/airlines/planes`.

- `STORAGE CREDENTIAL`: This is the identifier or name of the storage credential that contains IAM policies to allow access to our S3 path; for example, `airlines_cred`.

Bringing this all together, an example invocation of the command would be as follows:

```
CREATE EXTERNAL LOCATION airlines_loc URL abfss://dbsql/
airlines' WITH (STORAGE CREDENTIAL airlines_cred);
```

Altering external locations

An external location can be altered by changing the following fields:

- URL

- Storage credential

- Owner

- Name

The `ALTER` command syntax is as follows:

```
ALTER EXTERNAL LOCATION location_name
    { RENAME TO to_location_name |
      SET URL url [FORCE] |
      SET STORAGE CREDENTIAL credential_name |
      OWNER TO principal }
```

You can alter one or more fields in one command. The two options of note are as follows:

- Notice how the name change requires the use of the `RENAME TO` clause instead of the `SET` clause, which is typical to `ALTER` commands.

- Note the `FORCE` option when changing the URL. By default, if the external location is already in use, then altering the URL is not allowed. The `FORCE` option is used to override this behavior. At the time of writing, there is no way to enumerate where the external location is in use.

Altering storage credentials

An existing storage credential can be altered by changing the following:

- Name

- Owner

The `ALTER` command syntax is as follows:

```
ALTER STORAGE CREDENTAL credential_name
  { RENAME TO to_credential_name |
    OWNER TO principal }
```

You can alter one or both configurable fields in one command – that is, the name of the credential or the owner of the credential.

Dropping external locations

An external location can be dropped with the following command:

```
DROP EXTERNAL LOCATION [ IF EXISTS ] location_name [ FORCE ]
```

By default, if the external location is in use, then dropping it is not allowed. Use the `FORCE` option to override this behavior.

Dropping storage credentials

A storage credential can be dropped with the following command:

```
DROP STORAGE CREDENTIAL [ IF EXISTS ] credential_name [ FORCE ]
```

By default, if the storage credential is in use by one or more external locations, then dropping it is not allowed. Use the `FORCE` option to override this behavior.

DDL for Delta Sharing

One of the key capabilities introduced with Unity Catalog in Databricks is a feature called **Delta Sharing** (`https://databricks.com/product/delta-sharing`).

Simply put, Delta Sharing is a protocol for sharing your data assets with other organizations. Delta Sharing stands apart from other sharing technologies because of the following reasons:

- It is an open protocol, which means the recipients of the shared data can use any computing platform. It does not have to be another Databricks installation.
- It is a real-time share. This means that no copies of the data are made for sharing.

Databricks with Unity Catalog provides enterprise-grade security controls on Delta Sharing. The following diagram should clarify this:

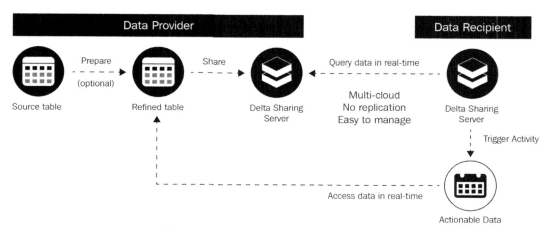

Figure 11.1 – Sharing data with Delta Sharing

As you can see, with Delta Sharing, the **Data Provider** creates a **Share** data object, which is a container for data assets that need to be shared. The **Data Provider** then creates a **Recipient** of this **Share**. The **Recipient** is the organization or individual who has requested this data. Finally, the **Data Provider** grants privileges on the **Share** to the **Recipient**.

Databricks does provide a UI to support this, which makes it extremely easy to configure data sharing between Databricks accounts. That said, let's look at the commands concerning the flights table in the airlines database we created in *Chapter 4, The Security Model*.

Bear in mind that shares and recipients can only be created, altered, and dropped by metastore administrators.

Creating data-sharing objects

As we discussed in the Delta Sharing flow, we must start by creating a data share. We'll learn how to create a share and a recipient in the following sub-sections.

Create a share

The CREATE command for SHARE has the following syntax:

```
CREATE SHARE [ IF NOT EXISTS ] share_name [ COMMENT comment ]
```

The following is an example of its usage:

```
CREATE SHARE IF NOT EXISTS airlines_share
```

Executing this statement will create a data sharing object called `airlines_share` that will hold all the data we want to share with recipients. Note that this data-sharing object is not shared with the intended recipients yet!

Next, we must create a recipient of the share.

Create a recipient

The `CREATE` command for `RECIPIENT` has the following syntax:

```
CREATE RECPIENT [ IF NOT EXISTS ] recipient_name [ COMMENT
comment ]
```

The following is an example of its usage:

```
CREATE RECIPIENT IF NOT EXISTS airlines_recipient
```

The thing to note here is the output. The output will contain an `activation_link` field that must be securely shared with the recipient. The recipient must follow the activation link to activate the sharing. Once activated, they can register the data assets in the share into their data catalog or use them directly.

Now, we can grant the select privilege to the recipient with the following command:

```
GRANT SELECT ON SHARE airlines_share TO RECIPIENT airlines_
recipient;
```

Executing this command will ensure that the intended recipient, `airlines_recipient`, has read privileges on the data shared in the `airlines_share` data sharing object. Note that without this bit of security programming, the recipient will not be able to access the shared data!

Altering data-sharing objects

The next step in the process is to add data assets to the `SHARE` object so that the recipient can access them. This can be done via the `ALTER` command, which has the following syntax:

```
ALTER share_name { alter_table | REMOVE TABLE clause }
```

The command has two possible operations, as discussed in the following sub-sections.

ADD TABLE

In this operation, a table or partitions of a table are added to the data share and hence made available to the recipient.

Here is an example:

```
ALTER SHARE airlines_share ADD TABLE airlines.flights
```

Our `flights` table does not have any partitions. But if it had partitions – for example, on the `Year` and `Month` columns – we could specify specific partitions to be shared. Partitions must be specified as a comma-separated list of `key=value` pairs; for example:

```
ALTER SHARE airlines_share ADD TABLE airlines.flights
PARTITION(year=2008, month=10)
```

Finally, we can specify an alias for the shared table with the `AS` clause, like so:

```
ALTER SHARE airlines_share ADD TABLE airlines.flights AS
shared_data.flights_shared
```

REMOVE TABLE

In this operation, the share is altered by removing a previously shared table object. This is not to be confused with dropping a share. The following is an example:

```
ALTER SHARE airlines_share REMOVE TABLE airlines.flights;
```

Executing this statement will remove the `airlines.flights` table from the `airlines_share` data sharing object. The recipients of this share will not have access to the `flights` table anymore. Any other tables that are a part of the share will continue to be accessible by the recipients of the share.

Dropping data-sharing objects

The `DROP` command for dropping a `SHARE` object is as follows:

```
DROP SHARE [ IF EXISTS ] share_name
```

The following is an example of its usage:

```
DROP SHARE IF EXISTS airlines_share
```

Simple.

The `DROP` command for dropping a `RECIPIENT` object is as follows:

```
DROP RECIPIENT [ IF EXISTS ] recipient_name
```

The following is an example of its usage:

```
DROP RECIPIENT IF EXISTS airlines_recipient
```

Executing this command will remove the `airlines_recipient` object from the data sharing system. The recipient will no longer have access to any data that was previously shared with them.

Working with data manipulation language commands

Databricks SQL supports the following common data manipulation commands:

- `INSERT INTO`
- `UPDATE`
- `DELETE FROM`

These are standard commands in the database and data warehouse world and do not require detailed unpacking.

Instead, we will learn about certain SQL commands in Databricks SQL that accommodate the data processing patterns specific to Lakehouse and Databricks SQL. Let's start with the very versatile `MERGE INTO` command.

MERGE INTO

`MERGE INTO` is technically not a Databricks-specific command, but it is an important command as it allows you to process **Slowly Changing Dimensions (SCDs)** and the **Change Data Capture (CDC)**, as well as perform data deduplication. Let's learn about this command concerning these processes. `MERGE INTO` is an advanced command which will appeal more to data engineers than data analysts. That said, if you are responsible for engineering data sets, you will find this section useful.

Data deduplication

Duplicate data in tables is undesirable. Duplicating data at a big data scale is even more undesirable as it can have disastrous performance effects. Consider one of the most commonly ingested forms of data in data lakes: logs generated from applications. However, logs are prone to having duplicates. Hence, our data ingestion process must cater to deduplicating data. Let's look at an example with the following architecture:

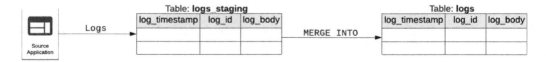

Figure 11.2 – Data deduplication architecture

In this architecture, our source application is generating logs that are prone to duplication. So, we receive all the logs in a staging area – the `logs_staging` table. Finally, we use the MERGE INTO command to write only the logs that are not duplicated into the logs table. We call a record a duplicate if the value of the `log_id` field is already present in the table.

Now, let's work through an example of data deduplication:

1. Initialize the `logs` table, as follows:

    ```
    insert into logs values(1, 1, '11');
    insert into logs values(2, 2, '12');
    insert into logs values(3, 3, '13');
    ```

2. Simulate a new log arrival by initializing the `logs_staging` table, as follows:

    ```
    insert into logs_staging values(2, 2, '12_dup');
    insert into logs_staging values(4, 4, '14');
    insert into logs_staging values(5, 5, '15');
    ```

    Here, we have a duplicate entry for `log_id = 2`.

3. De-duplicate the data with a MERGE INTO statement, as follows:

    ```
    MERGE INTO logs
    USING logs_staging
    ON logs.log_id = logs_staging.log_id
    WHEN NOT MATCHED THEN INSERT *
    ```

Here, the ON clause specifies the merge condition. In our example, we are specifying the merge behavior if `log_id` in a staging table record matches a record in the destination table.

The WHEN NOT MATCHED clause corresponds to the case when `log_id` of a staging table record does not match any record in the destination table. Since our task requires that we forward log records from staging to the destination if they are not already present in the destination, we use the WHEN NOT MATCHED clause instead of the WHEN MATCHED clause. As part of the clause, we instruct the command to insert the records into the destination table.

Now, this is only a toy example, and it can be expanded further on many lines. For example, how do we ensure that only new records in the staging table are processed instead of the entire staging table every time? You can take it up as an exercise to try that out or read on!

Change Data Capture and Slowly Changing Dimensions

Another common operation in data lakes is capturing change data from source systems – for example, capturing a change event that represents the creation of a new user entry in a source database, a change event that represents a user updating their email address, or a change event that represents the user asking to be forgotten (deleted) from the system. Let's look at an example with the following architecture:

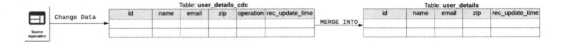

Figure 11.3 – Change Data Capture architecture

In this architecture, the source application is receiving new user sign-ups and modifications for existing user records. We assume there's a change event capture mechanism in the source system that emits the events as they happen. The events capture the operation type – `Insert/Update/Delete` – as well as the operation timestamp.

Now, let's work through an example of change capture:

1. Initialize the `user_details` table, as follows:

```
insert into user_details values(1,'User 1','user1@org.
com', 'Z1', 1);
insert into user_details values(2,'User 2','user2@org.
com', 'Z2', 2);
insert into user_details values(3,'User 3','user3@org.
com', 'Z3', 3);
insert into user_details values(4,'User 4','user4@org.
com', 'Z4', 4);
insert into user_details values(5,'User 5','user5@org.
com', 'Z5', 5);
```

2. Simulate new change event arrivals by initializing the `user_details_cdc` table, as follows:

```
insert into user_details_cdc values(1,'User 1','user1@
org.com', 'Z1-new-1', 'UPDATE', 6);
insert into user_details_cdc values(1,'User 1','user1-
new@org.com', 'Z1-new-1', 'UPDATE', 7);
insert into user_details_cdc values(3,'User 3','user3@
org.com', 'Z3', 'DELETE', 7);
insert into user_details_cdc values(6,'User 6','user6@
org.com', 'Z6', 'INSERT', 10);
```

```
insert into user_details_cdc values(7,'User 7','user7@
org.com', 'Z7', 'INSERT', 11);
```

Here, we have two updates for `User 1`. The first update changes their zip code, while the second update changes their email address. Hence, our change data capture must get the latest update to `User 1`. We also have an event for deleting the records of `User 3`. Finally, we have two new users in the system – `User 6` and `User 7`.

3. Capture the change data with a `MERGE INTO` statement, as follows:

```
MERGE INTO user_details target USING (
    select id, name, email, zip, operation, rec_update_time
    from (SELECT *, ROW_NUMBER() OVER (PARTITION BY id
ORDER BY rec_update_time DESC) as rank from user_details_
cdc)
    where rank = 1
) as source
ON source.id = target.id
WHEN MATCHED AND source.operation = 'DELETE' THEN DELETE
WHEN MATCHED AND source.operation = 'UPDATE' THEN UPDATE
SET *
WHEN NOT MATCHED AND source.operation = 'INSERT' THEN
INSERT *
```

As with the previous example, the `ON` clause specifies the merge behavior based on whether the ID matches the source table and the target table. The `WHEN MATCHED` clause handles the `Update` and `Delete` cases as any update or delete will require the existence of the ID in the target table. The `WHEN NOT MATCHED` clause handles the `Insert` cases. This is because if the ID matches, it is an update to an existing record, not a new record.

The case of slowly changing dimensions can be handled similarly. If we consider the preceding example, if we were to implement **Slowly Changing Dimension Type 2**, then we must have three records for `User 1` in our `user_details` table as we have the baseline record and then two updates to the record. Out of the three, only the third and latest record should be marked as current. This can be achieved by making small changes to the `MERGE INTO` statement. I will leave it up to you to complete this exercise. If you require hints, see `https://docs.databricks.com/delta/delta-update.html#slowly-changing-data-scd-type-2-operation-into-delta-tables`. Slowly changing dimensions are supported natively by the **Delta Live Tables** (**DLT**) product of Databricks. DLT is a mechanism to define data pipelines declaratively with SQL or python.

Incremental data processing with a Change Data Feed

One last use case of the MERGE INTO command is incremental data processing. Let's continue with the user details example from the previous section. The change capture from the source system to the data lakehouse was well implemented.

However, it's likely that the user_details table is also used to feed other tables on Lakehouse – for example, a marketing mailing list. Consider the case of updating the ZIP code and email address of User 1 and removing User 3 from the system. This must be captured in the user_details table and reflected in the mailing_list table. One way to achieve this is to have a periodic job that goes through each record in the mailing_list table and consults the user_details table if the email address and ZIP code are outdated and updates the record accordingly.

There are many flaws with this design. It is slow and inefficient, and it doesn't work in real time.

To this end, Delta Tables emit what is called a **Change Data Feed** or **CDF** (https://docs.databricks.com/delta/delta-change-data-feed.html). The **CDF** records all the insert, update, and delete events happening on a Delta table. We can use this change feed to identify *which user records have been changed* and *what has changed in those records*. This will enable us to propagate our changes incrementally. Let's apply this to our mailing list example, which has the following architecture:

Figure 11.4 – Incremental data processing

In this architecture, user_details_cdc receives change events from the source application. These change events are propagated to the user_details table with the MERGE INTO command. Finally, we use the CDF emitted by the user_details table to incrementally update the mailing_list table.

We will enable CDF on the user_details table by attaching the following clause to the CREATE statement of the user_details table:

```
TBLPROPERTIES (delta.enableChangeDataFeed = true);
```

This will ensure that the user_details table emits the CDF – that is, the updates to this table after every MERGE operation from the user_details_cdc table. We will use this feed to do the following:

- Insert new mailing targets if new user records have been inserted.
- Update existing mailing targets if user records have been modified.
- Delete mailing targets if the user records have been deleted from the system.

Let's simulate this with an example. Follow the same initialization and change the data simulation steps from the previous example:

1. Perform the initial data load.
2. Perform the CDC simulation.
3. Process the incremental data with the following MERGE INTO statement:

```
MERGE INTO mailing_list
USING (
  SELECT *
  FROM (SELECT *, ROW_NUMBER() OVER (PARTITION BY id ORDER BY
rec_update_time, _commit_version DESC) as rank FROM table_
changes('user_details',<start_timestamp>,<end_timestamp>))
  WHERE rank = 1
) AS user_cdf
ON mailing_list.id = user_cdf.id
WHEN MATCHED AND user_cdf._change_type = 'update_postimage'
THEN UPDATE SET *
WHEN MATCHED AND user_cdf._change_type = 'delete' THEN DELETE
WHEN NOT MATCHED THEN INSERT (id, name, email, zip) VALUES (id,
name, email, zip);
```

To understand how this MERGE INTO command functions, we must understand the use of the table_changes() function, which returns the CDF between two timestamps or commit versions.

Let's query table_changes after the CDC simulation, as follows:

```
SELECT * FROM table_changes('user_details', 0,10)
```

We will see the following output:

Table

id	name	email	zip	rec_update_tim	_change_type	_commit_versk	_commit_timestamp
1	User 1	user1@org.com	Z1	1	update_preimage	6	2022-05-15 14:14:32.000
1	User 1	user1-new@org.com	Z1-new-1	7	update_postimage	6	2022-05-15 14:14:32.000
3	User 3	user3@org.com	Z3	3	delete	6	2022-05-15 14:14:32.000
6	User 6	user6@org.com	Z6	10	insert	6	2022-05-15 14:14:32.000

Figure 11.5 – Change Data Feed

If we correlate this with the `MERGE INTO` query, we will see that the CDF provides a `_change_type` field that specifies the event type as an `Update`, `Insert`, or `Delete`. We can also use `_commit_version`, `_commit_timestamp`, or any user-defined field to calculate the most recent change event for any user. As we saw in the previous section, we can use the event type in the `MERGE INTO` statement to process the changes. You will notice that the CDF does not include rows for records that did not change. This is the key to efficient incremental processing.

COPY INTO

The `COPY INTO` command (`https://docs.databricks.com/sql/language-manual/delta-copy-into.html`) is best understood as a bulk load command for Delta tables. There are a lot of cases where organizations receive data files and they must be loaded into user-facing tables for further querying. There can be other such cases as well.

The `COPY INTO` command can pick up such files and then insert the records into the target table.

For example, our `airlines` dataset contains data up to the year 2008. Now, we receive the new data from the years 2008 to 2020 as a collection of CSV files. Here, we can run a command similar to the following:

```
COPY INTO airlines.flights
FROM (SELECT * FROM 'abfss://airlines-container@
airlinesstorageaccount.dfs.core.windows.net/flights_2008_2020')
FILEFORMAT = CSV
PATTERN = 'file_[0-9].csv'
FORMAT_OPTIONS('header' = 'true')
```

The syntax in the preceding code block is straightforward:

- `COPY INTO` requires the target table or target cloud storage location. In this example, we use the table name.
- The `FROM` keyword specifies the subquery that reads the data files that need to be copied into the target table. Here, we are running a blanket `SELECT` statement over the files present in the

ADLS location. As you may recall, this is the storage container we created in *Chapter 4, The Security Model*, in the *The internals of cloud storage access* section.

- The subquery must also supply options to FILEFORMAT, such as the file glob PATTERN to match the correct files and other FORMAT_OPTIONS such as the header and delimiter.

There is, however, the important consideration of access to the cloud storage location. If you are using Unity Catalog, you have the external location mechanism at your disposal to control access to the cloud location. You must have the WRITE FILES privilege on the external location. See the *Data definition commands* section for more details.

If you are using Hive Metastore, you can specify your credentials inline in the command, like so:

```
COPY INTO airlines.flights
FROM (SELECT * FROM 'abfss://airlines-container@
airlinesstorageaccount.dfs.core.windows.net/flights_2008_2020')
(WITH CREDENTIAL (AZURE_SAS_TOKEN = '…'))
FILEFORMAT = CSV
PATTERN = 'file_[0-9].csv'
FORMAT_OPTIONS('header' = 'true')
```

In this command, we are copying the new flights data, which was received in the flights_2008_2020 ADLS location, into our existing flights table. We are also specifying our credentials to be able to work with the ADLS location using the Azure SAS token specified in the WITH CREDENTIAL clause. Upon execution, our flights table will reflect this new data.

Working with the inbuilt functions in Databricks SQL

Databricks SQL has a very comprehensive list of inbuilt functions (https://docs.databricks. com/sql/language-manual/sql-ref-functions-builtin.html) to cater to a variety of processing needs. If you are coming from a database or data warehouse world, you might not find an exact 1:1 mapping for certain functions in their names. However, by and large, you should be able to find the function for your needs. Covering all the functions is not possible in a book, nor is it of any additional value. Instead, I am going to talk about two standout powerful function families.

JSON

JavaScript Object Notation (JSON) is a versatile semi-structured file format that is often found in the data lake world. However, this versatility often gets abused in the form of very intricate schemas and arbitrary levels of data nesting, and, at times, arbitrary schemas as well. This makes relation processing of JSONs difficult at times.

Databricks SQL provides a way to query this semi-structured data. This is a very powerful feature that often gets overlooked, which is why I am including a discussion here.

Returning to our tradition of finding new datasets to work with, this time, we will use the *Our World in Data* dataset on the COVID-19 pandemic (`https://ourworldindata.org/coronavirus`). It provides data about the pandemic in JSON format.

Attribution

This data has been collected, aggregated, and documented by Cameron Appel, Diana Beltekian, Daniel Gavrilov, Charlie Giattino, Joe Hasell, Bobbie Macdonald, Edouard Mathieu, Esteban Ortiz-Ospina, Hannah Ritchie, Lucas Rodés-Guirao, and Max Roser. Please attribute them as per `https://github.com/owid/covid-19-data/tree/master/public/data#license` if you are using this dataset.

You can download the dataset from `https://github.com/owid/covid-19-data/tree/master/public/data` and upload it to a cloud storage location of your choice to follow the discussion.

Note

Ensure that your SQL Warehouse has access to the cloud storage location. If you are using Unity Catalog, ensure that you have READ FILE permissions on the external location object referring to this cloud storage location.

For this discussion, we are going to suspend our knowledge of the JSON data source capability in Databricks, where we can just run the following line of code and Databricks SQL will infer the full schema of the JSON dataset:

```
select * from json.`abfss://covid19@owidcovid.dfs.core.windows.net/owid-covid-data.json`
```

Instead, we will read the JSON dataset as a text file and use the JSON path expressions to query and discover the data. Let's start.

Extracting values using identifiers

The dataset is organized by ISO codes of countries – that is, each country will have a nested JSON containing the data for that country. I am interested in the data for my home country, India, which bears the ISO code IND. So, I can extract the information for India by executing the following command:

```
select value:IND from text.` abfss://covid19@owidcovid.dfs.core.windows.net/owid-covid-data.json`
```

In this query, `value` is the default name of the column into which all the JSON data is read as text. By using the `:` delimiter, we are extracting the top-level field, which contains the IND key.

Since the top-level field is a field and not an array, we can also use `value:['IND']` to the same effect.

Upon executing this query, we will see that there are multiple nested fields, such as `continent`, `location`, and `population_density`, as well as an array called `data` that contains multiple JSON entries representing data for each date since the data about the pandemic was collected. Let's learn how to query them using JSON path expressions.

Extracting nested fields

One of the major causes of the massive spread of COVID is the population density of countries. We can extract the population density by executing the following command:

```
select value:IND.population_density from text.` abfss://
covid19@owidcovid.dfs.core.windows.net/owid-covid-data.json`
```

In this query, we used dot (`.`) notation to instruct Databricks SQL to follow the top-level `IND` field and extract the value for the `population_density` key. As mentioned previously, since this is a field, we can use the square-bracket notation (`value:['IND']['population_density']`) to the same effect.

Extracting values from arrays

The actual field we are interested in is the `data` field, which is an array. To extract the `data` array, we can execute the following command:

```
select value:IND.data[99] from text.` abfss://covid19@
owidcovid.dfs.core.windows.net/owid-covid-data.json`
```

In this query, we are using the index notation on the `data` element (which we now know to be an array) to retrieve the data from the 100th day of the pandemic (array indexes start from 0).

Of course, this query returns another JSON representation of the data, so we can execute further nested queries to retrieve the information, like so:

```
select value:IND.data[100].date, value:IND.data[100].new_cases
from text.` abfss://covid19@owidcovid.dfs.core.windows.net/
owid-covid-data.json`
```

And that's it. As you can see, the ability to query semi-structured data in a relational context with intuitive dot and index notations is a very powerful tool. You can use it to explore columns in tables containing free-form JSON text, or parse massive datasets and extract only the information you need. You can consult the official reference for JSON handling at `https://docs.databricks.com/sql/language-manual/sql-ref-json-path-expression.html` to check for new capabilities as and when they are added by Databricks.

Lambda functions

Databricks SQL has a lot of powerful functions that require the use of Lambda functions (https://docs.databricks.com/sql/language-manual/sql-ref-lambda-functions.html). In essence, Lambda functions are simple, short, inline, anonymous functions. They are best understood through an example.

Let's consider the `array_sort(array, lambda_function)` function. This function sorts the elements of an array for you. However, you must define how the sorting should happen. You must define this because it is plausible that your array is not an array of primitive data types, but a custom data type. You will need to define how to use the members of the custom data type to order the elements. This is where Lambda functions come in.

Let's work through an example invocation of `array_sort` to see Lambda functions in action. Consider the following SQL command:

```
SELECT
  array_sort(
    array(struct(1,2), struct(3,4), struct(-1,4)),
    (p1, p2) -> CASE
      WHEN p1.col1 = p2.col1 THEN 0
      WHEN p1.col1 < p2.col1 THEN -1
      ELSE 1
    END
  );
```

In this example, we have the following:

1. Our array, which we want to sort, consists of a custom data type with two columns – `col1` and `col2`.

2. We define our Lambda function in such a way that it receives two elements from the array at a time in the p1 and p2 parameters.

3. Then, it compares the values of `col1` in p1 and p2 and returns -1, 0, or +1, depending on whether p1 < p2 or p1 = p2 or p1 > p2. The `array_sort()` function uses this return value to perform the ordering. If you wish to reverse the ordering, just change the condition upon which -1 is returned.

As you can see, Lambda functions are very powerful. They are used across a lot of other function families such as aggregation, filtering, and more.

Summary

In this chapter, we learned how to consult the official SQL command reference for Databricks SQL. More importantly, we learned about some of the Databricks SQL-specific commands. We also learned more about Unity Catalog and the concept of Delta Sharing while learning about various data definition commands. After that, we learned how to implement real-life data engineering and BI engineering use cases while learning about data manipulation commands. Finally, we learned how to query semi-structured data and the power of Lambda functions.

In the next chapter, we will continue our investigation of Lakehouse-specific SQL commands – specifically, commands for administrating Lakehouse.

12
SQL Commands – Part 2

Maintaining and managing data and data access in any database system is a continuous process. The Lakehouse is no different. In this chapter, we will focus on the SQL commands that help us maintain and manage our Lakehouse. We will also learn about Lakehouse-specific SQL commands for discovering data assets. Finally, we will learn about advanced security programming techniques available on the Lakehouse.

In this chapter, we will cover the following main topics:

- Working with Delta Lake maintenance commands

- Working with data security commands

- Working with metadata commands

> **Note**
>
> This chapter is not intended as a complete SQL command reference. We will cover the practical usage of SQL commands that are specific to Databricks SQL and the Lakehouse. The rest of the standard SQL commands can be studied at `https://docs.databricks.com/sql/language-manual/index.html`.

Technical requirements

To complete this chapter, you must ensure the following:

- You have familiarity or experience with SQL and writing SQL queries.

- You have reviewed the official general reference (`https://docs.microsoft.com/en-us/azure/databricks/sql/language-manual/#general-reference`).

Working with Delta Lake maintenance commands

Like any system, be it hardware or software, Delta Lake also requires periodic maintenance. In this section, we will learn about some of the commands to use for different maintenance operations. These commands are relevant to data engineering and data science teams. Business intelligence users need not concern themselves with these activities.

Vacuuming your Delta Lake

As we learned in *Chapter 8*, *The Delta Lake*, with every data insert, update, or delete, new files are created. After each such activity, the transaction log of the delta table is updated to reflect the set of files that constitute the table's *current* or *latest* version. So, while the execution of user queries will ignore the non-current files, those files still exist on your cloud storage and are incurring costs. While these are not excessive costs, they can grow over time if left unchecked. This is where the VACUUM command comes in. True to its name, it vacuums these non-current files.

Now, before you go ahead and vacuum your Lakehouse, keep in mind that some retention is not a bad thing. The non-current files are a history of how your data table evolved. This allows Delta Lake tables to travel back in time and read data as of a particular time or version. They are required for transactional guarantees and are very helpful in audits, data fixes, and rollbacks.

Hence, selective vacuuming is the way to go. The command is as follows:

```
VACUUM table_name [RETAIN num HOURS] [DRY RUN]
```

The RETAIN clause in the preceding command defines how many hours of history to retain on the table; it specifies the not-current files from the inception of the table up to *current time – retention hours*.

If you wish to do a dry run, or just see a list of files that will be deleted should you run this command, include the DRY RUN clause.

It is worth noting that if you try to retain data for less than 7 days or 168 hours, Databricks SQL will deny your request. If you are running this command in the Data Engineering persona on a notebook, then you have the option of switching off this behavior by executing the following command:

```
%sql SET spark.databricks.delta.retentionDurationCheck.
enabled=false;
```

Consider the user_details table from *Chapter 11*, *SQL Commands – Part 1*. If we wish to dry-run our vacuum operation on it, we must execute the following command:

```
VACUUM user_details DRY RUN
```

Executing this command will list the files that will be vacuumed away, as shown in the following screenshot:

Figure 12.1 – Dry -running a vacuum operation

There are the following points you must make a note of concerning vacuuming:

- You must have an organizational policy on history retention. Databricks recommends at least 7 days of retention. You must gauge your requirements based on the uses of the data and the stability of the data pipelines. For example, consider the case of streaming data pipelines. They tend to create small files at an alarming rate. Even if you have optimized writes and automatic compactions are turned on (see *Chapter 8*, *The Delta Lake*), the files that make up the current state of the table are optimally sized, but the small files that were originally written are still around and you will want to keep cleaning them up at a faster schedule. Another scenario could be that you find a logical error in your data pipeline that was introduced by a code change 1 month ago. Now, if you have only 7 days of retention, you will not be able to restore your table to how it was 1 month ago. Instead, you will have to reprocess all your data instead of selectively reprocessing 1 month's worth of data.

- Vacuuming is not going to increase the performance of user queries since Delta Engine will automatically ignore the non-current files.

- Consider the cost of vacuuming versus the cost savings it drives. Vacuuming has a lot of fixed operations such as listing files, computing which files fall within retention versus outside of it, and more. So, if your tables do not receive frequent updates, consider running VACUUM at a lower frequency. On the flip side, if you have a streaming pipeline, the number of files generated and hence the cost associated with that can justify frequent vacuuming.

- Consider the other Delta Lake maintenance commands running in your Lakehouse. If you are running OPTIMIZE commands regularly, you can consider chaining the VACUUM command with it.

- Avoid running VACUUM before or in the middle of any data pipelines. It can slow down the processing. More importantly, it will only add time to the pipeline's execution and provide no performance benefits. Hence, it can be done as part of a separate maintenance activity.

Time -traveling in your Delta Lake

As we discussed in the previous section, non-current files represent the history of your table. This means you can time -travel and see the snapshot of the table as of a particular time or even restore the table to that snapshot.

Why would you want to do this? There can be many reasons, including when you want to roll back some logic changes in your data processing or roll back due to some logical errors.

First, we must view the history of the table and determine which time/version we want to view or restore.

Let's consider the user_details table from the incremental processing example from *Chapter 11, SQL Commands – Part 1*. We can run a DESCRIBE HISTORY command on this table, as follows:

```
DESCRIBE HISTORY user_details
```

This will result in an output similar to the following:

Table

version	timestamp	userId	userName	operation	operationParameters
6	2022-05-16 09:04:09.000	8899701884401733	vihag.gupta@databricks.com	MERGE	{"matchedPredicates":"[{"predicate":"(source.operation = 'DELETE')","actionType":"delete"},{"predicate":" (source.operation = 'UPDATE')","actionType":"update"}]","notMatchedPredicates":" [{"predicate":"(source.operation = 'INSERT')","actionType":"insert"}]","predicate":"(source.id = target.id)"}
5	2022-05-16 09:03:41.000	8899701884401733	vihag.gupta@databricks.com	WRITE	{"mode":"Append","partitionBy":"[]"}

Figure 12.2 – Viewing the table history

Here, we can see the exact **operation** that brings about a new commit version. **timestamp** and **version** are also recorded. We can use either of these two to time -travel or restore.

To view a particular version of the table, simply run the following query:

```
SELECT * FROM user_details VERSION AS OF 4
```

You can replace VERSION with your TIMESTAMP of choice as well.

To restore the table to a particular version, simply run the following query:

```
RESTORE user_details TO VERSION AS OF 4
```

Yes – it is that simple.

There are two things we must make a note of with regards to restoring:

- Restoring the table does not wipe out the history. Restoring just changes the current files listed in the transaction log (see *Chapter 8, The Delta Lake*, to read about the transaction log).

- The ability to restore depends on the available history. So, vacuum with care!

Repairing your Delta Lake

It is plausible that some of the data files are manually deleted from the table's location. Why would that happen? This could be due to human error, errant data pipeline logic, archival policies on cloud storage, and more. If this were to occur, our transaction log may point to non-existent files. This means that a user query may try to look up non-existent files and error out.

If this happens, you must run the FSCK REPAIR TABLE command. This removes the filename entries for the missing files from the transaction log. It has a very simple syntax, as shown here:

```
FSCK REPAIR TABLE table_name [DRY RUN]
```

Now, an argument can be made that if certain data files are manually deleted, then what is the point of repairing them?

For starters, at least you will be able to access the data that you have. Furthermore, perhaps a non-current file was deleted, say by some archival policies on the cloud storage. However, there could still be users using the past data versions of the table. In this case, the repair job makes some sense.

Now, the durability guarantees of cloud storage make an event such as this highly unlikely and we can minimize the remaining risk by reducing external access to the data. This can be achieved by using managed tables. Here, we can use the access control mechanisms to restrict external tooling from modifying storage locations. If you are using Unity Catalog, ensure that external tooling has read-only access to the location objects to minimize this risk.

Optimizing your Delta Lake

The OPTIMIZE command is a maintenance command that can be used to optimize the layout of data in your tables. As you may recall, we discussed the OPTIMIZE command concerning Z-Ordering in *Chapter 8, The Delta Lake*.

However, OPTIMIZE can be used without Z-Ordering as well. The following is the command syntax for the OPTIMIZE command:

```
OPTIMIZE table_name [WHERE predicate]
    [ZORDER BY (col_name1 [, ...] ) ]
```

If we do not specify the ZORDER clause, the OPTIMIZE command will try to recreate the data files in such a way that all the files are of an even size. This is especially useful when there are frequent updates to the data tables, and you have disabled auto-optimized writes to avoid write-time latencies.

Running the OPTIMIZE command is a compute-intensive activity, so you must ensure that you are running it as efficiently as possible. You can use the WHERE predicate to indicate the desired portions of the dataset that you want to run the OPTIMIZE command on.

Keep in mind that running OPTIMIZE on an already optimized partition will not have any effect.

This wraps up our discussion on maintenance commands for the Lakehouse. Next, we will discuss some advanced security programming techniques we can perform to protect our data assets.

Working with data security commands

We covered data security commands such as GRANT, REVOKE, and DENY (Hive Metastore only) in significant detail in *Chapter 4, The Security Model*. If you want to consult the official command reference for these commands, visit https://docs.databricks.com/sql/language-manual/index.html#security-statements. In this section, we will focus on an advanced bit of security programming and learn about row-level and column-level permissions in Databricks SQL.

Dynamic view functions

At the time of writing, Databricks SQL does not have table bindings for expressing row-level or column-level permissions for users and user groups. Instead, it uses the concept of views and dynamic view functions.

Databricks SQL exposes two dynamic view functions:

- Current_user(): This returns the username of the user executing the query.
- is_member(group_name): This returns a Boolean value indicating whether the current user is a member of the group.

For example, consider a user group called pii-group that only I am a part of. This means that the other user in my organization, Suteja, is not a part of this group:

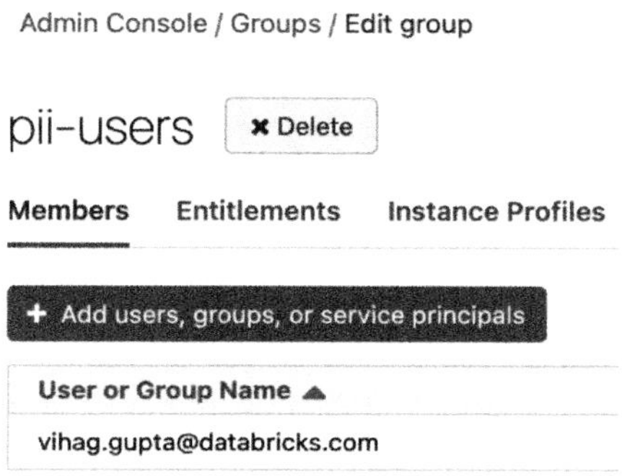

Admin Console / Groups / **Edit group**

Figure 12.3 – pii-users group members

If I execute the preceding dynamic view functions as the following query, the `is_pii_user` column will return `true`:

```
SELECT current_user, is_member(" pii-users" ) as is_pii_user
```

In contrast, if Suteja runs the same query, the `is_pii_user` column will display `false`, as shown in the following screenshot:

current_user()	is_pii_user
sutejakanuri@gmail.com	false

Figure 12.4 – Result of Suteja running the is_member() dynamic view function

Controlling access to columns

In this section, we will use a dynamic view function to create a view that selectively hides or shows columns. We will use the `people_db` database that we created in *Chapter 3, The Data Catalog*. For this discussion, we will tag the `ssn` and `birthDate` fields as **personally identifiable information (PII)** fields.

The following `VIEW` definition dynamically masks the PII columns in our data – that is, `ssn` and `birthDate`:

```
CREATE VIEW people_protected AS
SELECT
  id, firstName, middleName, lastName, gender, salary,
  CASE WHEN is_member('pii-users') THEN ssn
  ELSE 'REDACTED'
  END AS ssn,
  CASE WHEN is_member('pii-users') THEN birthDate
  ELSE 'REDACTED'
  END AS birthDate
FROM people
```

Note how we use the `is_member()` function to determine whether the user should receive redacted values for the PII fields.

Now, if Suteja selects data from this table, she will see redacted values for `ssn` and `birthDate`, as shown here:

Table

id	firstName	middleName	lastName	gender	salary	ssn	birthDate
3766824	Hisako	Isabella	Malitrott	F	58862	REDACTED	REDACTED
3766825	Daisy	Merissa	Fibben	F	66221	REDACTED	REDACTED

Figure 12.5 – Redacted values for non-members

In contrast, I, who am a member of the `pii-users` group, will see the plaintext values instead of redacted values, as shown here:

Table

id	firstName	middleName	lastName	gender	salary	ssn	birthDate
3766824	Hisako	Isabella	Malitrott	F	58862	938-80-1874	1961-02-12 05:00:00
3766825	Daisy	Merissa	Fibben	F	66221	971-14-3755	1998-05-19 04:00:00

Figure 12.6 – Actual values for non-members

And that's it! An argument can be made that creating such views for each table will not be scalable, especially if a lot of tables must be access controlled this way. That's fair. Unity Catalog has introduced a feature called attribute-based access control in its roadmap. This feature allows you to annotate columns and data assets with tags. Therefore, creating policies for access to these tags will be possible, thus making this process maintainable.

Controlling access to rows

In this section, we will use a dynamic view function to create a view that selectively hides or shows rows. We will continue building on the same example. Consider that there is a user group called marketing-users that is only allowed to see details of users who are 30 years or older. I am a part of this group; Suteja is not.

The following VIEW definition dynamically excludes the records that are not supposed to be read by marketing folk:

```
CREATE VIEW people_reachable AS
SELECT *
FROM people
WHERE
  CASE
    WHEN is_member('marketing-users') AND (months_
between(current_date,birthDate) > 360) THEN TRUE
    WHEN !is_member('marketing-users') THEN TRUE
    ELSE FALSE
  END;
```

Again, note the use of the is_member() function in the CASE statement to set the rule that marketing folks can only reach users who are older than 30.

Now, if Suteja, who is not part of the marketing-users group, selects data from this table, she will see all the records, as evident by the min and max birth dates:

Table

min(birthDate)	max(birthDate)
1951-12-31 05:00:00.000	2000-01-30 05:00:00.000

Figure 12.7 – All records can be viewed by non-members

In contrast, I, who am a member of the marketing-users group, will not see users who are younger than 30:

Table

min(birthDate)	max(birthDate)
1951-12-31 05:00:00.000	1992-05-15 04:00:00.000

Figure 12.8 – Limited records can be viewed by members

And that's about it. As mentioned previously, an argument can be made about the scalability of this approach. That said, there is a feature called attribute-based access control in the development roadmap that will allow a table-bound row access policy to be used.

This wraps up our discussion of advanced security programming. Next, we will discuss the metadata commands that are available with Databricks SQL to search for and discover our data assets.

Working with metadata commands

In this section, we will learn about metadata commands, which allow you to list and describe data assets, set configurations, and explore metadata about the data assets. You will be able to use these commands to search for and discover data assets and gain deeper insights into them.

Listing data assets

Two commands can be used to list data assets:

- SHOW
- LIST

The SHOW command is the standard SQL SHOW command. In Databricks, it supports the catalog, database, table, view, and function objects. For example, we can list the tables in the `airlines` dataset with the following statement:

```
SHOW TABLES IN airlines;
```

For an extensive discussion of the SHOW command for the data objects, please revisit *Chapter 3, The Data Catalog*.

The SHOW statement also supports listing users and groups. It also supports Unity Catalog-specific data assets – external location and storage credential. Please refer to *Chapter 11, SQL Commands – Part 1*, for a detailed discussion on them.

The LIST command, which is available with Unity Catalog, can be used to list all the files available in a cloud storage location. For example, to see the files in a hypothetical storage container where the airlines data is stored, we can execute the following command:

```
LIST 'abfss://flights@airlines.dfs.core.windows.net/'
```

If the user running this command has the READ FILE privilege on the external location data object referring to the ADLS URL, then the command will list the objects at this path.

The SHOW statement also supports Delta Sharing-specific data assets – that is, share and recipient.

Two specific SHOW statements stand out:

- SHOW PARTITIONS: This lists all the available partitions on a table. Alternatively, you can use it to list the exact partition as a key-value pair to check the existence of a particular partition.

- SHOW TBLPROPERTIES: This lists all the extra table properties we have enabled on a table. Recall that in *Chapter 11, SQL Commands – Part 1*, we enabled a table property to enable a change data feed on a table. Such table properties will be listed with this command. You can also list the value of a property by specifying it as a key-value pair in the command.

These are standard commands and very intuitive. If required, you can refer to the official command reference at https://docs.databricks.com/sql/language-manual/index.html#show-statements.

Describing data assets

The DESCRIBE command enables us to describe the details of a data asset– for example, the structure of a table, the location of a database, or the signature of a function.

The DESCRIBE statement in Databricks supports the standard catalog, database, table, and function data objects. Keep in mind that there is no DESCRIBE VIEW. Use DESCRIBE TABLE to describe a view.

The DESCRIBE statement also supports Unity Catalog-specific data assets, such as external locations and storage credentials.

The DESCRIBE statement also supports Delta Sharing-specific data assets, such as share and recipient.

Each data asset responds differently to the DESCRIBE command. Furthermore, some data assets can also have options such as DESCRIBE, FORMATTED, and EXTENDED, which control how granular information is displayed. For example, a DESCRIBE table will display column-level statistics if we enable the EXTENDED option.

Please revisit *Chapter 3, The Data Catalog*, for detailed usage examples of the DESCRIBE command.

Analyzing Delta tables

The final metadata command that I want to talk about is the ANALYZE command. This is because its existence is a bit counterintuitive to what we learned in *Chapter 8, The Delta Lake*. There, we learned that Delta automatically calculates statistics on data files to enable automatic file skipping.

The ANALYZE command also collects statistics on a specific table. It has the following syntax:

```
ANALYZE TABLE table_name [ PARTITION clause ]
    COMPUTE STATISTICS [ NOSCAN | FOR COLUMNS col1 [, ...] |
FOR ALL COLUMNS ]
```

Before we discuss the options available to this command, first, let's discuss how it differs from the automatic statistics collection in Delta tables. As you may recall, the automatic statistics collection in Delta tables only computes the minimum and maximum values of the columns where it collects the statistics. By default, the statistics are computed for the first 32 columns, and it is advisable to compute statistics only for columns of non-string primitive data types.

The ANALYZE command goes beyond that. It computes deep statistics about the table and the columns beyond the minimum and maximum values of those columns.

For example, it will calculate the number of rows with null values, the cardinality of the column, the average length of records in the column, the maximum length of records in the column, and more.

These statistics are used by the optimizer to come up with better query execution plans.

However, there is a big catch. The ANALYZE command must be run after every new batch of data is written. It is not automatic as it is computationally expensive. You must check whether this command applies to your databases and tables. This means establishing that the cost of performing the analysis is worth the gains in performance. If so, schedule a regular analysis job. If not, automatic statistics collection should suffice.

With that cleared up, let's look at the various options for the ANALYZE command:

- PARTITION: This clause specifies the partitions where the analysis must be performed. This can reduce the compute footprint of the analysis job.

- FOR COLUMNS: This clause specifies the columns where the analysis must be performed. This helps keep the analysis targeted to specific query patterns, especially in the case of wide tables.

- NOSCAN: This clause specifies that the analysis should only scan the file sizes and not the individual records. Hence, the deep analysis metrics will not be computed.

For example, if we were to analyze our favorite flights table, we would have to run the following command:

```
ANALYZE TABLE flights COMPUTE STATISTICS FOR COLUMNS year,
tailnum
```

Statistics make the most sense when they're read at an individual column level. Hence, you can run the following command:

```
DESCRIBE EXTENDED flights tailnum;
```

In the preceding command, we are asking the DESCRIBE statement to display EXTENDED information about the tailnum column in the flights table.

The observed output is as follows:

Table   ⋮

info_name	info_value
col_name	tailnum
data_type	string
comment	NULL
min	NULL
max	NULL
num_nulls	139774
distinct_count	12865
avg_col_len	5
max_col_len	6
histogram	NULL

Figure 12.9 – Computed statistics

And with this, we have finished discussing the available metadata commands of note.

Summary

In this chapter, we learned how to consult the official SQL command reference for Databricks SQL. More importantly, we learned about some of the Databricks SQL-specific commands. First, we learned about Delta Lake maintenance commands such as VACUUM and RESTORE. We also learned how to control user access at the row and column levels using dynamic view functions. Finally, we learned how to list and describe various data assets using metadata commands.

This brings us to the end of our discussion regarding the concepts, features, and functions of the Databricks SQL platform. In the next chapter, we will learn how to test these concepts, features, and functions at scale with the TPC-DS dataset.

Part 4:
TPC-DS, Experiments, and Frequently Asked Questions

This part focuses on putting the concepts learned in *Part 2* and *Part 3* to the test, using the TPC-DS benchmark. This part also rounds up the book with a compilation of commonly asked questions and uncertainties about what Databricks SQL is and what it can and cannot do.

This part comprises the following chapters:

- *Chapter 13, Playing with the TPC-DS Dataset*
- *Chapter 14, Ask Me Anything*

13

Playing with the TPC-DS Dataset

In this chapter, we will get acquainted with the TPC-DS dataset. Lakehouse platforms, including Databricks, use TPC-DS benchmarks to prove their capabilities. Hence, it is important to know about it. In this chapter, we will learn about the TPC-DS dataset, the TPC-DS benchmark, and how to use the TPC-DS dataset to validate some of the concepts we learned about in the previous chapters.

This chapter is only for advanced users who wish to build a larger dataset to test out Databricks SQL features. If you already have access to such a dataset, or you don't want to test with bigger datasets, there is no need to go through this chapter.

In this chapter, we will cover the following topics:

- Understanding the TPC-DS dataset
- Generating TPC-DS data
- Running automated benchmarks
- Experimenting with TPC-DS in Databricks SQL

Technical requirements

To follow this chapter, you must have the following:

- Working knowledge of Scala and Apache Spark
- Access to a Databricks workspace
- Access to an IDE with Scala plugins or familiarity with terminal-based commands for compiling Scala projects
- Have read *Chapter 8, The Delta Lake,* and *Chapter 9, The Photon Engine,* of this book

Understanding the TPC-DS dataset

Transaction Processing Performance Council (**TPC®**) is a non-profit corporation and a worldwide consortium. It was founded in 1985 and has major hardware and software vendors as full-time members.

Their mission is two-fold:

- Develop data-centric benchmark standards for various systems.

- Disseminate objective, verifiable benchmarking data to the industry.

TPC-DS (`https://www.tpc.org/tpcds/`) stands for **Transaction Processing Performance Council – Decision Support**. It is a benchmarking standard for creating verifiable, objective performance data about **decision support systems** (**DSSs**).

DSSs are software systems that sift and analyze massive amounts of data and can compile comprehensive information that can be used in decision-making. For example, a DSS can compile projected revenue or inventory management information for an enterprise operation.

TPC-DS consists of two things of interest to us:

- A software that allows us to generate data that is used for TPC-DS benchmarking at any scale. Please download the TPC-DS specifications from `https://www.tpc.org/tpc_documents_current_versions/current_specifications5.asp` and study the Entity Relation diagram of the TPC-DS data.

- A set of standard benchmarking queries that can be used against this data.

Databricks and Databricks SQL also come under the umbrella of decision support systems since organizations use them to store data and run business-critical data analytics on them to help make business decisions.

In November 2021, Databricks released a statement that it had broken TPC-DS records for data warehouse performance, and it was verified by the TPC themselves.

If you wish, you can read all about it at `https://databricks.com/blog/2021/11/02/databricks-sets-official-data-warehousing-performance-record.html`.

We are not interested in recreating those benchmarks – there is no point. We are more interested in seeing if we can get the TPC-DS data and use it to see some of the performance optimizations in action. As you may recall, in *Chapter 8, The Delta Lake*, I called out the fact that we do not have big enough example datasets. Well, TPC-DS is here to give you datasets of any size so that you can test the various performance-boosting features that we talked about in *Chapter 8, The Delta Lake*, and *Chapter 9, The Photon Engine*.

So, let's get right into it. First, let's learn how to generate TPC-DS data.

Generating TPC-DS data

We will stick to our tradition of finding tools within the Databricks ecosystem. The good folks of Databricks have created an open source project called **spark-sql-perf** (https://github.com/databricks/spark-sql-perf) that has everything we will need to generate the TPC-DS data. Let's begin.

Building the spark-sql-perf library

The first thing we must do is compile the spark-sql-perf library. I will be using the IntelliJ IDEA **Integrated Development Environment** (**IDE**). You can use any IDE of your choice or even compile the library from your terminal.

If you do not want to compile the library, you can head over to the GitHub repository for this book, download the JAR file, and move to the next step. However, note that the JAR file has been built for Spark 3.2.1 and Scala 2.12.10:

> **Note**
> Ensure that you install the necessary JDK and Scala versions onto your machine before commencing these steps. If you are using an IDE, it should guide you through the installation.

1. Import the spark-sql-perf library using the following Git web URL: https://github.com/databricks/spark-sql-perf.git.

2. Open the build.sbt file in the project's root folder and edit the scalaVersion and sparkVersion fields so that they match the Scala and Spark versions of the Databricks runtime you intend to use. The following screenshot is based on a cluster using DBR 10.4 LTS with Photon, which uses Spark 3.2.1 and Scala 2.12.10:

Figure 13.1 – Editing the build.sbt file

3. Build the package by running the `sbt +package` command in the terminal. The following screenshot shows the execution of the command in the terminal provided by the IDE:

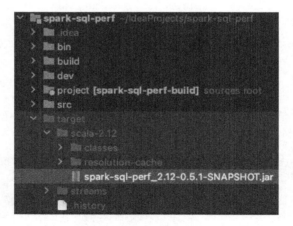

Figure 13.2 – Building the project

After successfully executing the `sbt +package` command, the built library – a Java JAR file – will be ready in the target directory in the project's root folder, as shown in the following screenshot:

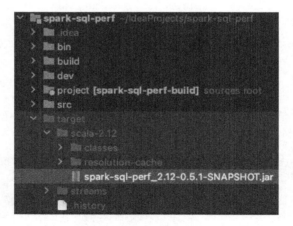

Figure 13.3 – The built library

Now, we must install this JAR file as a library in our Databricks workspace.

Installing the spark-sql-perf library

We must install the `spark-sql-perf` JAR file as a workspace library (`https://docs.databricks.com/libraries/workspace-libraries.html`). You must be in the **Data Science Engineering** persona view to do this:

1. Navigate to a folder of choice in your workspace and create a new **Library**, as shown in the following screenshot:

Figure 13.4 – Creating a workspace library

2. In the ensuing **Create Library** page, give your library an appropriate name and drop/select the JAR file we built in the previous section, as shown in the following screenshot:

Create Library

Library Source

| Upload | DBFS/S3 | PyPI | Maven | CRAN |

Library Type

| Jar | Python Egg | Python Whl |

Library Name

spark-sql-perf

Drop JAR here

Create   Cancel

Figure 13.5 – Installing the JAR file in the workspace library

Now, we must create a Databricks cluster that will be used to generate the TPC-DS data and install this workspace library onto it.

Creating a data generation cluster

In this step, we will create a cluster to create the TPC-DS data. For the sake of simplicity, I will reuse the same cluster to show the automated benchmarking process as well. You should create a different cluster with different specifications suited to the test you are undertaking. Follow these steps:

1. Create a new cluster, as outlined here: https://docs.databricks.com/clusters/ create.html. Ensure that you uncheck the **Enable autoscaling** checkbox. The **Workers** count should be based on the scale of data you wish to generate and how fast you want to generate it. The speed of generation will be directly proportional to the worker count. The following screenshot shows a cluster being created with a runtime suitable for the library:

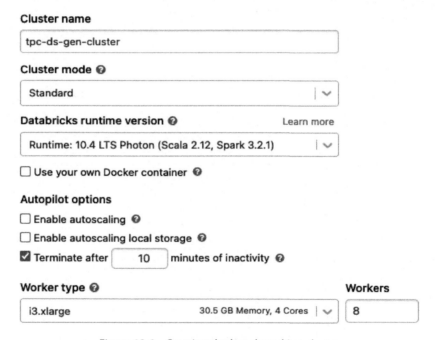

Figure 13.6 – Creating the benchmarking cluster

2. Install the workspace library in this cluster by clicking on the **Install New** button in the **Libraries** tab of the cluster you created in the previous step, as follows:

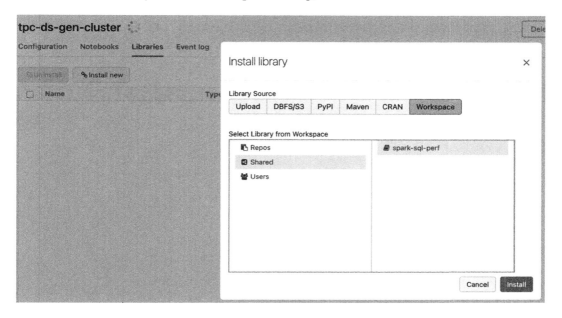

Figure 13.7 – Installing the workspace library in the cluster

Before we move on to the next step, why did I ask you to disable autoscaling? This is because we know the workload and that it requires a certain amount of compute power. Hence, it makes sense to configure the compute power right away.

The following are some pro tips for you:

- If you are looking to build TPC-DS datasets of higher scale factors, which will be a time-consuming process, consider using an all-on-demand cluster (no Spot VMs) so that you don't risk preemption of workers.

- Ensure that the workspace library is in an *Installed* state on the cluster before running the data generation commands. Otherwise, the commands will fail.

Importing the spark-sql-perf repository

The `spark-sql-perf` project on GitHub contains handy Databricks notebooks that we can use for performing the TPC-DS data generation. We will use the **Repos** feature (`https://docs.databricks.com/repos/index.html`) in Databricks to import the entire repository into our workspace. As shown in the following screenshot, click on the **Add Repo** button in the **Repos** menu and paste the **Git repository URL** details of the `spark-sql-perf` repository:

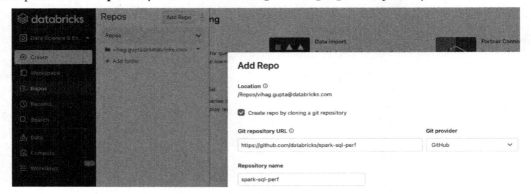

Figure 13.8 – Importing the spark-sql-perf repository

Running the data generation notebook

Once the repository has been added, navigate to the notebook at `spark-sql-perf/src/main/notebooks/tpcds_datagen`.

This notebook is a bit rough around the edges, as shown in the following screenshot, but don't worry – I will walk you through it:

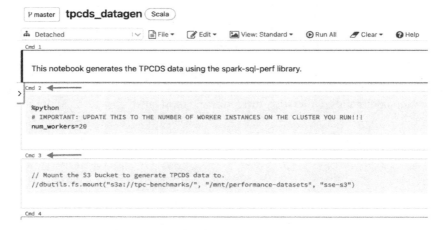

Figure 13.9 – The data generation notebook

Why Am I Not Creating Clean Notebooks for You?

Fair point. But I don't want to do that. I want you to be comfortable with the library as the Databricks team may add changes to the repository that you will want to use later. For example, the repository does not have automated benchmarking notebooks for SQL Warehouses. If they add it one day, I want you to be able to just consult this repository and get working instead of waiting on me to update my copy of things.

Let's go through the commands in the notebook, as shown in *Figure 13.6*, that you must work with. Keep in mind that the command numbers are true at the time of writing and may change in the future:

1. *Cmd 2*: Update `num_workers` to the number of workers in your data generation cluster.

2. *Cmd 3*: Mount a cloud storage location of your choice. To keep it simple, use the `/mnt/performance-datasets` mount point as it is hardcoded in other commands. To learn more about mounting, see `https://docs.databricks.com/data/databricks-file-system.html#databricks-file-system-dbfs`.

3. *Cmd 4*:

   - Update `scaleFactor` to the size of the desired TPC-DS dataset. Scale 1 means 1 Gb, Scale 10 means 10 Gb, and so on.

   - Update `format` to the format of choice. For example, if you want to test the performance of the Parquet format before testing the Delta format, set it to `parquet`.

   - Update `rootDir` if you selected a different mount point in *Cmd 3*.

   - Update `useDecimal` and `useDate` if you want to use decimal and date data types instead of strings. Using specific data types can bring about performance boosts that you may want to test.

   - Make a note of `databaseName` and optionally add a prefix to it. All the TPC-DS tables will be created in this database.

4. *Cmd 15*: Update `discoverPartitions` to `false` if you are creating the data in Delta format. This is because `discoverPartitions` is implemented as an `ALTER TABLE RECOVER PARTITIONS` command, which is not valid in Delta. Delta automatically discovers and tracks partitions.

5. *Cmd 17*: Comment out the `table.analyzeTables()` function if you are creating data in Delta format. This is because Delta automatically discovers and maintains table and column-level statistics.

That's it! Attach this notebook to the data generation cluster and run the notebook. Once completed, you should be able to see the TPC-DS data generated in the **Data** tab, as shown in the following screenshot:

Figure 13.10 – Generated data in the Databricks SQL Data Explorer

As you can see, I have prefixed my database name with vg_; the notebook automatically adds descriptive postfixes based on our configurations. Every new data generation activity will create a new database.

You can study the Entity Relation diagram of the data by downloading the TPC-DS specifications from https://www.tpc.org/tpc_documents_current_versions/current_specifications5.asp.

Keep in mind that the notebook creates external tables. So, if you want to delete any database or tables, make sure that you drop them in the Databricks portal and delete the actual files in the cloud portal.

Now, you have a TPC-DS dataset that you can use to run benchmarking exercises or just experiment in general. Let's start by seeing how we can run benchmarking tests.

Running automated benchmarks

The spark-sql-perf library allows you to run automated benchmarks against the queries of the TPC-DS specifications. If you are interested in studying the queries, you can study the query templates that are bundled in the specifications. If you are interested in studying the Databricks SQL versions of these queries, you can navigate to spark-sql-perf/src/main/resources/tpcds_2_4. The following screenshot shows how to navigate the IDE:

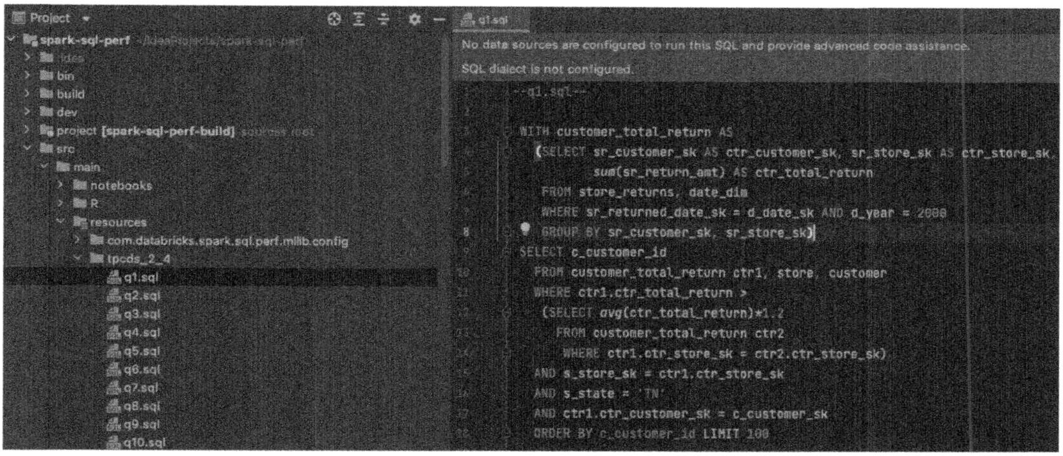

Figure 13.11 – TPC-DS benchmark queries

As we noted in the *Understanding the TPC-DS dataset* section, we are not interested in recreating benchmarks. However, if you do want to do so, you can do so by following the README file of spark-sql-perf. Let me quickly show you how to run a benchmark in a Databricks workspace.

> **Note**
>
> The spark-sql-perf library can only run benchmarks against a Spark cluster. It does not have provisions to execute the automated benchmark on SQL Warehouses.

We will use the bundled notebooks available in the spark-sql-perf project. Navigate to the notebook at spark-sql-perf/src/main/notebooks/tpcds_run.

You must update certain values based on what you set in the data generation step, as follows:

- *Cmd 2*:

  I.   Update scaleFactor to scaleFactor of the generated data.

  II.   Update the useDecimal and useDate fields to the values used in the data generation process.

  III. Add the filterNull variable if it's not present.

  IV.   Update databaseName with any custom prefixes.

  V.   Set the iterations to the desired number of iterations of the benchmark. This is important because subsequent iterations can benefit from caching and warm JVMs.

That's it! Now, you can execute the notebook. The last command, *Cmd 7*, will display the execution results of the benchmark, as follows:

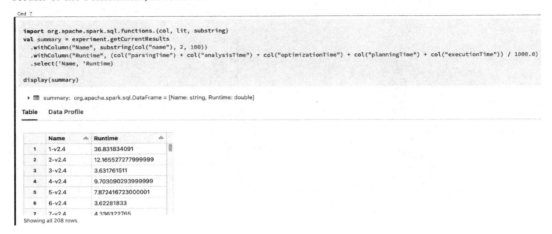

Figure 13.12– TPC-DS benchmark results

The benchmark results are self-explanatory. They are just the execution speeds of each query in the benchmark suite. The smaller the query runtime, the better. Of course, the runtime needs to be compared against that of an incumbent system.

Now that we know how to run the automated TPC-DS benchmarks, we can move on to experimenting with TPC-DS data by ourselves. Experiments could be of any form – you might wish to run your own benchmarking queries, or you may wish to test some Databricks SQL features. Let's see how.

Experimenting with TPC-DS in Databricks SQL

Now that we have the TPC-DS data generated and ready to query, you are free to experiment and validate everything that we've learned in the previous chapters – especially *Chapter 8, The Delta Lake*.

If you intend to use the TPC-DS benchmarking queries themselves, please note that you will have to import the Databricks versions of the queries into Databricks SQL manually. See *Figure 13.11* to learn how to obtain the queries. Otherwise, you can refer to the TPC-DS specification on the ER diagram and row counts to craft your own queries of varying complexity that test the features you want to test.

Keep the metrics you want to measure in mind. A measure such as speed requires that you keep the cluster configuration constant and account for the fact that Databricks SQL will cache table data and query results. Depending on the test, data skipping effectiveness might be a better metric to measure.

As we saw in the *Generating TPC-DS data* section, there are many possible TPC-DS dataset configurations, each of which can produce a different insight. Let's look at a few possible and relevant case studies for you to explore.

Case study 1 – the effect of file formats

In this case study, you should keep your `scaleFactor`, `useDecimal`, `useDate`, and `useNull` configurations constant and test the benchmark queries for file formats such as CSV, Parquet, Parquet with Analyze Tables and Columns, ORC, and Delta. You should observe how the performance of Parquet based tables and Parquet based tables on which statistics collection have been run, compare to Delta based tables. Recall that the `ANALYZE TABLE` command can be used to perform explicit statistics collection. This will help you validate the concepts of automatic statistics collection and data skipping.

An added variant would be to increase `scaleFactor` exponentially and see if a significant performance gap arises between the various file formats.

Case study 2 – the effect of specialized data types

Often, organizations will mark all the fields in tables as strings to avoid complex data quality enforcement engineering and faster availability of data for querying. However, this can have a detrimental effect on queries as automatic statistics collections and data skipping will be less effective.

You can keep the `scaleFactor`, `format`, and `useNull` configurations constant and toggle the `useDecimal` and `useDate` configurations to see the difference in the performance of filtering queries on columns with these data types.

An added variant would be changing the format and seeing if Delta still manages to collect meaningful statistics and improve performance over Parquet based tables upon which statistics collection has been performed.

Finally, `scaleFactor` can be increased exponentially to see if there is a significant performance disparity.

Case study 3 – the effect of NULLs

Nulls are notorious. They can proliferate very easily in Data Lakes as the data quality enforcement can be lax. They also can have very detrimental effects on querying by making data skipping and clustering methods such as ZORDER less effective.

You can toggle the `useNull` configuration to introduce null values in the generated dataset, while keeping everything else constant. You can also try to ZORDER certain columns while enabling null values and see if the data skipping is less effective.

A reasonable variant would be increasing `scaleFactor` to see if NULLs cause severe performance drops at higher scales.

Case study 4 – ZORDER and partitions

You can test the effects of ZORDER with and without partitions. The following tables are good candidates for partitioning due to their data volume: `inventory`, `web_returns`, `catalog_returns`, `store_returns`, `web_sales`, `catalog_sales`, and `store_sales`. You can run simple filtering queries on any of these tables at a high scale factor to see how the partitions and ZORDER change the data skipping performance. If you want a refresher on ZORDER and partitions, please see *Chapter 8, The Delta Lake*.

Case study 5 – Bloom filter indexes

You can test the performance of needle-in-a-haystack queries by toggling Bloom filter indexes on datasets with high scale factors.

Hopefully, these case studies will keep you busy for a long time. More importantly, I hope that they will help you test the various performance-boosting features of Databricks SQL to your satisfaction.

That said, before concluding this chapter, I want to say that benchmarks are great, but the real test of any product is against your data. Test Databricks SQL against your data and draw your own conclusions. And just as a cautionary note, even if you run the benchmarking suites as per the steps noted in the chapter, please do not consider them formal benchmarks. Formal benchmarks are a scientific exercise that requires a lot of preconditions, checks, and balances to be followed to ensure the fairness and reproducibility of results.

Summary

In this chapter, we learned about the TPC-DS benchmark and the TPC-DS dataset. We learned how to generate TPC-DS data at any scale. Then, we learned how to execute the automated TPC-DS benchmark suites in the `spark-sql-perf` library in our Databricks workspace. Finally, we discussed the various ways in which TPC-DS data can be used to test the performance-boosting features of Databricks SQL.

With this, we have come to the end of the primary topics of this book on Databricks SQL. I am sure that you still have some questions. Hence, in the next chapter, we will go through some of the most commonly asked questions about Databricks SQL!

14

Ask Me Anything

As we come to the end of this book, I thought it would be a good idea to compile a list of questions that get asked about Databricks SQL.

In this chapter, we will go through some of the common questions that we get asked about Databricks SQL and Databricks in general.

We will cover the following topic:

- Frequently asked questions

Frequently asked questions

Databricks SQL is part of an entirely new product category called the **Lakehouse**. The Lakehouse is an alternative to data lakes and data warehouses. This prompts a lot of interest and questions from prospective customers. I am sure that you will also have a lot of questions, even after spending time reading this book.

So, here is a list of such questions and their answers, in no particular order.

How does Databricks SQL define small, medium, and large table sizes?

If we think about defining the size of tables on traditional systems, it could depend on the number of rows, the length of the records, or the number of nodes that the table is sharded across.

Since the Lakehouse enables big data processing, it can accommodate all sizes of datasets. You do not have to provision computation resources separately for small, medium, and large tables. Tuning the warehouse's size is easy as well – if queries are running slow, increase the warehouse T-shirt size. If queries are getting queued, increase the maximum number of clusters in the warehouse.

That said, if we were to see current trends in performance, anything with a compressed data size of 1 GB or less is very small. Let me provide a sense of scale. When we run the OPTIMIZE command, it creates data files that are 1 GB each. It is not recommended to partition a table under 5 to 10 GB (this number keeps increasing as Databricks brings more innovations). The out-of-the-box data skipping is just fine for handling this.

If you were to ask me to give you table T-shirt sizes, I would say the following:

- Small: ~ 10 to 100 GB

- Medium: ~100 GB to a few TB

- Large: 100 TB+

How does Databricks SQL define long and thin tables and long and broad tables?

This is like the previous question. The Lakehouse is not bound by the traditional definitions of long, thin, and broad tables. It can accommodate data tables of all shapes and sizes with equal ease.

How does Databricks SQL support normalization and denormalization?

The Lakehouse inherits the flexibility of data lakes in terms of data modeling. In essence, it is modeling-agnostic. You can implement any modeling technique with Databricks SQL and the Lakehouse. For example, you can implement Kimball-style star schema data models, Inmon-style data marts, or a Data Vault.

This is because, at the end of the day, the data model is implemented via table DDLs or in semantic layers on the reporting side. Databricks SQL supports primary keys, surrogate keys, and foreign keys. That said, primary keys and foreign keys are currently not enforced – they are supported to allow interrogation from other tools.

ETL best practices for big data and **Online Analytical Processing** (**OLAP**) systems recommend disabling these keys for faster ingestion and independent ingestion of datasets. The key definition is mainly maintained in data modeling tools or semantic layers on the reporting side.

Databricks SQL fully supports SQL syntax, so loading a normalized or denormalized table will happen just like in any other SQL database. You can read about it further in Bill Inmon's e-book at `https:// databricks.com/p/ebook/building-the-data-lakehouse`.

How does Databricks SQL perform **Change Data Capture** (**CDC**)*?*

CDC is an essential activity on the Lakehouse. ETL processes on the Lakehouse conform to the medallion architecture pattern, which we discussed at length in *Chapter 10, Warehouse on the Lakehouse*. In the medallion architecture, the first data layer is an as-is replica of the source data systems. The CDC process defines how fast the changes on the source data systems are replicated on the Lakehouse. Databricks can support CDC as fast as the source data system can emit changes. This is made possible by support for real-time stream processing and ACID transactions with Delta. As per the medallion architecture, this data layer can be called bronze or raw. This layer contains data that has not been processed in any form. Hence, it is also a historical archive of source data.

> **Note**
>
> Keep in mind that the medallion architecture is just a design pattern. It is not an enforceable feature or framework. So, when we say bronze or raw data layers, it just means that the data is unprocessed.

Many CDC design patterns are supported:

- **Pull Pattern**: This uses JDBC/ODBC to connect to any database and extract new records based on a timestamp data column. Learn more here: `https://docs.databricks.com/data/data-sources/sql-databases.html`.

- **Push Pattern**: This uses CDC extraction tooling such as Oracle Goldengate or Debezium to push the captured change data as data files to cloud storage. You can use Databricks Autoloader to automatically process these files into the Lakehouse.

- **Databricks Partner Ingestion Hub**: Databricks has a large ecosystem of ISV partners that can simplify data ingestion from a variety of sources. The full list can be found here: `https://docs.databricks.com/integrations/partners.html`.

Landing the data is only one part of the process. The change data must also be processed into the rest of the medallion architecture. First, the bronze layer's data must be conformed and cleaned into a logical data model. These data models could be domain/industry-specific data models that represent standard definitions of key business entities and their relationships. This data layer is the silver layer. The silver layer is constructed by extracting source data changes, as captured in the bronze layer, and transformed into data models. These data models could be of the third normal form, similar to data models.

Most self-service analytics is served from the silver layer. This involves getting change data to this layer as fast as possible. Since this layer contains a data model that is often constructed with values from multiple bronze tables, there is always a wait for all related records to be captured before a row is written in the silver layer. This is made easy in Databricks by streaming change data between the bronze and silver layers with technology such as Change Data Feed. Finally, since this is a very write-heavy data layer, Data Vault-like write-performant data models can be used in this layer.

Finally, the silver layer's data must be moved to more consumption-ready "project-specific" denormalized and read-optimized data models. This is known as the gold layer. The gold layer's primary focus is on reporting use cases. The presentation layer of projects fits in this layer. Kimball-style star schema data models or Inmon-style data marts are best suited for data modeling in this layer.

Databricks has tools such as Delta Live Tables and Change Data Feed that allow you to efficiently process captured change data through the bronze, silver, and gold layers. See *Chapter 11, SQL Commands – Part 1* for detailed case studies on CDC.

You can learn more about Delta Live Tables here: `https://docs.microsoft.com/en-us/azure/databricks/data-engineering/delta-live-tables/delta-live-tables-cdc`.

How does indexing work in Databricks SQL?

Delta Lake automatically captures column statistics for every data file, which is used in effective data skipping. You can consider this the equivalent of automatic indexing. Then, there are tools such as ZORDER and Bloom filter indexes, which can be used for more pointed indexing. ZORDER is analogous to clustered indexes in the database world. Bloom filter indexes are useful for needle-in-the-haystack searches, especially for strings.

I recommend revisiting *Chapter 8, The Delta Lake,* for further reading on ZORDER and Bloom filter indexes.

How does Databricks SQL handle time series data?

You can create any data structure of your choosing, including temporal data structures. There are out-of-the-box functions that can help you process time series data. However, depending on your requirements, a specialized time series store may also be considered.

How does Databricks SQL partition data across nodes?

Databricks does not run on on-premise servers. Revisit *Chapter 3, The Data Catalog,* to see how storage and computation are decoupled in the Lakehouse. The storage is on cloud object stores, and the data processing clusters are provisioned ephemerally as required.

On the cloud object store, the data can be partitioned based on certain fields. When the data is processed for querying, the Apache Spark framework automatically distributes the data across the various nodes (workers) in the cluster. It is transparent.

How does Databricks SQL handle authentication and authorization?

Revisit *Chapter 4, The Security Model,* for a full discussion. In summary, you can program your data security with SQL security statements such as GRANT, REVOKE, and DENY. There are various authentication mechanisms, including SSO, Personal Access Tokens, and Azure Active Directory.

It is recommended that you stay updated with the Unity Catalog product in Databricks as that is poised to be the default catalog of the Lakehouse; Hive Metastore will be phased out. See `https://docs.databricks.com/data-governance/unity-catalog/` for more details.

Does Databricks SQL support business keys or surrogate keys?

Yes, it does. Databricks supports **identity columns**, which will be automatically assigned unique, statistically increasing values with new record inserts. You can learn more here: `https://docs.databricks.com/sql/language-manual/sql-ref-syntax-ddl-create-table-using.html`.

Does Databricks SQL support applications with ACID requirements?

Databricks Lakehouse does support ACID guarantees. This support enables the Lakehouse architecture to bring together the best of data lakes and data warehouses. However, since it is an analytics tooling, it is best used for **Online Analytical Processing (OLAP)** and not **Online Transactional Processing (OLTP)**.

Does Databricks SQL have drag and drop wizards?

No. However, you can use any of the Databricks partners for visual data ingestion, preparation, and transformation. You can find the list of available partners here: `https://databricks.com/company/partners/technology`.

Does Databricks SQL support cursor operations?

Cursors are an anti-pattern in Databricks SQL. Revisit *Chapter 9, The Photon Engine*, to learn how your data is processed in parallel across machines, without you having to manually loop over records. Databricks SQL can query petabyte scale data and express all ETL without creating and looping through cursors.

Does Databricks SQL support updates?

Yes – you can perform inserts, updates, and deletes with Databricks SQL. If you are curious about the mechanics of these operations on Delta Lake, please revisit *Chapter 8, The Delta Lake*.

Depending on your requirements, you can also consider the `MERGE INTO` statement, which merges a set of inserts, updates, and deletes from a source to a target table in one operation rather than one operation per transaction. It is faster and more efficient. We discussed practical uses of the `MERGE` command in *Chapter 11, SQL Commands – Part 1*.

Does Databricks SQL support real-time and streaming data?

Yes. The underlying big data processing framework, Apache Spark, supports batch, near-real-time, and real-time data processing. You can start your streaming journey here: `https://docs.databricks.com/delta/delta-streaming.html`.

Does Databricks SQL support primitive data types?

Yes. See `https://docs.databricks.com/sql/language-manual/sql-ref-datatypes.html` for more details.

Does Databricks SQL support complex data types?

Yes. See `https://docs.databricks.com/sql/language-manual/sql-ref-datatypes.html` for more details.

Does Databricks SQL support query federation?

It does. You can connect to multiple data sources directly and use them in a federated query. The question is, why would you want to do that? Querying source transaction systems can be a very bad idea as it may affect the performance of live systems. You can make a case for querying other specialized analytical data stores in a federated mechanism – but again, you must be careful when mixing data from potentially non-relational data with relational data as it may mess up the semantics of the query and the results.

Does Databricks SQL support materialized views?

Support for materialized views has just been announced. It will be built on the Delta Live Tables product to accelerate queries and reduce infrastructure costs with efficient and incremental computation.

Does Databricks SQL charge for Photon Query Engine?

No. It is enabled by default on SQL Warehouses.

What are the performance limits of Databricks SQL?

I recommend revisiting *Chapter 6, SQL Warehouses*, to learn how to scale Databricks SQL to queries of any size at any concurrency level. In short, the Apache Spark big data processing framework, which forms the basis of Databricks SQL, can easily scale to petabytes of data and any number of joins.

Of course, as with all software systems, you must define the precise metrics of performance that you are interested in to correctly gauge a system.

What is the learning curve for existing data warehouse users?

Virtually none. Databricks SQL is ANSI-SQL compliant, so your existing SQL skills are transferrable. Similarly, database administrators will find standard data definition statements and data security statements, making their skills transferrable as well.

Some recalibration might be required to move away from the cursor-oriented processing of stored procedures and adapt to different utility functions, but these can easily be found in the Databricks SQL Reference.

How can I write stored procedures in Databricks SQL?

You cannot write stored procedures in the traditional sense. One of the reasons for this is that stored procedures tend to be cursor-driven and process records in a loop, which is not suitable for big data workloads. What you can do is define user-defined functions, or create Python code that achieves the same effect. You can learn more at `https://docs.databricks.com/sql/language-manual/sql-ref-syntax-ddl-create-sql-function.html` and `https://docs.databricks.com/dev-tools/pyodbc.html`.

How can I create a star schema in Databricks SQL?

Please revisit *Chapter 10, Warehouse on the Lakehouse* for details on this. Another good resource is this official blog by Databricks: `https://databricks.com/blog/2022/05/20/five-simple-steps-for-implementing-a-star-schema-in-databricks-with-delta-lake.html`.

Use Delta tables for your fact and dimension tables to get the best performance. For further performance improvements, ensure that your fact tables are Z-ordered. Also, Z-order your dimension key fields. Ensure that your fact tables are Z-ordered. Finally, make use of the primary and foreign key support so that your BI tools can interrogate the data for the relationships.

How can I connect Databricks SQL queries to my VCS/Git?

You cannot at the time of writing.

How can I handle slowly changing dimensions in Databricks SQL?

Many mechanisms can be employed. See `https://docs.databricks.com/data-engineering/delta-live-tables/delta-live-tables-cdc.html` for more details. In summary, an SCD of any type can be achieved with a combination of inserts, updates, deletes, and merges along with using a Change Data Feed of Delta tables.

I already have Spark SQL; why do I need Databricks SQL?

Do not confuse SQL on Spark with Databricks SQL. SQL on Spark is simply a SQL layer over Apache Spark. Databricks SQL is a full product that caters to business intelligence workflows. Furthermore, the topology of compute clusters is very different in Databricks SQL versus traditional Spark clusters meant for data engineers and analysts. See *Chapter 6, The SQL Warehouses*, for more information.

Are column names case-sensitive in Databricks SQL?

No, they are not.

Summary

In this chapter, we covered some frequently asked questions about Databricks SQL. Hopefully, this answered any remaining questions you may have had about Databricks SQL. That said, Databricks SQL is constantly evolving, so I recommend staying updated with the latest documentation and release notes. And if these are not enough, reach out to your Databricks representative!

Index

Symbols

10-Query Rule 159

A

access
  denying 83
  revoking 82
access control
  with Apache Hive™ Metastore 65, 66
  with Unity Catalog 66
access control lists (ACLs) 65
access control, SQL Warehouse
  about 170
  chargeback 173-175
  operations 171
  privileges 171
  programming access control 172, 173
Active Directory application
  creating 93
ADLS Gen2
  storage location, creating 94, 95
aggregate operator 234
Alerts page 24, 25
Amazon Web Services (AWS)
  about 12, 97

cloud storage access 97
ANALYZE command
  about 286
  FOR COLUMN clause 286
  NOSCAN clause 286
  PARTITION clause 286
Apache Hive™ Metastore
  about 34
  access control 65, 66
Apache Spark 153
Apache Spark™ execution model
  about 223, 227
  analysis 223, 224
  code generation 225
  execution 225, 226
  logical plan, optimizing 224
  physical plan 224, 225
append-only file formats 197
application programming interface (API) 196
artifacts
  administration, by account
    administrator 148, 149
  administration, by owner 148
  governing 148
asset Metadata
  exploring 80, 81

assignment strategy criteria, SQL Warehouse
projects and groups 170
resources, sharing 169
workload type 169
atomicity 197, 206
authentication modes, validated
BI tools connection
Azure Active Directory 182-184
configurations 182
Databricks personal access token 182
Databricks username and password 182
Autoloader
reference link 242
automated benchmarks
running 300-302
Auto Stop function 158
auxiliary statements
about 72
reference link 51
AWS console, instance profiles configuration
reference link 97
Azure Active Directory 92
Azure Active Directory authentication
using 182-184
Azure Databricks 12
Azure Data Lake Storage (ADLS) 4
Azure side configuration
reference link 92
Azure storage account
reference link 92

B

Bloom filter indexes
about 217
testing 217

bottom of sidebar
about 14
Help option 14
Partner Connect option 14
Settings option 14
Workspace selector option 15
bronze layer, Medallion architecture 242, 245
built-in performance-boosting
features, Delta Lake
about 207
automatic caching 212, 213
Automatic Compaction 211, 212
automatic statistics collection 207- 210
Optimized Writes 211, 212
business vault 246
bytecode
reference link 225

C

calendar-based selection tool 114
cataloging technology
selecting, implications 37
catalogs
about 35
altering 255
creating 254
dropping 255
Catalyst optimizer 223
Change Data Capture (CDC) 262, 306
Change Data Capture (CDC), design patterns
Databricks Partner Ingestion Hub 307
Pull Pattern 307
Push Pattern 307
Change Data Feed (CDF)
about 266
reference link 266
Choropleth 128

cloud storage access 89-92

cloud storage access, in Amazon
    Web Services (AWS)

  about 97

  Databricks instance, configuring
      to use IAM role 99

  Databricks SQL, configuring to
      use instance profile 99

  instance profile, configuring 98

  instance profile, creating 98

  S3 bucket, configuring 98

  S3 bucket, creating 97

  stages, configuring 97

  storage container, testing 100, 101

cloud storage access, in Microsoft Azure

  about 92

  Active Directory application, creating 93

  storage container, testing 96, 97

  storage location, creating on
      ADLS Gen2 94, 95

cluster tags and tag propagation

  reference link 175

code generation 228

cohort analysis 133-135

cohort visualization 133-135

comma-separated values (CSV) file 145

Conference on Innovative Data
    Systems Research (CIDR) 5

configurable performance-boosting
    features, Delta Lake

  Bloom filter indexes 217

  CACHE SELECT 218

  z-ordering 214-216

consistency 198, 206, 207

COPY INTO command

  about 268, 269

  reference link 268

Cost Analysis tool

  reference link 174

Cost Optimized policy 158

Create menu 25, 26

CREATE privilege 84

cursors 309

D

dashboards

  alerts 146-148

  composing 139-143

  creating 139

  interacting with 145

  publishing 139

  scheduling with 145

  users access, obtaining to 144, 145

  using 143

Dashboards page 23, 24

data

  organizing, on Lakehouse 240

data assets

  describing 285

  listing 284, 285

database

  about 34

  exploring 78-80

  sharing 77, 78

database administrators (DBAs) 63

Databricks

  about 5

  overview 4, 5

  reference link 12

Databricks, cataloging technologies

  Apache Hive™ Metastore 34

  Unity Catalog 35

Databricks CLI and utilities

  reference link 12

Databricks Help Center
  reference link 14
Databricks instance
  configuring, to use IAM role 99
Databricks, instance profiles configuration
  reference link 97
Databricks Lakehouse platform
  overview 9
Databricks Partner Connect
  about 187
  accessing 188, 189
  data source file 190
Databricks partners
  reference link 307
Databricks personal access token
  reference link 182
  using 182
Databricks pricing
  reference link 174, 222
Databricks Secrets
  reference link 93
Databricks side configuration
  reference link 92
Databricks SQL
  about 178, 269, 306, 310
  configuring, to use instance profile 99
  data organization model 34
  data types 123
  inbuilt functions, working with 269
  three-level data organization model 35
  TPC-DS data, experimenting 302
Databricks SQL, instance profiles
      configuration
  reference link 97
Databricks SQL, JSON path expression
  reference link 271

Databricks SQL security model
  about 64
  access control, with Apache
      Hive™ Metastore 65, 66
  access control, with Unity Catalog 66
  query execution model 67, 68
Databricks Technology Partners
  reference link 309
data catalog
  about 33, 65
  three-level namespace 36
data catalog, for exploring data visually
  about 41-43
  catalogs, navigating 43
  databases, exploring 45
  databases, navigating 44
  tables, exploring 46-49
  views, exploring 50
data definition language (DDL)
  catalogs, altering 255
  catalogs, creating 254
  catalogs, dropping 255
  Delta Sharing 258, 259
  external locations, altering 257
  external locations, creating 256, 257
  external locations, dropping 258
  for catalogs 254
  for external locations 255, 256
  statements 72
  storage credentials, altering 257, 258
  storage credentials, dropping 258
data definition language (DDL) commands
  working with 254
data engineering, post Delta Lake
  about 204
  append-only file formats, solving 206
  data, extracting 205

data, writing 205
   object store limitations, solving 206, 207
data engineering, prior to Delta Lake
   data, extracting 197, 198
   data layout, optimizing 198
   data warehouses, synchronizing 201
   data, writing 197, 198
Data Explorer 17, 41
Data Explorer, hierarchy
   catalog 17
   database 17
   tables and views, within database 17
data generation cluster
   creating 296, 297
data generation notebook
   running 298-300
Data Lake
   about 34
   data abstraction hierarchy 37
data layout optimization
   about 198
   clustering 199
   optimal file sizes 200, 201
   partitioning 199
   statistics collections 200
data manipulation language commands
   COPY INTO 268, 269
   MERGE INTO 262
   working with 262
Data Manipulation Language
      (DML) statements 72
data marts 241
data modeling techniques
   implementing 244
data object privileges
   reference link 87

data organization model
   about 34
   example 38-41
data retrieval statements 72
Data Science and Engineering persona
   about 29
   features 30
data security commands
   column access, controlling with 281
   dynamic view functions 280, 281
   row access, controlling with 283
   working with 280
data-sharing objects
   altering 260
   creating 259
   dropping 261, 262
   recipient, creating 260
   share, creating 259
   TABLE, adding 260, 261
   TABLE, removing 261
data skipping 207
Data Vault
   about 247
   reference link 245
Data Vault, entities
   hubs 246
   links 246
   satellites 246
DDL, for Delta Sharing
   data-sharing objects, altering 260
   data-sharing objects, creating 259
   data-sharing objects, dropping 261, 262
Delta caching 212
Delta Engine 18
Delta Lake
   about 18, 240, 308
   built-in performance-boosting features 207

configurable performance-
    boosting features 214
guidelines 247
optimizing 279
repairing 279
storage format 201-204
storage format, fundamentals 196
time traveling 278, 279
URL 16
vacuuming 276, 277
Delta Lake maintenance commands
    DESCRIBE HISTORY command 278, 279
    FSCK REPAIR TABLE command 279
    OPTIMIZE command 279
    VACUUM command 276, 277
    working with 276
Delta Live Tables
    reference link 308
Delta Sharing
    about 258
    reference link 258
Delta tables
    about 311
    analyzing 285-287
DESCRIBE command 285
DESCRIBE HISTORY command 278, 279
directed acyclic graph (DAG) 236
distributed filesystem (DBFS)
    about 38
    reference link 38
dropdowns
    Dropdown List option 117
    Query Based Dropdown List option 118-120
    using 116
durability 198, 207
dynamic value selection tool 115, 116

dynamic view functions
    current_user() 280
    is_member(group_name) 280

E

enterprise data warehouse (EDW) 241, 242
enterprise deployment patterns
    reference link 14
entity-relationship (ER) diagram 246
Excel format 145
executor 225
external Apache Hive metastore
    reference link 37
external locations
    about 84, 255
    altering 257
    creating 256, 257
    dropping 258
external locations and storage credentials
    reference link 85
Extract, Transform, and Load (ETL) 6

F

FSCK REPAIR TABLE command 279
funnel visualization 135-137

G

generic data warehouse system
    components 240, 241
gold layer 307
gold layer, Medallion architecture
    about 243, 247, 248
    guidelines 248
Google Cloud Platform (GCP) 12
Google Cloud Storage (GCS) 4

H

Hive Metastore 75

I

IAM role
  used, for configuring Databricks instance 99
Identity and Access Management (IAM) 64
identity columns 309
inbuilt functions, in Databricks SQL
  JSON 269, 270
  Lambda functions 272
  reference link 269
  working with 269
instance profile
  configuring 98
  creating 98
  used, for configuring Databricks SQL 99
Integrated Development
    Environment (IDE) 293
isolation
  about 197, 206
  Serializable level 206
  WriteSerializable level 206

J

JAR file 73
JavaScript Object Notation (JSON)
  about 269, 270
  nested fields, extracting 271
  values from arrays, extracting 271
  values using identifiers, extracting 270
Java Virtual Machine (JVM) 153, 232
job 225
Just-in-Time (JIT) 225

L

Lakehouse
  about 305, 306
  data, organizing 240
Lakehouse architecture
  implementation 8
  issues 7
  issues, solving 8
  overview 5-7
  reliable data management 8
  SQL performance 9
  visual representation 8
Lambda functions
  reference link 272
least privilege 73, 74
LIST command 284
Live Autocomplete 106
logical plan 224

M

machine learning (ML) operations 4
Machine Learning persona
  about 26-29
  icons 28
  reference link 28
managed MLflow service
  reference link 29
Map Marker 128-132
map visualization
  about 128, 129
  styles 128
materialized views
  reference link 50
Medallion architecture
  about 241, 244
  bronze layer 242

gold layer 243
    reference link 242
    silver layer 242
MERGE INTO command
    about 262
    Data Capture, changing 264, 265
    data deduplication 262, 263
    Dimensions, changing slowly 264, 265
    incremental data processing, with
        Change Data Feed (CDF) 266-268
Meta, Amazon, Netflix, Google,
    and Apple (MANGA) 4
metadata commands
    ANALYZE command 285, 286
    DESCRIBE command 285
    SHOW command 284
    working with 284
Metastore
    about 35
    reference link, for design and concepts 34
Microsoft Azure
    cloud storage access 92
middle of sidebar 15
minimum-maximum (min-max) ranges 214

N

non-validated BI tools connection
    about 184
    driver, downloading 184
    driver, installing 185
    SQL Warehouse connection,
        configuring 186
numbers query parameters
    using 109-112

O

Online Analytical Processing (OLAP) 309
Online Transactional Processing (OLTP) 309
operational data store (ODS) 241, 242
operations
    executing 72
optimistic concurrency control
    reference link 206
OPTIMIZE command 279
    reference link 216
optimized logical plan 224
ownership 77

P

personally identifiable information
    (PII) fields 281
Photon
    about 153, 222, 223
    for data engineering 237
    reference link 222
Photon Engine 221
Photon product roadmap 234, 236
Photon runtime
    reference link 222
Photon vectorized DAGs
    versus traditional code-generated
        DAGs 233, 234
physical plan 224, 225
pivot table visualization 137, 139
point-in-time parameters 115
Point-in-Time Query Parameters 114
Power BI™ Desktop 179
principle of least privilege 82
privileges
    about 72
    ALL_PRIVILEGES 72

CREATE 73
CREATE TABLE 73
MODIFY 73
MODIFY_CLASSPATH 73
READ FILES 73
READ_METADATA 73
SELECT 72
USAGE 72
WRITE FILES 73

Q

queries
    developing 104-106
    working with 103, 104
Queries page 21
Query Based Dropdown List option 118-120
Query Editor 19, 21
query execution model
    about 67, 68
    authorization events 67
    authorizing 67, 68
Query History page 22
query parameters 109
query profile
    reference link 167
query results, chart visualizations
    error bars 126, 127
    grouping 125
    stacking 126
query results, specialized visualization types
    about 128
    cohort analysis 133-135
    cohort visualization 133-135
    funnel visualization 135-137
    map visualization 128-132
    pivot table visualization 137, 139

query results, visualization type
    about 120
    charts 123, 125
    tables 120-123

R

raw vault 246, 247
read access 83-86
recipient
    creating 260
Reliability Optimized policy 158
return on investment (ROI) 210

S

S3 bucket
    configuring 98
    creating 97
S3 IAM role, adding to EC2 policy
    reference link 99
Sample trips Taxi query 21
schema hints 106
schemas 34
securable objects 64, 71
Security Credential 255
security model
    about 75, 76
    summarizing 86
Security statements 72
SerDe
    reference link 50
Serverless SQL
    using 175
service principal 71
SHOW command 284
SHOW PARTITIONS statement 285
SHOW TBLPROPERTIES statement 285

sidebar navigation
  about 12
  bottom of sidebar 14
  middle of sidebar 15
  top of sidebar 13
silver layer, Medallion architecture
  about 242, 245
Simple Storage Service (S3) 4
Single Instruction Multiple Data (SIMD) 231
sizing scenarios, SQL Warehouse
  CPU-bound workloads 163
  memory-bound workloads 162
Slowly Changing Dimensions (SCDs) 262
solid-state drives (SSDs) 212
spark-sql-perf library
  building 293, 294
  installing 295, 296
  reference link 293
spark-sql-perf repository
  importing 298
SQL commands 108, 275
SQL databases, using JDBC
  reference link 307
SQL persona
  about 15, 16
  Alerts page 24, 25
  Create menu 25, 26
  Dashboards page 23, 24
  Data Explorer 17
  Queries page 21
  Query Editor 19, 21
  Query History page 22
  SQL Warehouses 18, 19
SQL reference, for Databricks SQL
  reference link 59

SQL statements, for exploring
    data programmatically
  about 51
  databases, exploring 52-54
  functions, exploring 59, 60
  tables, exploring 55-57
  views, exploring 58
SQL Warehouses
  about 18, 19
  access control 170
  assignment strategy 169
  Auto Stop function 158, 159
  cluster autoscaling 159
  cluster size, selecting 156, 157
  creating 154
  details, configuring 180, 181
  downscaling rules 162
  governing 168
  organizing 168
  query routing 159
  queuing 159
  running state 160
  scaling 157
  sizing 159, 162
  spot instance policy 158
  starting state 160
  stopped state 160
  upscaling rules 160, 162
SQL Warehouse, signals
  concurrency of queries 164
  concurrency of queries, cases 165
  execution speed of queries 166-168
staging area 241, 242
standard plan optimization techniques 224
Star schema
  about 247
  reference link 247

statistics collection (stats collection) 207
storage container
    testing 96, 97
storage credentials
    altering 257, 258
    dropping 258
storage location
    creating, on ADLS Gen2 94, 95
Structured Query Language (SQL) 199

T

Tableau Desktop™ 180
tables 34
tab-separated values (TSV) file 145
temporal query parameters
    calendar-based selection tool 114
    dynamic value selection tool 115, 116
    using 112, 113
text query parameters
    using 109-112
third normal form 241
three-dimensional (3D) space 215
top of sidebar
    about 13
    Data Science & Engineering 13
    Machine Learning 13
    SQL 13
TPC-DS data
    data generation cluster, creating 296, 297
    experimenting, in Databricks SQL 302
    generating 293
    spark-sql-perf library, building 293, 294
    spark-sql-perf library, installing 295
    spark-sql-perf repository,
        importing 298, 299, 300
TPC-DS dataset 292

TPC-DS in Databricks SQL, case study
    Bloom filter indexes 304
    effect, of file formats 303
    effect, of NULLs 303
    effect, of specialized data types 303
    partitions 304
    ZORDER 304
traditional code-generated DAGs
    versus Photon vectorized DAGs 233, 234
Traditional Indexes 198
Transaction Processing Performance
        Council - Decision Support (TPC-DS)
    about 292
    URL 292
tree data structure 223

U

UI-based user-facing table access control
    about 87
    current permissions, displaying 87, 88
    privileges, granting 88
    privileges, revoking 89
UI tools
    using, for schema selection and
        sampling 107, 108
Unity Catalog
    about 17, 35
    access control 66
    consideration 84, 85
    reference link 308
    URL 35
Unity Catalog identities
    reference link 69
Unity Catalog product
    reference link 35
unmanaged tables
    reference link 39

unresolved logical plan 223
user and group administration
    reference link 69
user-facing table access control
    about 69
    access, denying 83
    access, revoking 82
    asset Metadata, exploring 80, 81
    database, exploring 78-80
    database, sharing 77, 78
    groups principal 69-71
    least privilege 73, 74
    operations 72
    ownership 77
    privileges 72
    read access 83-86
    securable objects 71
    security model 75, 76
    security model, summarizing 86
    service principal 69-71
    users principal 69-71

V

VACUUM command 276, 277
validated BI tools connection
    about 178
    authentication details 182
    examples 179, 180
    programmatic connection 187
    SQL Warehouse details 180, 181
vectorization
    about 227-229
    code generation 228
    volcano model 228
    working 229

vectorization, operators
    about 230
    aggregate 230
    filter 230
    scan 230
    tree evaluation 231, 232
vectorized query engine 222
volcano model 228

W

well-designed query 167
WholeStageCodeGen tag 236
WholeStateCodeGen tag 225, 236

Z

Z-order curves 216

Packt.com

Subscribe to our online digital library for full access to over 7,000 books and videos, as well as industry leading tools to help you plan your personal development and advance your career. For more information, please visit our website.

Why subscribe?

- Spend less time learning and more time coding with practical eBooks and Videos from over 4,000 industry professionals

- Improve your learning with Skill Plans built especially for you

- Get a free eBook or video every month

- Fully searchable for easy access to vital information

- Copy and paste, print, and bookmark content

Did you know that Packt offers eBook versions of every book published, with PDF and ePub files available? You can upgrade to the eBook version at packt.com and as a print book customer, you are entitled to a discount on the eBook copy. Get in touch with us at customercare@packtpub.com for more details.

At www.packt.com, you can also read a collection of free technical articles, sign up for a range of free newsletters, and receive exclusive discounts and offers on Packt books and eBooks.

Other Books You May Enjoy

If you enjoyed this book, you may be interested in these other books by Packt:

Simplifying Data Engineering and Analytics with Delta

Anindita Mahapatra

ISBN: 9781801814867

- Explore the key challenges of traditional data lakes
- Appreciate the unique features of Delta that come out of the box
- Address reliability, performance, and governance concerns using Delta
- Analyze the open data format for an extensible and pluggable architecture
- Handle multiple use cases to support BI, AI, streaming, and data discovery
- Discover how common data and machine learning design patterns are executed on Delta
- Build and deploy data and machine learning pipelines at scale using Delta

Microsoft Power BI Cookbook - Second Edition

Greg Deckler, Brett Powell

ISBN: 9781801813044

- Cleanse, stage, and integrate your data sources with Power Query (M)

- Remove data complexities and provide users with intuitive, self-service BI capabilities

- Build business logic and analysis into your solutions via the DAX programming language and dashboard-ready calculations

- Implement aggregation tables to accelerate query performance over large data sources

- Create and integrate paginated reports

- Understand the differences and implications of DirectQuery, live connections, Import, and Composite model datasets

- Integrate other Microsoft data tools into your Power BI solution

Packt is searching for authors like you

If you're interested in becoming an author for Packt, please visit authors.packtpub.com and apply today. We have worked with thousands of developers and tech professionals, just like you, to help them share their insight with the global tech community. You can make a general application, apply for a specific hot topic that we are recruiting an author for, or submit your own idea.

Share Your Thoughts

Now you've finished *Business Intelligence with Databricks SQL*, we'd love to hear your thoughts! Scan the QR code below to go straight to the Amazon review page for this book and share your feedback or leave a review on the site that you purchased it from.

https://packt.link/r/1803235330

Your review is important to us and the tech community and will help us make sure we're delivering excellent quality content.

Printed in Great Britain
by Amazon

12121373R00201